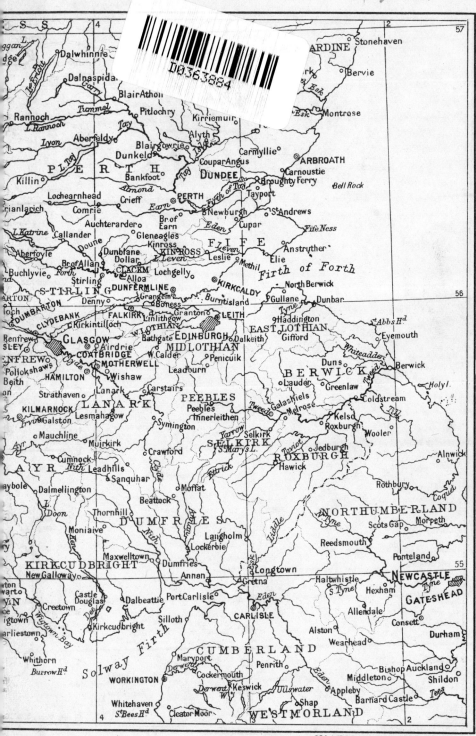

15

57

SS
L

Dalwhinnie
Dalnaspida

PL. Tummel
Rannoch
L. Rannoch

Lyon
Aberfeldy
Killin

PERTH
Lochearnhead
Comrie

Blair Athou
Pitlochry
Kirriemuir
Alyth

Blairgowrie
Dunkeld

ARDINE
Stonehaven
Bervie

Esk
Montrose

Carmyllie
Coupar Angus
ARBROATH
Carnoustie
Broughty Ferry

DUNDEE
Bankfoot

Almond
Crieff
PERTH

Firth of Tay
Tayport

Bell Rock

Trianlarich
Auchterarder
Gleneagles

Callander
L. Katrine
Doune
Aberfoyle
Dunblane
Br of Allan
Buchlyvie
Dollar
Forth
Stirling
Denny

Earn
Br of
Earn
Newburgh
St Andrews

Eden
Cupar
Fife Ness

KINROSS
Leven
Kinross
L. Leven
Leslie

FIFE
Anstruther
Elie

CLACKM
Alloa
Lochgelly
Methil
Firth of Forth

DUNFERMLINE
KIRKCALDY
North Berwick

Grangem
Boness
Burntisland
Gullane
Dunbar

DUMBARTON
Clydebank
Kirkintilloch
FALKIRK
Granton
LEITH
Tyne
Haddington

RENFREW
SLEY
Glasgow
Airdrie
COATBRIDGE
Kirkintilloch
W LOTHIAN
Bathgate
EDINBURGH
MIDLOTHIAN
Dalkeith
EAST LOTHIAN
Gifford
St Abbs Hd
Eyemouth

Pollokshaws
Beith
HAMILTON
MOTHERWELL
Wishaw
W. Calder
Leadburn
Penicuik
Duns
Whiteadder
Berwick

Strathaven
Lanark
Carstairs
PEEBLES
Lauder
Greenlaw
Coldstream
Holy I.

KILMARNOCK
LANARK
Lesmahagow
Peebles
Innerleithen
Tweed
Galashiels
Melrose
Kelso
Roxburgh
Wooler

Irvine
Galston
Mauchline
Muirkirk
Symington
Crawford
Yarrow
St Marys L.
SELKIRK
Ettrick
Teviot
Jedburgh
ROXBURGH
Hawick
Alnwick

AYR
Cumnock
Nith
Leadhills
Sanquhar
Clyde
Moffat
Liddle
NORTHUMBERLAND
Tyne
Rothbury
Coquet

aybole
Dalmellington
L.
Doon
Thornhill
Beattock
DUMFRIES
Langholm
Lockerbie
Reedsmouth
Scots Gap
Morpeth
Ponteland

KIRKCUDBRIGHT
New Galloway
Moniaive
Maxwelltown
Dumfries
Annan
Longtown
Gretna
Haltwhistle
S Tyne
Hexham
Reedsmouth
NEWCASTLE
GATESHEAD
55

rton
warto
WIN
igtown
arliestown
Castle
Douglas
Creetown
Dalbeattie
Port Carlisle
Eden
CARLISLE
Alston
Allendale
Consett
Durham

Wigtown Bay
Kirkcudbright
Silloth
CUMBERLAND
Wearhead

Whithorn
Burrow Hd
Maryport
Derwent
Cockermouth
Penrith
Eden
Bishop Auckland
Middleton
Appleby
Barnard Castle
Shildon

WORKINGTON
Derwent
Keswick
W
Ullswater
Shap
Tees

Whitehaven
St Bees Hd
Cleator Moor
WESTMORLAND
2

Solway Firth

4

56

4

2

W. & A.K. Johnston, Limited, Edinburgh & London.

VIEW OF LOCH AFFRIC AND SNOWCAPPED RIDGE OF MAM SOUL

S. P. B. MAIS

I RETURN
TO SCOTLAND

WITH 15 PLATES AND 11 MAPS

Dunvegan Castle.

CHRISTOPHER JOHNSON LONDON

To
GILLIAN
my
companion
in
all my
wanderings
with
love

PRINTED IN GREAT BRITAIN
BY WESTERN PRINTING SERVICES LTD., BRISTOL
FOR CHRISTOPHER JOHNSON, PUBLISHERS, LTD.
FIRST PUBLISHED 1947

CONTENTS

3

PLATES

MAPS

These sketch-maps are intended as a guide
to illustrate the text

5

I wish to express my gratitude to the Editor of S.M.T. magazine for permission to reproduce those chapters in this book which originally appeared in that periodical.

S.P.B.M.

INTRODUCTION

EVERYONE, I imagine, had his own private wish that he intended to fulfil to celebrate the end of the long, dour, exhausting struggle to preserve our freedom that remorselessly stole six of the best years of our lives.

Both my daughters had long ago made me promise to give them a pony when the war ended. They never deviated from that decision.

My wife and I also made a vow from which we never deviated. While the rest of the world proposed to fly over to the United States or cruise round the Mediterranean, we had but one ambition, to revisit a country that is much more accessible and in our view much more worth while.

For six years we had to forgo our annual visit to Scotland. We had six years' leeway of enchantment to make up. We had no desire to see anything new. All we wanted was to stand where we had stood of old, meet again the friends from whom we had been too long parted, and recapture an old rapture—indeed, a whole succession of raptures.

Scotland had something to give that we could get nowhere else, infinite variety of colour and contour packed into small space, romance and legend and blood-curdling reminders of ancient clan feuds, herds of deer on heather-covered moorland, the golden eagle soaring above the great bens, and wide green straths where the great amber-coloured rivers wind their way from the deep blue lochs to the wide firths and the sea. There was so much that I wanted so desperately to see again that I wanted to be everywhere at once. I planned my tour in detail. I devoted so many days to this place and so many days to that in order to taste again as many as possible of the plums of this prodigiously prolific pie.

It would be grand to take the sleeper again for Inverness and look out from my bunk in the early morning across Strath Spey to the mighty mass of the Cairngorms as the train raced through Kingussie and Aviemore, but I knew perfectly well that if I made a beeline for the Highlands I should stay in the Highlands, and there were other places I wanted to visit on the way. So I would make my way as fast as I could to the Border at Berwick-upon-Tweed, and there meander from east to west with the ballads of Thomas the Rhymer and Chevy Chase ringing in my ears as I crossed by way of Carter Bar or Deadwater into the land of my heart's desire. There was much that I wanted to see again here, Flodden Field, Roxburgh, Jedburgh, Dryburgh, Melrose, Abbotsford, the Eildon Hills, the Lammermuirs, Tweedsmuir, and the whole land of Buchan and Scott.

It is curious, in view of the veneration in which the great majority of Englishmen still hold Sir Walter, that so few ever visit his Tweedside home, and even more curious that scarcely any of the million or so readers of *The Thirty-Nine Steps* ever visit the lonely open moors over which Richard Hannay was chased by that desperate gang of Huns. It must sound sacrilege to a Scot to hear me say so, but I find it even easier to recapture the atmosphere and spirit of the moors from reading Buchan than from reading Scott who, with more labour, achieves a less vivid picture.

8

More curious still is the Englishman's ignorance of the romantic land of the Covenanters that S. R. Crockett made his own, because that view across the Solway Firth of the mountains of Galloway and Carrick is the first that the Southerner gets of the mysterious magic heights that guard the Border.

And how enchanting are its recesses when you get up to Loch Trool and the Loch of the Dungeon, the land where Robert the Bruce took up his stand and first defied the invader.

This wild, beautiful hill country is no more like the Highlands than it is like Wales. It is, like its inhabitants, intensely individualistic, and not to be mistaken for any other land. It is, of course, only a stone's throw from the fertile valley of the Doon and the rich fields of Ayrshire.

It seems astonishing that Burns with his passionate love of wild beauty should have failed to explore the high land south of Dalmellington, but so far as I know he makes no mention of it, and Crockett remains its sole chronicler.

I am no more a lover of birthplaces than Keats was, and I do not feel specially drawn to Kirk Alloway. There is more of the spirit of Burns in the Tam o'Shanter Inn in Ayr, a city I certainly proposed to revisit, if only for the fact that, like Aberdeen, it manages to combine the advantages of a fine seaside resort with those of a thriving academic and shopping centre.

At first the architecture of most Scottish towns strikes harshly on an eye accustomed to more colourful stone and less angular contours, but there is a strength and dignity about these stark buildings that I find exhilarating and extraordinarily revealing of the

A*

Scots character inasmuch as the dour exterior gives no indication of the astonishing warmth and cosiness within.

I have often looked out to sea from Ayr and promised myself the climb over Goat Fell and a holiday in Arran, but on this tour I was going to turn my back resolutely on the unknown and content myself only with reviving old memories.

The average Englishman, for instance, will be surprised to hear that from Ayr I proposed to make a beeline for Glasgow.

This turbulent great city has, like Aberdeen, got a totally undeserved reputation in the South. The truth is, and there is real Scots humour in this, that Aberdonians are the most generous-hearted people in the world, and Glaswegians among the most cultured.

That there should be intense rivalry between Glasgow and Edinburgh is only natural, and the first score goes naturally to Edinburgh, because its layout is infinitely more attractive.

Every traveller emerging from the train at Princes Street or Waverley gapes open-mouthed at the glory of the Castle and Europe's loveliest street, but whereas Edinburgh has to be content with Arthur's Seat and the Pentland Hills, Glasgow is right in the shadow of the great bens of the Trossachs. The glory of Glasgow is an entirely different glory from that of Edinburgh.

The Clyde is the heart and soul of Glasgow while the Firth of Forth is only an adjunct to Edinburgh, and the proximity of great ships in the making all along the yards of Clydebank seems to link up Glasgow with the great world in a way that I never feel in Edinburgh. Glasgow is cosmopolitan; Edinburgh, by comparison, parochial.

I would rather live in Edinburgh, but I find Glasgow fuller of surprises and more exciting. And I have never been able to understand the slurs cast upon Sauchiehall Street, which I find as exhilarating as Broadway and infinitely kindlier. That probably is Glasgow's secret. It lacks shape. It sprawls uncomfortably on steep slopes that would make it easier to ski down than to cycle. It has great pockets of unbelievably sordid slums, but it is tremendously alive and in every quarter is packed with warm-hearted citizens who combine the strangest of assets: a love of literature and of the lonely hills with a knowledge of marine engineering to be found nowhere else in the world.

And it is, for its size, astonishingly easy to get out of. The Dumbarton Road leads so quickly to Helensburgh that you have to rub your eyes before you can believe that you are really once more on the threshold of the Highlands.

But there, high above you, stands the Cobbler almost as rugged as the peaks of the Cuillin, to assure you that this is no fancy.

From Edinburgh the way to the Highlands is long. There seem to be many false starts before you get to Pitlochry. Gleneagles, for instance, is pleasant enough moorland, but not a place to loiter in if you want arduous climbs and awe-inspiring vistas.

I am no great lover of the Trossachs, because they are over-exploited, but nobody could deny that Loch Lomond deserves all the panegyrics that have been lavished on it, and Loch Lomond is on Glasgow's doorstep.

You remember what Coleridge, Wordsworth, and Sir Walter Scott said about Loch Achray, and they were certainly connoisseurs. You may remember too the effect of the view from the top of the Cobbler on the two young men who were so impressed by its magnificence that they knelt down and dedicated their lives from that moment to the service and glory of God.

So it would be absurd to join in the chorus of detraction of the Trossachs. The worst that can be said about them is that they are accessible, and to the Glaswegian that is their great asset.

For those of us, however, who have come a long way and want to enjoy our Highland fastnesses in quietude, the extra step to Crianlarich is more than worth while.

It was when I caught my first view of Ben More that my Highland holiday would really begin, for Loch Tay was the first loch I visited as a child, and it was to the banks of Loch Tay that my mind had so often strayed during the previous six years. Not that I proposed to make my headquarters at Lawers where you look down on the blue waters, or even at Fearnan where you can hear the waves lapping against the jetty and the little beach. My favourite hotel lies just over the hill at the entrance to Scotland's longest and perhaps least known glen.

I have enjoyed so much happiness at Fortingall that it was difficult to believe that I could ever again recapture such peaks of ecstasy, and when I once again made contact with that Elysium, I doubted whether I should ever be able to drag myself away to continue a tour which would scarcely have begun; but I risked that, because there were certain excursions that I had to take, whatever else I missed. One was the 'bus drive along Glen Lyon to the Bridge of Balgie and the walk over the deer forest to Loch Rannoch. I have never rambled over this rough wet forest without encountering at least two herds of deer who seem to have been at least as anxious to see me as I have been to see them. At least, they have never run away.

Another cherished plan of mine was to continue up the glen past Meggernie to Loch Lyon which I still believe to be the most isolated loch in Scotland, and thence through the gap in the mountains that the Campbells passed on their memorable foray over Rannoch Moor to Glencoe. A third track that I meant to take from the Bridge of Balgie is the one that climbs southward to Loch Larig, under the shadow of Ben Lawers, where I hoped once again to see the golden eagle soaring in solitary state, high over the great peaks, and so down to rejoin the 'bus from Killin that would take me home along the northern shores of Loch Tay.

Whether I should ever again reach the top of Ben Lawers and scour the rocks for those rare Alpine plants that the botanists treasure so highly, or scale the razor-edge of the fairies' mountain of Schiehallion, would depend on the weather and my physical condition. As the years increase I find not equal exhilaration, but complete serenity in looking up at the peaks that I used to scale at incredible speed and with so much exhaustion, and after all, so far as Ben Lawers is concerned, there is always the pony.

I hoped at any rate to climb high enough to flush my capercailzie and ptarmigan, and put up a white hare, if not a wildcat. One of the compensations one gets, after the passion for scaling the highest peaks at the greatest speed has subsided, is the joy of exploring at leisure the rowan-fringed cataracts of the mountain burns.

I know no other part of Scotland where one can get

such rich and various reward for so little effort. And
the interest in Fortingall and Glen Lyon is not confined to the scenic. There are reminders at Fortingall
of Rome (it is claimed as the birthplace of Pontius
Pilate), and all along the glen are relics of prehistoric
occupation, and reminders of clan feuds, and ancient
legends.

Indeed, once having got back, the trouble would
be to tear myself away from the good food, the good
companionship, and the inexhaustible wealth of wild
moors, water, and heather-covered hills. This is the
parting of the ways. Fortingall stands in the very
heart of Scotland. I had a vast tract still to cover.
Should I go west or east?

Last time I had made a dash for Oban, and so rich
are my memories of that excellent centre that I decided to make the journey that way round again.

Of Oban itself I remembered best its sunsets over
Kerrara and the changing lights over the mysterious
island of Mull.

One excursion that I particularly looked forward
to was the day's sail in the *Loch Fyne* round Mull,
which crams more diverse enchantment and excitement into a few hours than we could hope for in
weeks in a foreign cruise.

There are, first, the ever-changing contours of the
brooding mountains and desolate moors of the island
itself, the view up Loch Linnhe towards Ben Nevis
and over the wild land of Morven. Then comes the
first port of call at Tobermory with its memories of
the sunken treasure-ships of the Armada. Then, as a
change from the quiet waters of the Sound of Mull,
there is the open sea beyond Loch Sunart, with the
low-lying islands of Coll and Tiree far out on the

western horizon, and near by to the north, the terrifying coast beyond Ardnamurchan.

I, as an indifferent sailor, am glad to see the ship turn south to hug the coast of Mull until we are put ashore in small boats to explore Fingal's colourful cave on the tiny rocky islet of Staffa. These polygonal basalt pillars are supposed to resemble those at the Giant's Causeway which I have not seen. They certainly resemble nothing else that I have seen. The cave is not deep or wide, but it is of tremendous height, and the rocks under the clear water are pink and blue and green, and make a far more exciting memorial to the great Gaelic hero than the poems of his son Ossian, which I find turgid and almost unreadable.

Just south of Staffa lies our third and most impressive port of call, the holy island of Iona. There is a Gaelic proverb which says that if you go to Iona once you will go there thrice. I hoped that proverb would hold true in my case, for I certainly wanted to see at least once more the home of St. Columba, the restored cathedral and the burying-place of those fifty-two Scottish kings.

Iona is a pleasant unassuming little island, a sort of Sicily at Mull's toe, rising to a height of only just over 300 feet. It wears so serene and happy a look that it is difficult to remember that the Vikings five times descended upon it to burn and murder the defenceless monks. It is just beyond Iona that we run past those treacherous rocks where David Balfour was shipwrecked and marooned before setting out on his great trek across Appin. The return journey along the southern coast of Mull provides more glimpses of the lively heights and gullies of the misty islands that I propose to explore—but not on this trip.

An almost equally exciting day's round tour that I
meant to take this time was the steamer trip up Loch
Etive under the lee of Ben Cruachan, by coach up the
wild glen round the foot of the giant Shepherds of
Etive to the white inn on King's House Moor and
then down into the sombre depths of Glencoe, which
still remains to me the most terrifying of all Scots
glens by reason of the black overhanging corries of
the great bleak crags into which the luckless Mac-
Donalds fled to escape the treachery of the Campbells,
250 years ago. Last stage of this memorable outing is
the evening cruise from Ballachulish down Loch
Linnhe, with the sun setting behind Morven.

From Oban I would make my way to Fort William,
not to climb Ben Nevis, which I shall probably for
ever leave unscaled, but to take the train past Glen-
finnan, Loch Shiel, and Arisaig with their haunting
memories of Prince Charles Edward, to take the
steamer at Mallaig up the Sound of Sleat towards
the misty isle of Skye, to smell again the sweet scent
of the bog-myrtle with which the whole island is
impregnated.

There are many places that called me with great
urgency in this island, first that chaos of water and
rocks known as the Quiraing where the echo used to
give back my daughter's name as I called it across the
vast abyss. I hoped this time that she would be with
me to call out herself in person.

I wanted to visit again the ruined castle of Duntulm,
once the main stronghold of the MacDonalds, Lords
of the Isles, to see the house where Flora MacDonald
gave sanctuary to the prince, and the churchyard of
Kilmuir where she lies buried, and so by way of
Tallisker to see if they still distil that wonderful whisky,

and on to the seat of MacLeod to gaze on the faded fairy flag and the famous Dunvegan Cup.

Then as fitting climax I proposed to spend a night among the climbers at the Sligachan inn before scrambling over the menacing bare crags of the Cuillin to peer down into the dragon-haunted depths of the inky-black waters of Loch Coruisk.

Several of the Cuillin peaks are over 3,000 feet high, but it is not their height but their shapes that are so forbidding.

On a misty day they can be dangerous. Even on a clear sunny day they are frightening. Here is Nature in her most elemental mood, raw, stark, and malevolent, but everybody who visits them feels the same fatal fascination. They both beckon and threaten. They dare you to essay their conquest, and they reward their conquerors not by a smile of welcome, but with a savage-toothed leer, betraying craggy chasm after craggy chasm into which a false step will pitch you headlong. The Cuillin hills are the only hills I know that are equally terrifying whether seen from far away or from their very heart.

From Portree I would cross the Minch to Stornoway, not to climb hills but to revisit the wonderful stone circle at Callernish, perhaps even to hear again what I have heard only once in my life, the authentic notes of fairy music, and certainly to visit some of those gentle, hardy, hospitable crofters who have solved the art of being completely self-supporting. It is amazing to discover how few are man's needs and with what skill he is able in that unfertile land to build his own black house, provide his own food, and send out children into the great world fully equipped to make their mark in almost every walk of life. If I had time I would then set sail for the rich fertile land of Orkney to wander round the ancient burial-ground of Maeshowe, explore the Stone Age village of Skara Brae, and watch the golden plover wheel above the Stones of Stennes.

I would go to Rousay to see the eider-duck, the tern, and the puffins, and perhaps again encounter a shark, and having got so far I would doubtless succumb to the temptation to go on to Lerwick and revisit the bird-haunted cliffs on the Holm of Noss and watch the great auks swoop down on the flying gulls and force them to disgorge their prey. There can be few sights in the world more impressive to the bird-lover than that 600-feet-high cliff face with every ledge filled with kysties, skuas, gannets, and every other imaginable sea-bird. And I hoped to return the richer by a Shetland jumper or so, and perhaps even bring back Shetland ponies for the children.

But I should not be able to dally long among the islands, fascinating as they are, for there remained a great slice of the mainland that my heart yearned to see again at the first possible moment.

So from Lerwick I would sail straight back to Aberdeen, that enchanting scintillating city of shining granite, which is architecturally the most homogeneous of all cities, and in generous hospitality quite outstanding. Aberdeen is the sort of city where you must arrive with one suitcase empty because the Aberdonian is not only prolific in generosity, but makes it a point of honour to see that his gifts are not only acceptable but accepted.

Here are vast stretches of sand to bask on, a clear sea to bathe in, a constant procession of fine ships to watch coming into and going out from the great

harbour, alluring shop windows, smiling and courteous shop assistants, luxurious hotels, an atmosphere
of great intellectual activity, and an electrically in-
vigorating keen air. And, most unexpected of all,
the nightingale. I have never heard the nightingale
sing in Berkeley Square, but I have often heard him
in the night-watches sing between the Brig o' Don and
the Brig o' Dee. And the word Dee reminds me of
my main reason for going back to Aberdeen. It was,
of course, to explore again what is generally acknow-
ledged to be the bleakest, bonniest, and boldest of all
Scottish rivers.

Deeside above Ballater is quite incomparable. First
there is the noble sweep of the broad river through
the densely wooded, gracious country that surrounds
Balmoral below the cone-shaped Craigendorrach, the
magnificent dark Lochnagar and the huge mass of
Morven.

Then comes the great Keep of Invercauld and
Braemar with its memories of great Highland Gatherings. I supposed the Highland Games would come
back, but whether they did or not, there would always
remain the great walk over the Larig under the shadow
of Braeriach and Cairn Toul down into the forest of
Rothiemurchus and so into the sweet wide strath of
Speyside.

Two wild rough mountain walks over crag and
through stream cried out to be repeated, that of the
Larig, and the way Prince Charles Edward took to
outwit the pursuing Hanoverians over the Corrie-
arick. I meant to conquer both those lovely fastnesses, but if I might have only one, I would choose
the Larig because it would take me right into the
heart of the Cairngorms, the most richly rewarding

of all the high ranges. Here I would be certain of my stags and my golden eagle, as well as of my capercailzie and ptarmigan.

Here I would be certain of having that sense of humility in the presence of great majesty that comes to one only in the presence of such fierce and savage heights as Ben Macdhui. I had never passed through the narrow gorge at the top of the Larig without a sense of awe and fear, and I wanted to recapture again that strange exhilarating feeling of the unimportance of one's own personal anxieties and ambitions and the importance of the continuity of the eternal hills, unscarred and unaffected by the petty strife of man. It is certainly good for us to lift up our eyes to the hills whenever we get the chance. It is certainly essential for our soul's health. The grandeur of these heights impresses even those who only pass by in the far distance in the train. I never met anyone who has come into close contact with them who does not speak of them with reverence. They can be, as J. J. Bell once said, terrible in their desolation, woeful where they are most wonderful, but they inspire us also with a sense of the sublime and sometimes even of godlike serenity. And what a superb contrast is provided when we descend on the farther side into the soft mossy gracious glades that lead to the enchanted tree-fringed little Loch-an-Eilean where Captain Knight tried to reintroduce the osprey. To cross this great divide between Dee and Spey is to run through the whole gamut of human emotions, and for this reason alone I put the Larig walk as the climax of the whole tour.

My way now lay north by way of Culloden Moor, which always wears a stricken look, to the gay and lovely northern capital of Inverness, the most consciously Scottish of all Scots towns in spite of the purity of the English that is characteristic of all the natives when they are not speaking Gaelic among themselves.

The Victorian tourists used to sail down the whole length of the Caledonian Canal.

I had never done that, and did not propose to do so now. I would probably stand on the tower of Castle Urquhart and scan the waters of Loch Ness in vain for a sight of the monster of whose existence I have never been in doubt, but there are glens hereabout that would call me away from the great glen, notably Glen Garry, Glen Moriston, Glen Affric, and Glen Cannich, and how was I to find time (I meant to!) to get back to the white inn of Clunie and gaze once more upon the Five Sisters of Kintail? There are times when I think that Compton Mackenzie was right when he sent me off from Strath Glass to explore what he called the finest glen in all Scotland, and so far as tumbling cataracts and a wealth of trees are concerned, I think the palm must be conceded to Glen Affric. The contrast here is so vivid between the great bare shoulders of the snow-capped austere Mam Soul and the gentleness of the loch below, that one remembers this setting long after better known vistas have faded from the mind.

But comparisons between the various lochs and glens of the Northern Highlands are invidious. Somehow I meant to find time to get back to Loch Torridon, Loch Maree, Loch Broom, and Loch Assynt, and though their very inaccessibility may have something to do with the glory that we attach to them, I still think that each of these four is in its own kind unbeatable. The first three are of course sea-lochs, which means that their shores are fringed with a golden hem of seaweed. And there are unforgettable islands jewelled in Loch Maree, and the great bare massive cliffs of granite that overhang them are as intimidating as the Cuillin.

Most impressive of all are the rough-hewn black Quinag and the narrow serrated ridges of the sharp hump of Suilven, rising up like the Matterhorn, the most eerie in shape as it is the most difficult of access of all Highland mountains.

Having seen these I would be content to return as speedily as may be to Edinburgh, my last port of call.

It is unnecessary to enlarge upon the fascination that Edinburgh possesses, not only for all Scotsmen, but for visitors from all over the world.

The memories evoked during a stroll along the Royal Mile take us back to Mary Queen of Scots, Darnley, Prince Charles Edward, John Knox, Robert Louis Stevenson, Deacon Brodie, Burke and Hare, and a host of other notable and notorious persons of the past. No other street is so packed with legend and history.

And in Princes Street it is not only the spaciousness and grace that draw us. The lure of the shops is as strong as the lure of the gardens, for it would be un-thinkable to go south without loading ourselves up with tins of Edinburgh Rock and the famous short-bread, and adding yet another tartan to our array of kilts to which we have no legitimate claim. Then there are those brogues. I haven't bought a pair of shoes outside Scotland for over twenty years.

I am no lover of shops, but I make an exception of Edinburgh. Even its bookshops seem to contain better books than the London shops. But Edinburgh's glory is insidious and not easily definable. Something of its secret is to be found in the dignity of George Street and Charlotte Square where you feel that you are a member of a friendly family circle, and might at any moment see De Quincey, Scott, Burns, Dr. John Brown, Sydney Smith, Raeburn, or Carlyle emerge from one of these stately porticos which have altered scarcely at all since their day. The atmosphere of this part of Edinburgh is sedate and leisurely, redolent of the century in which its spacious houses were built. I am no lover of towns, but I would willingly live in Edinburgh, and I have never yet stayed in it without being entertained so lavishly as to make me extremely reluctant to face the southern journey.

I hope I have made it clear why my main peace-time project was to return to Scotland. It was because I would be sure of gaining intense æsthetic and physical delight in climbing well-loved hills, wandering by the side of rippling burns, watching birds that I hadn't seen for six years, and cementing old friendships. The rest of the world could wait. For me the call was insistent and clear. It was to lie in the heather, listen to the 'whaups', and rest my eyes upon the distant peaks. There I would find the spiritual refection for which I had pined for so long.

If in the outcome my actual physical performance fell short of what I had promised myself, well—what is a man's aim for, if not to exceed his grasp? The exigencies of time and space cramp and limit our bodies, but the spirit roams free. What I have not been able to visit in the flesh, I have returned to in my memories. If my inspiration has led me to disconnected experiences rather than a continuous itinerary, I hope none the less that I have given a fair picture of the better parts of Scotland, and that my return will inspire readers to make the journey for themselves and see how right I am.

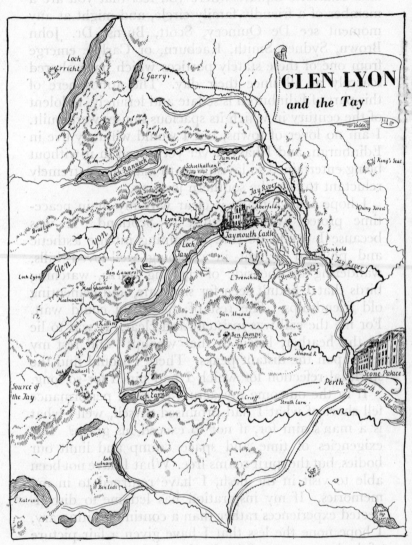

GLEN LYON
and the Tay

Loch Urricht

L Garry

Velda

King's Seat

Loch Rannoch

Schiehallion

L Tummel

Cluny Forest

Tay River

Aberfeldy

Brae Lyon

Lyon R

Glen

Lyon

Glen

Taymouth Castle

Loch

Tay

Dunkeld

Tay River

Loch Lyon

Ben Lawers

L Frenchie

Strath Bran

Meal ghaordie

Mealnazow

Glen Almond

Glen Lochay

Killin

Ben Chonzie

Almond R

Glen Dochart

Loch Dochart

Scone Palace

Source of
the Tay

Perth

Firth of Tay

Loch Earn

Crieff

Strath Earn

Loch Dome

Loch
Lubnaig

Ben Ledi

L Katrine

The Trosachs

CHAPTER ONE

Back to Glen Lyon

PRACTICALLY never in life does the reality of a good thing come up to one's memory or anticipation of it. Scotland alone always exceeds my most sanguine expectations.

I left Euston on a very foggy, cheerless night, but my sleeper was not on the wheels. I slept. I ate a prodigious breakfast at the Station Hotel, Perth, and being for once in my life in no hurry, gave myself up to a perfect orgy of shopping in the first city where I have met civility in shop assistants for six years. I bought a compass (I'm a mountain climber by passionate instinct and know how much depends on the possession of a compass), two pipes with square bowls that make equilibrium easy from the urbane and knowledgeable Mr. Rattray, one sporran for my nine-year-old daughter, a fountain pen, a diary, a copy of Allan Ramsay, a copy of James Fergusson, a copy of Waterton, and an exquisite edition of Isaak Walton full of magnificent engravings. I then had lunch in the sun at the Royal George (have I mentioned that I had run into a heat wave, in October?), and then lay on a bench in the South Inch looking down on the cairngorm-coloured waters of the Tay listening to the

25

prattle of two young repertory actors who were resting between bouts of *The Cherry Orchard.* Two Black
Watch soldiers sold me a scarlet hackle, a pleasant
souvenir for a Flag Day, and somewhere in the
distance I heard pipes. At 3.50 the top-hatted station-
master was promising me a sleeper for my return
journey, and at four o'clock I was on my way to see
Birnam wood yellowing before its annual pilgrimage
to Dunsinane.

It was just forty years ago, when I was an undergraduate, that I was first introduced to Glen Lyon.
I was callow and a Sassenach, but after all I am a
hillsman. I should have known better. I fell into
the common trap of believing that Perthshire must
be less worth while than Sutherland because it is more
accessible.

Since that far-off day I have seen many glens and
climbed many hills in many parts of the world, but
I've never climbed a hill that gave me a richer reward
than Ben Lawers, and I've never walked a glen more
filled with beauty than Glen Lyon. Don't tell me that
Glen Affric is wilder. I know that. Many glens are
wilder. No glen has for me more atmosphere.

It had become even more precious to me because I
never expected to see it again. After six years of war
it is I who have changed, not the glen. I came back
battered in body, soul, and mind. I left it after a
fortnight a whole man again. Let me tell you what
I did.

At 5.9 I was met by my host at Aberfeldy station
and I entered my dream land. There wasn't a cloud
in the sky to hide the razor-like edge of Schiehallion
or the awe-inspiring massif of Ben Lawers. We drove
through the grounds of Taymouth Castle, full of

convalescent Polish soldiers, past Kenmore, along the banks of Loch Tay in the still waters of which the trees on the fringe of the loch were so brilliantly reflected that it was impossible to distinguish the real from the mirage.

We arrived at the white thatched-roofed hamlet of Fortingal at the sinking of the sun.

There was no sound at all beyond the call of the curlew, the chewing of the cud by the beasts, the chirping of the birds, and the ripple of a burn.

Rooks were homing along the sides of Drummond Hill. We had venison and red-currant jelly for dinner, and a bottle of 1929 Château Mouton Rothschild. Do you wonder that I slept soundly?

You may be surprised to learn that I spent my first morning shopping in Aberfeldy. You will be less surprised when I tell you that I have long ago ceased to enter shops in England. I have no time to join queues. I spent all my coupons for four years in one shop in an hour. Ever since I can remember I have bought all my clothes in that shop. I like being reminded in my overcoat, coat, trousers, scarf, cap, and stockings that the colours of the sphagnum moss, the russet bracken, the bare trunks of beech trees, the scarlet of the rowan, and the green of the bog myrtle are still flourishing in Scotland. In English cloth they give, or rather sell us at very high price, when they have any, colours that never were on sea or land and blend with nothing except the primitive Technicolor films.

Furthermore, I am met with courtesy and warm friendliness by the shopkeepers of Aberfeldy. I need that inner warmth badly after battling with the vulgar shambles of southern shops. But it is disconcerting.

27

It is so long since anybody seemed pleased to see me. If you are English you will scarcely believe me when I say that I left the bicycle that I was able to hire (fancy being able to hire a bicycle) resting by the kerb outside shops without locking it.

Bus drivers leave parcels and papers on the walls and in the hedges in the sure knowledge that they will be picked up by their rightful owners. To me that is so staggering that I have to pinch myself to assure myself that I am still alive. Perhaps I am dead and this is Heaven. If it is Heaven, I am well content. I have no wish to return to the earth that is post-war England.

The day continued cloudless. Our host drove us to Lawers where my wife rode with Mr. McLellan, the soft-voiced ghillie, up to the top of Ben Lawers while I trailed along slowly on foot behind, bewildered and enchanted in a sea of golden bracken. She saw an eagle and I mistook a stone for a stag. I picked some golden saxifrage and star-shaped cudweed. After three and a half hours we were standing on the summit, 3,984 feet above sea level, and looked down on a quite unbelievable world.

I first climbed Ben Lawers thirty-eight years ago. I have climbed it many times since. As it stands right in the centre of the central Highlands you would expect the view to be exceptionally good even for Scotland, but with all my experience of it the view on this cloudless October day far transcended anything that I could have hoped for or ever imagined. There was, in spite of the still heat in the valley, a slight but icy blizzard coming in from the north-west, but at 4,000 feet up you do not expect stillness or heat.

When I say that every peak for fifty miles round in

28

every direction stood up as clear as hills on a relief map, you will get no idea of what I was looking at. The Paps of Jura stood up out of a wreath of white; but elsewhere there was no veil of any kind except in the far south-east where a gauze-like heat-haze dimmed a little the Bass Rock and Arthur's Seat. The Cobbler clearly showed the nearness of Glasgow; Ben Macdhui, Cairntoul and the Cairngorm guarded the approach to Deeside. The elephantine mass of Ben Nevis seemed only a stone's throw from the yawning gap where the Shepherds of Etive guarded the portals of Glencoe. There was very little water to see, just the snaky track of blue Loch Tay at our southern foot, the silver Dochart stealing away under Ben More, and an unexpectedly light green patch on the north side of Rannoch that revealed Loch Ericht.

It was like standing in the middle of a giant-tumbled quilt. No, it wasn't. It was like standing on top of the world. It was on top of the world. I found it very difficult to believe that I was there. I now find it very difficult to believe that I have ever been there. It was so stupendous that I had to pretend to look for Alpine plants, and my wife, in white-rimmed sun-glasses looking as if she was a Vogue cover girl, began weighing herself down with lumps of quartz under the pretence of looking for cairngorms. That is the plain truth of it. It was so nearly sublime that, coming up from a world where sublimity is never even approximated to, it seemed quite unreal. We felt like Adam and Eve back in the Garden of Eden after being expelled. We needed more notice of this revelation of God's glory. No wonder the disciples talked nonsense on the Mount of Transfiguration. We felt quite un-worthy of the vision. I couldn't go on saying "Isn't

29

it wonderful?" I took a lot of photographs only to find that the camera wasn't working. That seems to me to be fair. I still have my eyes. I lay in a crevice on the south side of the summit, in the sun and out of the wind (just imagine!), munched venison sandwiches and drained a whole flask of whisky. The only place where whisky tastes as whisky should is on the top of a mountain. I lay there for one blessed golden hour by the clock. It was a lifetime of healing bliss. I have never known anything like it. I shall never know anything like it again. I was faintly surprised by the complete absence of other climbers on such a day. Just below the top razor-edge where the screes run steeply down to the sinister black lochan nan Cat I met a black-haired, black-eyed girl in a yellow jumper and shorts accompanied by a boy and a collie. She told me that she was a Hellene, and had but lately landed from Greece. She agreed that Lawers on this October day eclipsed the Parnassus, Olympus, Pelion, Ossa, and Athos. I was not surprised. She went on her way singing. If Wordsworth had been there we should have had a memorable lyric. "Will no one tell me what she sings?" It was Greek to me, but very, very lovely. An oread on the slopes of Lawers. I watched her gazelle-like movements as she sped upwards. For a moment I felt like following her. My wife, Mr. McLellan, the boy, and the collie might have misunderstood my impulse. I refrained, but I feel that I have missed something. I have an affinity with the Greeks, and with Scotland. I believe the oread would have been sympathetic. Feeling restless I strode over the boulders, and tumbled about the peat bog far ahead of the pony and the ghillie. I wanted to be by myself. Except for three and a half brace of

30

grouse I had the world to myself for the next two and a half hours. I moved as if in a dream, a dream in which the Greek girl took a curiously prominent part. When, therefore, I reached the little hotel at the foot of Lawers and found the oread already in possession I felt that my vision of the day was being a little too good to be true. It was only when the Glaswegian girl in charge of affairs said that the hotel was closed (we were standing inside it), that she didn't serve teas (I could hear the kettle singing on the hob) and then charged 1s. 6d. for two cups unaccompanied by food, served with surly grimaces, that I realised that we were down from the Mount of Transfiguration. So passed my first day. I shall not lightly forget it.

The next day was Sunday. It was cloudless. My wife and I set off with two baskets (we always take a basket each) to collect sloes. We spent one hour gossiping with two farmers about the following day's sheep-dipping. I was, as usual, mistaken for a rich English farmer and told that I must be making a lot of money if I could afford to come up to Scotland and pay £80 for a heifer.

My wife disappeared to pick sloes. I slept like a lizard on a hot stone till noon when the Sassenach Sunday noon-tide instinct woke me sharply. The shimmering ripples on the vast loch below the hill reminded me of the fact that the Tigh-an-Loan Hotel at Fearnan was but a step. Within ten minutes I was quaffing a quart of ice-cold beer in the sun on the jetty. I was very nearly late for luncheon. Sunday luncheon at Fortingall is something of a ritual. There were thirty-seven different varieties of hors d'œuvre. There were pickled apricots, Roquefort cheese, mush-rooms, grapefruit . . . I forgot the glory that was

Greece in the gourmet that was me. There was omelette de l'Estragor, there was more venison, there was Yorkshire mint pasty, and if you've never tasted Yorkshire mint pasty you've got something coming to you that will make your mouth water. At three o'clock I was in the kirk. I just had time to notice the good taste in tweeds of the village girls and to find difficulty in tracing the Paraphrase in my Prayer Book before sinking into a profound sleep. Four times during the sermon I was summoned back from the waters of Lethe by my patient wife who dislikes my snoring in church, poor wretch.

My dreams that night were confused. I was wearing a kilt, carrying a sgur dhu, and I was attempting to scale overhanging cornices to get away from dark figures who were searching for me in the heather far below. I remember being filled with a sense of elation because I knew that they had missed me and could never scale the crags that I had scaled. I was, I need scarcely add, accompanied by a most fascinating, understanding, fleet-footed oread.

My dreams at home are seldom dreams of triumph. If I have to run my legs are clogged with mud, but now my movements were as light as air. Perhaps the hors d'œuvre had something to do with it.

But I set out to tell you about the Glen. After all, it is the scenery and the people whose happy lot is cast in this fair ground that have restored me to sanity. Each morning at 11.30 Donald draws up at the hotel door in the 'bus bound for Killin. Each morning at 10.10 George (accompanied by Rita) passes on his way up the Glen over the Bridge of Balgie.

Donald has a happy gift of being able to throw

32

BRAEMAR CASTLE

RIVER DEE NEAR BRAEMAR

out papers with his right hand that land exactly on the front-door steps or the garden gates of the crofts while his left hand turns the steering wheel. Donald doesn't stop much. George and Rita stop at every house.

Let me tell you about George and Rita. Their mail van arrives earlier, as I told you. Their destination is halfway up the largest and I believe the finest glen in all Scotland. At the entrance the hills fall so steeply and fold over so neatly above the river that you can't believe that there is a glen. It's exactly like the entrance to the caves in Cheddar Gorge. You get no premonition of the magnificence to come. But almost at once the hills fall back to give light and air to the fertile, wide strath, and the Glen begins.

George is a wit. George is God's gift to the Glen crofters. He has not only a paper or a letter for each of them, but a smile and a wisecrack too. Need I tell you that he calls each of them of whatever age or sex by his or her Christian name? I don't believe they have surnames in Glen Lyon.

Rita is sixteen. She is trim, slim, small-featured, pink and white, smiling, and lovely. Some day if I ever stop working I am going to run away with Rita, but we shan't run far, only to the tops of these enchanting hills. Rita is an oread of the Highlands.

She wears a dark-blue coat trimmed with silver buttons, a green frock, green handkerchief with yellow spots over the rich brown hair that is 'snooded abune her brae', and pure silk stockings encase her comely legs. Like the view from the top of Ben Lawers, Rita has to be seen to be believed. I don't believe there is a Rita. I believe that I dreamt her. She is as good a dream as ever Coleridge dreamt.

At Inverar there is a daily parade of seven or eight

B   33

ghillies, stalkers, and their families. They stand at attention, waiting on George's pleasure. Ultimately he calls the roll, Donald, Stuart, Jean, Ian, and the rest. They are then allowed to step out of the ranks and claim their precious post.

Rita, my darling Rita, leaves us, silent as a stag, at Camusvrachan to deliver the letters on a bicycle on the south side of the Glen where is no road. As at this point I am always lost in wonderment at the colours of the birks and the rowans, I never see her go until it is too late, and she is just a slim, trim figure of a solitary Highland lass on a bicycle. At Innerwick I myself leave George, not unobtrusively, though I usually forget to pay him. There is no coin adequate enough to pay this ferryman. I have no obols. At Innerwick I take the wet, stony, winding track up the Larig to descend on Loch Rannoch by way of the woods of Carie.

On the way up on this occasion I met Colonel Wills stalking what he called the greatest stag in all Scotland. I saw it. He didn't. On the way down I encountered Sir Ambrose Guise, followed by a pony dragging three dead stags whose faces and bodies were bedewed with the wet heather. He agreed that they looked more imposing alive. So do we all.

The 'bus terminus is a few hundred yards beyond Innerwick, at the Bridge of Balgie, where there is a double choice of route, but only one man to give you eggs and bannocks for tea, the kindly Mr. M'Connel, whose talk is a clear Pierian spring.

A winding track takes you up into the hills under the Cuillin-like crags of Ben-nan-Eachan, a truly fearsome sight, to rest at the cairn that looks down on Loch-an-Larig and then fall down to the shores of Loch Tay

on the Killin road at Edramucky. As George doesn't
reach the Bridge of Balgie till 11.30, and Donald
passes Edramucky at 3.10, and as I have to stop when
I see an eagle perched on a boulder within one
hundred yards of me, it needs more stamina than I
possess to make the contact. I know the distance to
be a mere ten or eleven miles, and the climb a paltry
1,800 feet, but I am growing old. I missed the 'bus
by twenty minutes.

As I was immediately picked up by a farmer in a
fast car, I was in on it, for it gave me time for tea at
the Tigh-an-Loan at Fearnan before trekking over the
pass at Easter Achtar to Fortingall for my Lucullan
dinner.

But perhaps the cream of all the walks is straight
on up the glen, past the white castle of Meggernie,
towards Loch Lyon, where you can thread your way
past the burial grounds and take the way that Captain
Robert Campbell took across Rannoch moor when he
went to massacre the MacDonalds of Glencoe.

But that is quite a trek. I am content to poke about
among the giant ant-hills where the myriad ants
imported from Brazil make whoopee for the pheasants.
There is furthermore a hazardous swinging angler's
bridge that spans a deep waterfall that I cross and
recross to gauge how near I am to being cured. I am
quite cured to-day, thank you. I find it less exciting
but much more beautiful (*pace* Wordsworth) than
Westminster Bridge.

Have I made it clear that I quite like Glen Lyon?
Good. Then why not see it for yourself? After all,
you live only just round the corner. I've got to come
all the way from Oxford. Perhaps that explains
something.

CHAPTER TWO

Between Spean and Spey

THEY always tell me at home that I'm just crazy about
Scotland. If anybody previously ignorant of what
Scotland has to offer could have been with me on
this occasion—it was the 18th October 1945—he
would, I think, have gone crazy too. Writing, as I
am, under the grey lowering clouds of a winter day
in Oxford, I find it hard to believe that I saw what I
saw. It came as a fitting climax to a cloudless fortnight
in Glen Lyon.

The morning, as I drove along the shores of Loch
Tay, was so misty that I saw neither the waters of the
loch nor any part of the slopes of Ben Lawers. A veil
had been drawn over the scenes of my delectable
wanderings. The fog was so dense that the driver kept
having to stop. He couldn't see the wall on either
side of the road. I felt that it was just as well. So, for
all I cared, beauty might as well veil herself once
more. At Killin there was just time to call in at
Grant's, the antique shop that had been closed when
I visited Killin the week before. How low the fortunes
of Killin have sunk since I was a boy was evident from
the number of shops that now seemed to be permanently closed. Even the hotel had been burnt out.

37

But I found a little lurid oil-painting of Glencoe, and as I was about to drive down Glencoe I thought it would prove a permanent memento of the occasion, so I bought it. I then made a dash for my train. I changed at the junction and then entered a much too hot, overcrowded train bound from Glasgow to Oban. I found shelter in a first-class carriage containing a young black-haired Adonis, dressed as a Tyrolean peasant, accompanied by a lovely blonde ballet-dancer.

"You are," I said, "an artist."

"You," he replied, "too?"

"You do me too much honour," I said. I looked out of the window. The mist was lifting. The leaves on the trees were yellow and shining like ripe apricots.

"An artist has been at work here," I went on.

"My hat!" said my Adonis.

"Golly!" added his companion.

There seemed to be nothing that I could add to those heart-felt panegyrics. After all, what would Wordsworth have said? I went on looking.

"I've never been here before," said Adonis.

"It's like waiting for the curtain to rise on Pavlova in *Les Sylphides*," I said to the ballet-dancer as we ran once again into the white pall of fog.

Suddenly a loch with tiny wooded islet appeared under the white mist, and the leaves of the trees were saffron-yellow.

"It's more exciting than Pavlova," said the ballet-dancer.

"I've never been here before," repeated Adonis. "I'd no idea."

"Where's your Tyrol now?" I asked as we passed under the shadow of Ben More and Stobinian, the

38

tops now suddenly clear under a perfect azure sky. It was a most wayward, tantalising mist, now hiding the whole world, now revealing only the low ground and then for a second or two the peaks.

"Why has nobody told me about this before?" asked Adonis.

"Where are you going?" I asked.

"Loch Awe—for the day," said Adonis.

"Majesty and awe, you'll get both," I said. "But you'd get something more if you came with me. It's going to be a day in a million."

The clouds then disappeared as if by magic. They didn't roll away. They just melted before our eyes. Suddenly there wasn't a cloud in the sky. Range upon range of high peaks were revealed in clear-cut detail in full glory.

"If you can reproduce this on canvas," said Adonis, "you'll be immortal."

"My painting," I retorted, "has to be done in words."

"And mine in music," he said. "One might be a setting for the other. What a symphony! What a lyric!"

"I'm not even going to try," I said. "I've come to rest my eyes, to heal my heart."

The train drew in to the bare platform of Tyndrum. I got out, leaving Adonis as rapt as Paris was on first seeing Helen of Troy. One solitary climber, weighed down with ropes, climbing-irons, and nailed boots, with a copy of *Convoy* sticking out of a pocket, stood waiting for the 'bus.

"Shepherds of Etive?" I asked.

"Just that," he smiled.

"Good climbing," I said.

39

"It ought to be," he replied. "What a bit of luck hitting a day like this."

I was being met. The chauffeur was young. I hoped he was not a Londoner.

"Where are you from?" I asked.

"Ardgour," he said.

"Good," I replied. "I've not been back for fifteen years, so I want to see what there is to see. Not too fast."

"I understand. Tell me when you want to stop."

"I don't want to start. I want to stay here for ever and just look. I don't believe I'm here."

"I understand. It's looking bonny to-day. But it gets better as we go along, and we've a long way to go."

Reluctantly I got into the car.

The road stretched endlessly into the distance. There was neither man nor vehicle nor human habitation in sight, only bare hill upon bare hill, a wide waste moorland of mahogany- and russet-coloured bracken and dark peat-bog. "The best road in Scotland," said the chauffeur, admiringly.

"I'm not worrying about the road," I replied.

A narrow defile between grim heights to the east marked the track that the Campbells took from Glen Lyon on that winter day 250 years ago to massacre the unsuspecting MacDonalds at the foot of Glencoe. I got a fleeting glimpse of the Orchy winding its way down to Dalmally, and soon we were on the bleak unwooded shores of Loch Tulla watching a lonely red-painted royal mail van speeding towards the Big House. It looked rather like an exotic scarlet bird darting over the dark moor.

Then we began climbing towards the hairpin bend

above Darybeg, towards Black Mount and the waters of Loch Ba and Loch Laidon.

I suppose there are wilder stretches of high land in the world than Rannoch Moor, but there are none that I know where I feel such a sense of emptiness and desolation.

And yet the grass by the hedgeless roadside was both golden and velvety. Far, far away to the east beyond Loch Rannoch stood the peak of Schiehallion, sun-kissed. The road turned away suddenly to the west under Clach Leathad towards the grim rocky heights of the Shepherds of Etive towering above the shining Kingshouse Hotel, now standing a little aloof and lonely away from the new road. Each separate inaccessible crag of the Shepherds was so heavily etched that it looked like an engraved copy of them etherealised.

Below us the road wound down between grimmer and grimmer hills, closing in and folding over the Glen o' Weeping.

Glencoe has the reputation of being always sinister, and indeed it is a Dantesque chasm, but on this day of unclouded blue skies its majesty inspired serenity rather than awe. As I looked up to Ossian's Cave, instead of feeling terror, as I usually do, I felt a strong desire to get out of the car and essay the climb. Down and down we went into the depths of the gorge. The old road down the glen is now as grass-covered and derelict as any prehistoric track or disused Roman road. I had no idea that roads went back as quickly as derelict fields. I had forgotten how long the glen is and the way it becomes gentle and wooded as it approaches the scene of the massacre.

On this colourful, sunny October morning the small

white cottages of Glencoe village looked gay, and the villagers carefree and cheerful. Swans and gulls were swimming on the surface on the sea-loch. I had even forgotten that Glencoe was a coastal village. It wore the look of a seaside holiday resort. Ships were serenely steaming up towards the Caledonian Canal, ships that might possibly have just reached this heavenly haven from the Atlantic. We drove on along the seaweed-girt Loch Leven, past the red-roofed busy industrial town of Kinlochleven, and were soon nestling under the shadow of the elephantine Ben Nevis that towers above Fort William.

I was in no mood to climb mountains. The sun was too hot for that. I was well content to explore the fascinating shops of this busy town, and then to sit on the quay-side and watch the changing colours on the hills on the other side of the loch as the sun gradually declined.

There was one moment when their slopes were rose-pink, another when they had changed to crimson velvet, then back they went to pearl-grey and so to jet black. As my bedroom in the house where I was staying also looked out on the water I was able next morning, before proceeding on my way, once more to watch the change of colour on these slopes from dark blue to pearl-grey and russet-brown.

I had the great good fortune to have as guide on the second stage of my journey a native who was as enthusiastic as he was knowledgeable.

Our way lay past Spean Bridge, near which we passed some Celtic resting-places for biers. According to my guide these bodies often had as many as four hundred followers, each of whom had to place a stone on the cairn that was built, wherever the body rested

42

on its journey, to prevent the ghost of the dead man or woman from haunting the scene.

There were silver birches, yellow maples, and elders all along the route. The elders were not yellow. Their leaves had turned a dirty brown. At Brae Roy we came to a stronghold of the Catholic MacDonalds. The big church that we passed was, I was told, built by the Irish Catholics who helped to build the famous tunnel that runs through the hills to take water from Loch Treig to the aluminium works at Fort William. This tunnel, which is over fifteen miles long, and has a diameter of 15 feet 2 inches, was begun in 1926 and finished three years later. It is a magnificent piece of engineering, and has left no disfiguring mark whatever on the scenery. On my way up to see the men at work on Loch Treig we passed a butcher who, my informant told me, took a toll of over 50,000 deer from the forests every year. When we got out of the car at the foot of Loch Treig we boarded an open trolley which took us up to the engineer's hut. Here we stood in a high wind and watched a crew of men attempting quite in vain to row a heavy barge towards a spot in the middle of the loch where work was going on to clear a rock that had fallen into the opening of the tunnel, which was 145 feet below the surface of the water—an unenviable job for the divers. The geological stratum here is of extraordinary interest. I kept on picking up pieces of shining stone, black mica, yellow topazes, and so on. I also passed the remnants of the ancient Caledonian oak forest that had been burnt down in 1565 to clear the robbers and wolves from their hide-out.

As we drove back down the rough track to regain the main road, we passed a millstone by the side of a burn bearing the inscription 'To the memory of Angus, 15th chief of MacDonald of Keppoch'. My guide told me that the water here in Drumly is green in summer and red in winter. If he told me the reason I've forgotten it. He also entertained me with a story of a lorry driver with a neat turn for apt metaphor. "Pull?" this man Cameron is reported to have said about his recalcitrant engine. "Pull? She couldn't pull a drunken woman downstairs backwards."

We came to a halt at the granite dam that holds up the waters of the Laggan, which has a most substantial balustrade specially constructed for one of the directors of the scheme because he feared heights.

The drive under the trees alongside the blue waters of Loch Laggan reminded me of the time when we used to picnic there in the far-off days when I used to spend my summer holidays on Speyside.

We cut over the hill to Loch Crunachan to see the most romantic track in all Scotland, the road cut by General Wade over the Corrieyarack, the pass that Prince Charles Edward and his followers crossed to outwit the English army in 1745. It is more years than I care to remember since I last flogged my weary way over that watery, stony track. On this occasion I was content to stand on the Spey dam and look down on the ingenious and expensive concrete fish-ladders especially constructed to satisfy the Spey Fishing Board, who demand that forty-eight salmon a year should be permitted to get up the river.

This used to be a great cattle country in the days of Cluny Macpherson. On the knoll above I saw the monument to his wife, who stood on this spot to see her house in the strath below burnt to the ground after the '45. And so we came to the two churches at

44

Laggan Bridge and Cluny Castle, where the Macphersons spent so much of their patrimony entertaining royalty. In spite of the fact that there was a price of £30,000 put on the head of old Cluny, he was hunted without avail for nine years, hiding in a cave in his own grounds and protected by his clan.

As we looked across the Spey to the distant Cairngorms my guide said, with a gasp of horror, "The witch's apron of snow has gone. There'll be a terrible disaster." He refused to commit himself further, so we drove in silence through Newtonmore and at last came to the end of our journey at Kingussie. I had not been here for thirty years, but it seemed to me not to have changed at all. It still looked solid and prosperous. The hotels were, even in October, full. The shops were inviting. The station platform, as I stood in the moonlight waiting for the night mail to take me back to Glasgow seemed to me to be like the gate of the Garden of Eden from which I was soon to be exiled.

CHAPTER THREE

The Tay

WHAT the Tweed was to Sir Walter Scott the Tay is to me. It is the first Scots river I knew, the first I swam in, the first I fished, the first I saw. It represents to me the border between one land and another, the threshold of enchantment.

It is exactly fitting that the magic woods of Birnam should stand above this river, for the whole course of these peat-brown waters is magical.

Other rivers, the Thames for instance, have their source in a tiny trickle or spring. The Tay, like the Lyon, has its source in a loch, fifteen miles long and in some places 500 feet deep.

There may be a river Tay flowing into the loch at the western end at Killin, but if there is I have not yet found it. I am told that the source lies twenty-five miles beyond the loch. But where?* The Dochart as everyone knows dashes wildly down past the burial ground of the MacNabs in its haste to mingle with the gentle Lochy and from that union springs the great loch which at its farther end emerges as the river Tay. And here, too, stands Taymouth, not as at Dartmouth, Tynemouth, and Teignmouth, at the junction of the

* *The map on page 24 supplies a possible answer, but this surely is the source of the Dochart.*

46

river and the sea, but near the junction of the loch and river.

Our starting-point then for our journey down the Tay begins at Killin, that solid, ancient country town below which the bubbling Dochart races so noisily.

Killin is set in surroundings that are not to be paralleled for variety even in the Highlands. The place itself is a medley of fir trees, high rocks, torrents, mills, bridges, and grey stone houses with the shining waters of the loch filling the middle distance, rugged peaks rising to great heights on every side. It is a fitting resting-place for that greatest of all Gaelic warriors, Fingal.

But its chief glory is its ancient bridge from which there is a grand view of the sugar-loaf of Ben More in the distant west and of the turbulent Dochart in the immediate foreground, cascading over mighty rocks and encircling a high rocky wooded island in which lie buried generations of the Clan MacNab.

At the entrance to the loch stand the little pier and the ruins of Finlarig Castle, the ancient seat of the Campbells of Breadalbane, where you may still see the dungeon, gallows-tree, and place of execution of those who were axed.

The Campbells now live near by at Auchmore, a house that cost £70,000 to build. They also own Kinnell, once the seat of the MacNabs, famous for a vine which is said to be the largest in Europe, as its one-time owners claimed to be the tallest in the Highlands.

You can still see anglers in small boats patiently waiting for the famous Loch Tay salmon which have been known to weigh up to fifty pounds, and are rarely found much under twenty.

There are two little islands in this loch, one near the north shore, and the other near Killin, containing the ruins of a twelfth-century priory. The nuns of this priory gave themselves one day's holiday in the year, on 12th June (some say 26th July), when they marched in procession from the ancient stone pier at Port-na-Ban, the port of the women, to Kenmore, where a fair is still held annually under the name of Feill-na-Naomh, the fair of the holy women.

When Montrose made his historic raid against the Campbells in 1645, they took refuge here, but according to one account he beat them out of it.

I have known sudden storms sweep over the loch and raise waves worthy of a fierce sea, but it has never been known to freeze. It is the clearest water I know, and there is no trace of weed in any part of it.

Now that the steamers are no more (only temporarily, I hope) we have the choice of two ways to Killin, by the road that skirts the more desolate south shore or the more popular road that runs under the base of Ben Lawers on the north side.

Before leaving Killin, however, you will be wise to climb Stronachlachan and get a bird's-eye view of the loch to recall the fight that took place on this spot between the Campbells and MacDonalds of Glencoe, when the Campbells suffered that heavy defeat which they later avenged by the massacre in the Glen. It was in this fight that Menzies of the Herns distinguished himself by cutting off the head of Angus MacDonald of Keppoch, and protected himself from the arrows of the enemy by carrying a dead body on his back. The north shore road first runs alongside the wooded banks of the gentle meandering Lochy. It turns sharply eastward over the bridge near the

entrance to Glen Lochy and climbs through woods
towards Morenish and the rough mountain track on
the left-hand side that climbs to the lonely Lochan
na Lairig and thence down to join Glen Lyon at the
Bridge of Balgie. This is one of the wildest and most
splendid walks in the Highlands, and leads past one
of the main ski runs in Perthshire.

The main road now draws nearer to the mighty
bulk of Ben Lawers with its long gentle slopes and
sudden abrupt rocky summit where botanists find the
Alpine forget-me-not, purple saxifrage, gentian, and
other rare plants.

Just by Milton Farm there lived, about 350 years
ago, a Stewart of Appin known as the Lady of Lawers,
whose prophecies are still spoken of with awe in the
neighbourhood. She planted an ash tree near the
old church when it was built, and said that when it
grew to the height of the church, the church would
fall, and that whoever cut down the tree would die
untimely. Both these predictions were fulfilled. She
also foretold that the Breadalbane lands would break
up like an old bootlace, and that a man on horseback
would one day carry all that belonged to the Breadal-
banes over the ridge of Alba. Another local worthy
or unworthy was the minister, Robert Stewart, who
acquired great wealth by meanness. He used to
promise his children a penny if they would go to
bed without supper and then steal it from them when
they were asleep.

The next village after Lawers is Fearnan, a very
pleasant hamlet set right on the shores of the lapping
waters of the loch with a small pier, a most attractive
little hotel, and the site of an old church dedicated to
St. Ciaran.

The roads diverge here, one climbing inland to join the Lyon at Fortingall, and so to Aberfeldy along the left bank, the other continuing under the thick woods of Drummond Hill to Kenmore. This last stage of the loch-side journey is enchanting, for the road runs high above the loch and there are colourful gardens among the woods on either side, with frequent exquisite little vistas of crags above and shining water below, and across the loch of the tracks winding over the hills from Ardtalnaig and Ardeonaig.

From Ardtalnaig, where Malcolm II built his castle of Tay and the Carthusian monks lived and worked the mills, there is a grand wild walk over the hills to the Sma' Glen, and from Ardeonaig there is a track leading into Glen Lednock and Comrie.

Nearer Kenmore is Acharn, where there is a third mountain walk to Amulree.

Kenmore is a picture-postcard village, with rows of neat, white-washed, thatched cottages lined up to face a wide square with a church on a knoll at the loch end and the imposing gates of the private drive to Taymouth Castle at the other.

On the chimney-piece of the very attractive inn you may read in his actual handwriting what Burns thought of this district:

> The outstretching lake, embosomed 'mong the hills,
> The eye with wonder and amazement fills;
> The Tay meandering sweet in infant pride,
> The palace, rising on its verdant side;
> The lawns, wood-fringed in Nature's native taste;
> The hillocks, dropt in Nature's careless haste;
> The arches, striding o'er the new-born stream;
> The village, glittering in the noontide beam.

This catalogue is not in the poet's happiest vein.

He is more at ease and more inspired when he writes in the vernacular.

The old road follows the left bank of the Tay, but in 1786 the fourth Earl of Breadalbane built the magnificent tree-fringed road that follows the right bank.

But first we follow the private drive that leads to the astonishing battlemented castle of Taymouth, built of green-grey chlorite slate from a local quarry just in time for Queen Victoria's memorable visit a hundred years ago.

This visit, which lasted three days, attracted ten thousand visitors. A special bodyguard of two hundred men, in addition to a hundred clansmen and a hundred ghillies, attended the twenty-three-year-old Queen. Bonfires were lit, guns fired, a ball held, and even a specially made barge built to carry the royal party away.

It is little wonder that she was able to recall the occasion with deep emotion, even twenty years after.

The castle is more like a museum than a house, with its enormous stone staircase, ornate woodwork, stained glass, banner hall, and Italian ceilings, but whatever you may feel about the house you can scarcely fail to fall under the spell of the lovely spacious park with the fine trees, the broad, deep, clear brown river, and the views of the surrounding hills, notably that of the grand peak of Schiehallion peeping over the tops of the lesser mountains to the north. There is a royal spaciousness about this park which more than compensates for the pretentiousness of the rather grim palace. And in any case it still breathes the atmosphere of past glories of the Campbells.

51

As we take the road to the south of the Tay we cannot but agree that, compared with the noisy Dochart, the Thames-like placid Tay is well named 'Tatha', the silent one.

Just after you emerge from the castle gates on to the road you will see on the right-hand side of the road, at Croit Mhoraig, one of the finest stone circles in Scotland. The stones stand in three concentric circles, the largest stones, eight in number, making up the innermost circle.

There is also a long slab, hollowed out into cups, which is generally accepted as the sacrificial stone.

In all there are fifty-four stones in the circle, which is known as the Styx, a corruption of 'stuic', meaning pillars.

The road now becomes an avenue running alongside the broad, shallow, quiet river, and the sun is hidden behind a canopy of magnificent beeches, planes, oaks, and ash trees.

The river here is increased in volume though not in speed by its junction with the Lyon, and the valley is wide and green, giving a fine view of the village of Dull and the gaunt derelict skeleton of Castle Menzies standing below the bare grey rocks, to the north. This keep, built in 1571, once harboured Prince Charles Edward as well as serving as headquarters to Montrose, Argyll, Mackay, and Mar in their sorties in the Highlands.

Near the castle is the old church of Weem, the glass of which is now shattered, but there are still relics of the clan Menzies and old sanctuary crosses.

A fine avenue of tall poplars, planted by Sir Robert Menzies, marks the line of the old road which crosses the Tay over General Wade's Bridge, a most pic-

turesque affair of five arches and four obelisks, serving
as a reminder of the great roads and forts built by this
enterprising soldier for his armies to bring the Highlanders into subjection. In all Wade built forty
bridges, and this one, built in 1733 to replace the
ferry, was considered by him to be his best. There is
a certain irony in the fact that these roads and
bridges have been since used by countless sightseers
to bring them into final subjection to the most
fascinating holiday ground in the world.

Close by the bridge is an unusually striking cairn
surmounted by the figure of a Highlander, Farquhar
Shaw, which commemorates the raising in 1739 of
the 42nd Highlanders, better known as the Black
Watch.

We are now in the flourishing market town of
Aberfeldy, one of the best centres for tourists in all
the Highlands.

It is also a busy shopping centre, and few tourists
fail to succumb to the entrancing combinations of
colours that are produced in the famous tweed mills
of Provost Haggart. Above the town stand the famous
Falls of Moness in a setting that inspired Burns to
write his lovely lyric 'The Birks of Aberfeldy'. But
'the foaming stream' rarely 'deep-roaring fa's' these
days. Too often in the summer it is a bare trickle.
When they are in full spate, however, the tumbling
waters crash down with imposing roar and violence.

Aberfeldy is admirably set out with its clean streets
and fine market square leading off to public gardens,
lawns, and golf course along the river bank.

Again, after leaving Aberfeldy, we have the choice
of two fascinating roads along the strath, one on the
right bank by the side of the railway line that links

up with Ballinluig, and the other along the north
bank of the Tay.

From whichever bank you look at this fine stretch
of water, you cannot fail to be struck by the beauty
of the deep pools alternating with the swifter shallows.
Everywhere the clear water shines like polished
mahogany below the gravel or grassy banks, and on
all these banks there is a wealth of trees.

On the south road we pass Grantully Castle and
Castle Daw; on the north Cluny House and Logierait.

Both roads are beautiful, and from both roads you
get the impression of many good estates, all obviously
well cared for.

At Grantully the old church, built in 1533, still
stands, but is no longer used. It occupies the site of
the older church of St. Eonan, and on an adjoining
knoll, from which there is a magnificent view of the
gentle wooded strath, once stood the saint's house.
Below it are the remains of a stone circle.

Grantully House, a finely restored sixteenth-century
Highland keep, once the home of Lady Stewart, was
later rented by the late Earl Beatty who entertained
the present King and Queen there. Just over the other
side of Dunfallandy, a notable hill with magnificent
views of wild moorland, lie the Tummel valley and
Pitlochry. The gardens of the many big country
houses hereabouts are particularly colourful.

On one of these estates was born just two hundred
years ago the boy, Daniel Stewart, who rose to be rich
enough to endow the College that now bears his name
in Edinburgh. At Pitnacree there still stand the ruins
of an old lint-mill to remind us that in more flourishing
days there were over a hundred of these mills in this
strath.

54

Above Ballechin, once the home of the Stewarts, who fought at Killiecrankie, are the remains of an ancient fort known as the Black Castle. Below lies the village of Balnaguard with its burn, fine waterfall, and gallows mound.

Close by is Eastertye with its remains of a stone circle and dog's-leg-shaped ford.

Logierait, which looks impressive on the map, is only a shadow of its former self, for there was a time when this parish sent more Peter's Pence to Rome than were contributed by St. Giles' in Edinburgh.

The old castle that once stood on the wooded knoll overlooking the Tummel has been supplanted by a great cross put up in memory of the sixth Duke of Athol.

A court of regality sat in the seventy-foot-long club-house which once sheltered 600 prisoners taken at Prestonpans, and close by was the hangman's house and hanging knoll.

The ash tree, over a thousand years old, on which the last hanging took place may be seen in the garden of the hotel. Rob Roy was imprisoned here, but of course, as usual, escaped.

The churchyard at Logierait contains a prehistoric cross and other ancient stones to remind us of the monastery that once stood on these slopes.

The railway crosses the river here to join the main line at Ballinluig, but the ferry has gone and there is no road bridge, which means that between Grantully and Dunkeld, a distance of fourteen miles, you have to keep on the same side of the river.

It is here that we take our last look westward at the wild, lovely mountains that stand sentinel over Loch Tay and Glen Lyon before we turn southward at the junction of Tay and Tummel to pursue our way to Dunkeld and Birnam.

The road now runs among thick woods high above the broad river which becomes more and more irritatingly invisible as we get farther south.

The bridge that links Dunkeld and Birnam was built by Telford in 1809.

From the ninth century Dunkeld was for a time the religious centre of North Britain. Here a missionary in St. Columba's day had set up his chapel of clay and wattle, and in 848 King Kenneth built a church and shrine to preserve the bones of the saint. In 1318 came the cathedral which was purged by the Reformers in 1560, and used as a citadel by the Covenanting Cameronians in 1689 in their victorious fight against the Highlanders, who outnumbered them by four to one. Sir Donald Currie restored it and you may still see in it the large stone effigy of 'the Wolf of Badenoch', the fourteenth-century iconoclast who burnt down Elgin Cathedral.

The estate of Dunkeld House, a seat of the Duke of Athol, is covered with vast plantations of larch, which remind us of the coming of Birnam's woods to Dunsinane which stands some twelve miles south-east.

After Dunkeld the hills and the woods give place to low-lying pastureland, and the Tay peacefully meanders away to the east past Murthly Castle and Caputh before turning south again at Cargill to Stanley, Scone, and Perth. Of old Scone (pronounced 'Scoone'), where the famous stone rested for 300 years, nothing remains but its market-cross and the gateway of the old palace.

Few towns in Scotland and none outside it possess quite such a distinctive atmosphere as Perth, which was Scotland's capital before Edinburgh, and even before Stirling. You feel it at once in the busy station, the threshold of wild romance. You feel it again in St. John's Kirk, one of the earliest stone churches in Scotland. You feel it again on the spacious avenues and greens of North and South Inch, which provide such a glorious breathing space for the workers in the distilleries, dye-works, and factories. Not for nothing is it known as 'the Fair City'. On the North Inch was fought that trial by combat of thirty men a-side between the Clans Chattan and Kay in 1328, known as the Battle of the Clans. Only nine remained to tell the story that Scott retold in *The Fair Maid of Perth*.

It was in the monastery of Blackfriars that James I was murdered in 1437, and in Gowrie House, now demolished, that James VI witnessed the murder of the Ruthven brothers. It was before the altar of the Church of St. John the Baptist that Edward III slew his brother John.

Not all Perth's memories are so grim. In the Salutation Inn, built in 1699, we see the oldest-established hotel in Scotland. It still retains a min-strels' gallery and the bedroom in which Prince Charles Edward slept. A slight climb up Kinnoull Hill provides a fine panorama of the city and of the Tay which here widens out into a tidal firth and exchanges the character that it bore above the city for a quite different one. It has still thirty-one out of its 117 miles to run. Did I mention that the Tay is the longest river in Scotland? Above the bridge of Perth, the salmon fishing is private, commanding rentals of anything up to £1,000, but below it the public are allowed to fish by rod in the autumn when the nets are taken off. As the banks are muddy and sedge-grown this necessitates wading. Some thirty-five years ago a Perth angler took a salmon of 61½ lb. weight, the head of which may be seen in the Perth museum.

The meeting of the river with the open sea can best be appreciated from the Tay Bridge, which is over two miles long, opened in 1887 to replace the earlier bridge that had been destroyed by a gale and involved the loss of a train-load of seventy passengers. This bridge is the second largest in the world, being surpassed only by that which spans the lower Zambesi.

It is fitting that this grand river should reach the sea under so imposing a bridge, and that its seaport should be so vigorous and individual a town as Dundee, famed not only for its cakes and marmalade, but also for its shipbuilding, engineering, and jute.

There are witnesses to its great age in the old steeple in the Nethergate, a fifteenth-century massive tower with battlements standing 156 feet high, and a fine hall. Close by are the old Town Cross and three churches under one roof.

Farther down the river, at the very mouth of the sea, is the popular watering-place of Broughty Ferry, which also boasts a sixteenth-century castle which has been very adequately restored. We are now at the end of a journey that has led us through the very heart of Scotland, from its wildest and most rugged heights, through wide straths and historic woods, to gentle fertile pastures and a land of prosperous and various industries. In a word, we have seen the whole glory of Scotland.

58

CHAPTER FOUR

Deeside

WHENEVER I am in Aberdeen I take the tram from Brig o' Don to Brig o' Dee, one of the cheapest and most worth-while drives that I know, but my thoughts on these drives always revert to the very different walk that connects the source of the Don with the source of the Dee.

I am more at home with the sources of most rivers than with their junctions with the sea, and when I hear the word Dee or see it in print, I think first of days on Braeriach, looking down into the dark chasm of the Larig Ghru or westward over the wide strath of Spey to the snowcapped Monadhliath.

I have come on the Dee from a number of angles; on foot down the boulder-strewn Larig from Aviemore, by motor charabanc up Glen Shee to the Devil's Elbow and down Glen Clunie to Braemar, by sea from Shetland to Aberdeen, and from the air.

Always it has surprised me: now by its wildness, now by its tameness; now by its almost suburban smugness, now by its quite awe-inspiring isolation.

I have been in Braemar for the Gathering and felt exactly as if I were in the Royal Enclosure at Ascot, meeting exactly the same people in much more com-

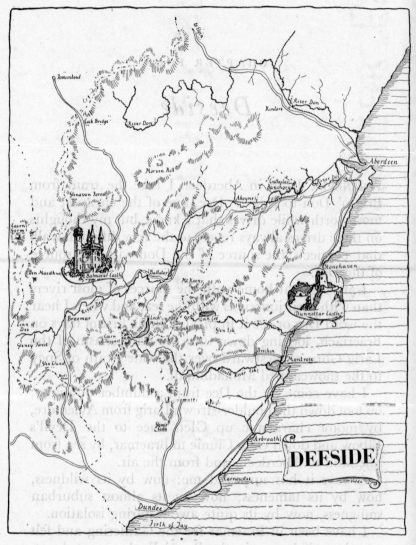

Tomintoul · to Inch · River Don · Kintore · River Don · Loch Bridge · River Don · Aberdeen · Morven Hill · Crathes Banchory · River Dee · Glenaven Forest · Aboyne · Cairn Gorm · Ben Macdhui · Balmoral Castle · Ballater · Stonehaven · Mt Keen · Dunnottar Castle · River Dee · Glen Muick · Angus · Braemar · Loch Muick · Dog · Bunchog · Braes · Loch Lee · Linn of Dee · Cairn Taggart · Glen Esk · Glenly Forest · Glen Clunie · Brechin · Montrose · South River Esk · Stonehaven Castle · Arbroath · Carnoustie · Dundee · Firth of Tay

DEESIDE

59

fortable and far more picturesque clothes. I have
been in Braemar in mid-winter and felt as much out
of the world as if I were on the Carpathians or the
Ural mountains. Few people know just how wild the
Deeside country can be. Glencoe has nothing on it
for savage isolation.

I have seen things in the gardens of Balmoral that
have made me rub my eyes before I could believe
in their existence, and I still find it difficult to believe
in that black-haired waitress in Ballater who, in
answer to my request for China tea said, "We only
serve Scots tea here". I also associate the Dee with
antique shops (Balmoral and Aberdeen), with dense
pine woods, and most of all with Queen Victoria,
who curiously enough seems to come more alive on
Deeside than in Windsor or any other royal palace.

The journey begins in Aberdeen, to my mind one
of the most fascinating cities in the world. My first
visit to Aberdeen was far too long ago for me to remember the date, but I remember being immensely
impressed as I flew over it, with the homogeneity of
the city compact of granite, clear-cut, ascetic, beautiful. My last visit to it was when I arrived at dawn
after an exciting journey spent mainly in trying to
recapture some of my youthful delight in a coast-line
that has changed hardly at all since I was a boy.

My mission on this occasion was to broadcast in
the company of Mr. Macpherson, the keeper from
Invercauld, who entertained me with stories of pole-
cats, pine-martens, and wild-cats.

All Scottish cities are full of character; St. Andrews,
Edinburgh, Glasgow, Perth, Inverness, all have their
own strikingly individual atmospheres. By far the
most individual is Aberdeen. You could not possibly

mistake it for any other city in the world. It must be easily the cleanest and the most enduring. Most of us know granite only on tombstones. It has for us rather grim associations. The granite of which Aberdeen is built sparkles in the sun and after rain resembles a sea of diamonds, so you get at once a sense of tremendous durability, and with it a sense of scintillating light which takes away all possible feeling of heaviness.

Compare with it the banality of the red-brick houses of Reading, and you will see what I mean when I describe Aberdeen as one of the most dignified cities of the world, and Union Street as worthy of comparison with Princes Street, Edinburgh, and High Street, Oxford.

It is quite true that at certain times the smell of fish that assails you as you leave the station is disconcerting, but you soon get used to it, and in any case it is a useful reminder that Aberdeen is the chief seaport in the north of Scotland and the headquarters of a great industry.

If you get the opportunity you ought certainly to explore the fish market and the harbour, whose north pier, built partly by Smeaton and partly by Telford, extends nearly 3,000 feet into the North Sea.

Even more exciting than the harbour, except for my memorable first voyage to Orkney and Shetland, is to my mind the vast granite quarry some three hundred feet deep and about three hundred years old from which has been hewn the stone that made the city.

But perhaps Aberdeen's best known industry is education. The famous university has two colleges: King's College, founded in 1494, and Marischal College, founded in 1593, rebuilt about a hundred years ago and extended again about forty years ago.

The sixteenth-century twin-towered cathedral of St. Machar is the only granite cathedral in the world, and is a fine example of the æsthetic appeal of stark simplicity.

This site had been consecrated by St. Machar a thousand years before the cathedral was built. The story goes that St. Columba told him to go north through the land of the Picts until he came to a place where a river made a curve like that of a bishop's crozier. This the Don does here, as you can easily see.

The old bridge over the Don, Brig o'Balgownie, is the most famous sight in Aberdeen. Its single Gothic arch, high above a dark pool, is very striking. It was built by Bishop Cheyne in the early part of the fourteenth century and is the oldest bridge in the north.

I have every reason to remember Aberdeen with gratitude.

The *Aberdeen Free Press* was the first paper to speak well of my early books. I have always been royally entertained by private hosts, and when I have stayed in the hotels I have been particularly struck by the courtesy and affability of the staffs.

I am unable to say whether the tram fares are cheaper than they are anywhere else, but they certainly give better value for money than anywhere else I know. Or can you suggest a more worthwhile two-pennyworth than from the Brig o' Don to Brig o' Dee?

The ninety-mile journey up Deeside is, as Hugh Quigley says, full of magic names: Aboyne, Banchory,

Kincardine O'Neil, Ballater, Morven, Hill of Fare and Glentanar.

When I was broadcasting from Aberdeen the majority of my Aberdeenshire colleagues sang the praises of Bennachie, and this chorus was swollen by the landscape artist, Mr. Simpson. So highly and well did they praise it that I shall always remain under the spell of this ben that I have never seen.

There was obviously a feeling among those devotees that the Don country had been less exploited, and in consequence retained its virgin beauty unsullied, whereas the Dee has been ruined beyond hope.

Mr. Quigley would obviously agree with this judgment because he says, 'Deeside itself has become commercialised to such a degree that one can only pass through it as rapidly as possible, content with an occasional climb to a near hill, such as the Table of Morven beyond Ballater and the Hill of Fare behind Banchory'.

On the other hand we have J. J. Bell's evidence that he has met people who declared the Dee to be the finest river in the world.

However that may be, I have felt moods of exaltation comparable to those inspired by the Lakeland hills in Wordsworth as I have stood on a stormy day at the Great Divide above the Devil's Elbow with Meall Odhar menacing me from the clouds on my right and the Cairnwell leaning over me from the heavens on my left, and I have felt my exaltation ooze out of me quickly as I have passed out of the wilderness of Glen Clunie by the only too well-worn track that leads to Balmoral.

So the wise traveller, wishing to end on a high note, should emphatically travel up, not down, Deeside.

BALLACHULISH, VIEW FROM BEN VAIR

BEN NEVIS IN WINTER

There are two roads, one on the north bank and the more popular on the south bank, reached by the old brig of 1527, which has, of course, been widened and reconstructed many times since then. At Blair you will see St. Mary's Catholic College, famous for the portrait of Mary Queen of Scots, copied from the miniature given by her on the eve of her execution to her attendant, Elizabeth Curle. At Culter we get the reminder of yet another of Aberdeen's famous industries, that of paper.

The tower of Drum Castle brings back memories of Robert the Bruce who gave this stronghold to his armour-bearer, Sir William Irvine.

We are now in the well-wooded country of the Burnett family, who have lived at Crathes for six hundred years.

Most people are familiar with the carved figure in three-cornered hat and gold-laced coat that stands on top of Crathes Castle. Near by is the old Bridge of Feugh under which road the waters of a river that is always turbulent flows over what Ernest Baker aptly calls a 'ruckle of tumbled rocks'.

We are now in Banchory, described by somebody as 'perhaps the prettiest spot on Deeside'. The adjective may well stand. It must be pretty because it made no impression on me at all. I do not go to Deeside, indeed I do not come to Scotland, for prettiness. I can get a surfeit of prettiness in the south. So let Banchory vie with Strathpeffer for the title of the prettiest inland health resort in Scotland. It makes an admirable centre not only for walkers but for archæ-ologists, for here once stood St. Ternan's house and the church in which until the Reformation his relics were cherished. These relics included his embalmed head, one volume of his book of the Gospels enclosed in a book-shrine, enriched with silver and gold; and a miraculous bell called Ronecht or Gongster.

You may learn something of the ecclesiastical importance of Banchory in medieval times, and of her prehistoric importance, from Dr. W. Douglas Simpson's admirable Rhind lectures of 1941 on *The Province of Mar* published by the Aberdeen University Press.

Then you will probe beneath the modern veneer of Banchory's 'prettiness' to the real Banchory of Scotland's earliest inhabitants whose relics of cairns, sculptured stones, forts, crannogs, and the rest are still to be seen hereabouts.

The railway runs away from the river after Banchory to make a turn round by Lumphanan, the scene of Macbeth's death:

> O'er the Mounth they chased him
> Intil the woods of Lumphanan;
> This Macbeth slew they there
> Intil the woods of Lumphanan.

On its way to regain the river the railway also passes the sheet of water known as Loch of Auchlossan.

It misses Kincardine O'Neil, once a place of great importance, for here the Dee was crossed by the Cairnamounth road which was the principal route from Strathmore into Mar.

Thomas the Durward, who died about 1231, built a bridge here, and his son founded a hospital by the side of the bridge. The church of Kincardine O'Neil was the most important in Deeside, and its beautiful ruins remain as a perpetual memorial to the Durward family. There is a very remarkable doorway which Dr. Simpson, who dates it as early fourteenth century, describes as 'exceedingly good of its kind, delicate and refined in every detail'.

The east and west gables of this fascinating kirk still stand, the west gable surmounted by an attractive bell-tower.

The mountains begin to close in as we come to Aboyne, 'the place where the white cow took a drink'. What most of us remember best about Aboyne are the games held every autumn on that very spacious and pleasant green round which the town is built.

Aboyne is the home of the head of the Huntly clan. Their moated, many-turreted castle is mainly modern, unlike the neighbouring castles of Corse and Coull (once the home of the Durwards), which are ancient and in ruins. Whenever a Durward of Coull died the bell of the neighbouring kirk rang of its own accord.

At Ballater, where the railway ends, I begin to feel for the first time that I am in the Highlands. Here are the queer hills of Craigendarroch, cone-shaped and wooded; dark Lochnagar, 'besmirched', according to Hugh Quigley 'in a poem of disgusting banality', but to my mind still impervious in its white crown to the vulgarisations that have gone on in the strath below, and big-nosed Morven.

Balmoral lies nine miles west. It is difficult to believe that it is nearing the centenary of its building. 1855 was not a period in British architecture of which we are proud. It is easy to cast ridicule on its pretentiousness, and in comparison with Invercauld House and the small but exquisite seventeenth-century Braemar Castle, it is a grotesque anomaly in this lovely, wild, wooded valley, but the gardens and surrounding woods make up for the garishness of the castle.

It is pleasant to come to the simple and appropriate

Cairn of Remembrance, the gathering-place of the clansmen of Clan Farquharson bound for battle and the disbanding place afterwards. Every man brought a stone to the cairn and took it away if he returned alive. The size of the pile shows how few came back.

Five miles farther on Craig Clunie rises almost perpendicularly from the glen, and it was in a cleft of this crag, some 600 feet above the road, that the Invercauld title-deeds were hidden after the Jacobite Rising of 1715.

The fifteenth-century Invercauld House, standing tall, gaunt and defiant on a green terrace half-circled by the Dee, stands to me as an emblem of all that is best in these Highland fastnesses.

The village of Braemar, just beyond, is an unexpectedly cosy place of good hotels, one of them, the Invercauld Arms, built on the mound on which the Earl of Mar raised the standard in 1715. It is sheltered, wooded, and rather sophisticated in its antique and tea shops. The Highland Gathering is the most famous of all gatherings, and causes a good deal of fury among those who do not contemplate with pleasure the sight of all London society dressed in Highland costume.

It was in a Braemar cottage that Robert Louis Stevenson wrote *Treasure Island*. The real Deeside, from my point of view, lies in these upper reaches to the west of Braemar.

The road stops at Inverey, but the thirty-mile walk up Glen Dee, past the Linn of Dee, under the mighty shadow of Ben Macdhui and Braeriach, down the Larig Ghru and across the forest of Rothiemurchus to Aviemore, is one of the two epic walks in Scotland. The other is the Corrieyairack, and to my mind the

68

Larig walk is the fiercer and more worth doing. But the excursions from Braemar are innumerable.

There is a grand view of the best part of Deeside to be got from climbing Craig Leek, behind Invercauld House. It is little more than two thousand feet high, but it provides a glorious view to the south to the summit of Lochnagar.

Hugh Quigley selects for special praise a view which 'comes at the end of a mountain walk over the peaks which stretch in a series of abrupt switchbacks to the east of the Clunie Water and Glen Callater. One can stand at the edge of the deep valley beside Loch Phadruig, a small blue gem, set in a narrow pass between steep hills, and look down on the deer crossing in hundreds the waste of Ballochbuie Forest and across a wide uneven barrier of grey stone, interrupted only by heather which sweeps up to a wilderness of rock with no definition, either of corrie or peak, to relieve its insignificant immensity.' That ridge walk is one of the finest short expeditions from Braemar.

A profitable and easy walk from Braemar is by way of Morrone Hill (2,819 feet), and thence over the heather moors to An Socach (3,059 feet) where you look out over some of the wildest country in the Grampians.

It is an easy descent by way of Baddoch burn to the road in Glen Clunie.

Running parallel to and east of the Glen Shee road is Glen Isla, at the top of which you come to a very wild country indeed under the high precipices and almost perpendicular walls that seem to present an impenetrable barrier to the would-be conqueror of Glas Maol.

A walk that I have always wanted to take is eastward from the summit of Glas Maol by way of Tol-

mount, Cairn Bannoch, the whole of the White
Mounth, and then down to Loch Muick and Glen
Muick to Ballater.

Hugh Quigley has only done it once and never
wants to repeat the walk, because he says that Lochnagar is better enjoyed at a distance, except of course
by the rock-climbers who like pitting their skill and
strength against its terrific corries.

We all have our special preferences, most of them
indefensible, and the part of the Dee that I know and
love the best is not the high country to the south
known as Belmorse Forest, but the higher and wilder
country of the Cairngorm where the Dee rises.

That preference may be due to the fact that I first
came to the Dee by way of the Spey, that I first met
the Dee in the company of a golden eagle and several
hundred stags, having encountered on the slopes above
a number of capercailzie and ptarmigan.

But when I begin to look more closely into the map,
and recapture again memories of great days in Glen
Lui, Glen Derry, and Glen Quoich; assaulting the
Cairngorm from the south; of softer days in Glen
Tanna and the Forest of Birse, of the approaches from
the south-east by way of Glen Esk and Loch Lee to
Glen Mark, to Mount Keen, I am hard put to it to
defend my earlier prejudice.

It would be wiser and fairer to say that all the hill
country above Deeside both north and south is calcu-
lated to satisfy man's desire for loveliness and majesty.
It is all awe-inspiring as soon as you get off the beaten
track, and I for one would be content to let Scotland's
glory be judged from this one stretch of water and the
watershed that contributes to it. It is to my mind
unbeatable.

70

Let the map speak. Take down your Bartholomew half-inch map of Deeside. Most maps are a sea of green, with a few divine splodges of brown. Deeside is, in the half that matters, one glorious canvas of brown, with generous splashes of the rare whites and greys that betoken the presence of heights and peaks that will never beckon in vain to the adventurous.

Here is a land of solemn majesty, untameable by man, changeless through the ages, at once man's solace in sorrow, inspiration in doubt, and glory in conquest.

For those who know how to enjoy it Deeside still remains one of the wonders of the world.

CHAPTER FIVE

The Perth Bull Show

SCOTLAND, in spite of my frequent visits, invariably springs a surprise on me. On this occasion I set out accoutred for ski-ing and prepared for extreme cold.

I ran into a February foretaste of spring that reminded me of the Isles of Scilly. Birds sang, snowdrops and even primroses lit up the gardens, the snow melted almost before my eyes on the upper slopes of Schiehallion and Ben Lawers. Glencoe alone, of all the places I visited, retained her grim and wintry look.

It was the weather that was the determining factor in my decision to visit the Perth Bull Show. I have reached an age when even the offer of a free seat at Murrayfield for the Calcutta Cup Match would not tempt me. I have given up stamping my feet and blowing on my fingers to restore my circulation at a Rugger match. The day of the Shorthorn Show was a day that might, as far as temperature was concerned, have been borrowed from June. I have watched many races at Ascot and many runs being scored at Lords on far colder days.

Indeed, many of those who led their bulls in slow, stately procession up and down Caledonian Road before the judges wore neither cap nor coat, and it wasn't wholly excitement or apprehension that kept them warm, though those emotions were naturally present where so high a prize was at stake.

During the previous week the world had been startled by the price paid for the champion Aberdeen-Angus bull by Bovril, Ltd. As I wandered round the pens where the competitors were being combed and brushed as carefully as debutantes before their coming-out ball, I tried to find out what sort of price they expected the champion Shorthorn to fetch. No one dared to suggest that it would come anywhere near the 7,500 guineas paid for Erwin of Harviestoun. If I had then prophesied that not only the champion but also the runner-up among the Shorthorns would fetch nearly double that sum, I should probably have been turned out of the pens.

In point of fact, I had so many other things beyond the fantastic prices to occupy my attention that I soon forgot their value in their beauty and their number. I had never seen 400 pedigree bulls assembled together before, and they all looked so amazingly symmetrical in form and physically fit that it did look to me as if the verdict might well depend upon a single curl or combed-out tail.

Never for a moment was a single bull allowed to move in the slow procession before the judges without a touch of the comb here or a slight brush there. It was like a mannequin parade except for the fact that mannequins generally do all their titivating, powder-ing, painting, and so on in retirement. These bulls were unblushingly painted, oiled, and preened under the very eyes of the judges. But while their dressers had no eyes for any bulls but their own, the owners scarcely gave their bulls a glance. Their eyes were riveted covetously, anxiously, but seldom contemptuously on the bulls behind and before.

The eyes of the bulls themselves struck me as roguish and roving. They eyed the crowd rather than each other. They seemed to realise that they were the cynosure of neighbouring eyes, and in consequence stalked or rather rolled along with an affectedly nonchalant air, like the man who broke the bank at Monte Carlo. Their voices, however, betrayed their eyes. Their bellowings, which were voluminous and never-ending, betokened an anxiety for the pastures they had left and a sense of indignity at being led by the nose. Don't misunderstand me. No bull showed any sign of indecorum. Indeed they were all so well behaved that I am quite prepared to believe that they had all been doped. Perhaps the introduction of a heifer or two might have lightened up the scene. But this was essentially a stag party. Even the spectators were pre-eminently male.

It is, I hope, casting no aspersions on the beauty and majesty of the bulls when I say that I was in the end even more excited by the ringside than by the beasts inside the ring. The onlookers were by far the most interesting I have ever seen. This, you must understand, was no Royal Show at Olympia with grandstand seats. It was not, as Ascot or Lords or the Braemar Gathering are, a Society function. The judging took place in one of the main streets of a town. There was therefore no charge. There was no distinction of person. The spectator who saw most was a ginger-haired errand boy who stood on the saddle of his bicycle, his eyes flashing, his errands all forgotten as he surveyed the noble head, wide stern, and short stumpy legs of Pittodrie Upright who was so soon to

74

change masters and continents, R. L. Smith of Pitcaple for R. L. Smith of Missouri, U.S.A.

Round the ring and in the pens I kept on encountering men with faces as noble as those of the bulls, dressed for once not in the standardised uniform of Ascot or Lords or Braemar, but in the distinctive undress of the farm, deer-stalker, fisherman's hat, check cap, bowler, Tyrolean Hombug on the head, regimental, college or school scarf round the neck, Service greatcoat or dingy mackintosh loosely covering limbs that were nearly always loose and long, and only partially hidden by kilt, plus-fours and riding breeches. Some wore leggings and nailed boots, others stockings to match the peat and heather, with brogues. Many carried the tall stick that we Sassenachs call the shepherd's crook. I wouldn't say that, apart from the kilt, of which I saw less than a dozen, their clothes betrayed their nationality. They came from Ireland, Wales, England, Argentina, and North America, but it was their faces and build that gave that fact away, not their dress. Farmers the world over wear these loose-fitting, comfortable, serviceable checks.

But the Highlander has his own high cheekbone and lanky frame, the Welshman his black hair, sallow face, and small neat figure. The English farmer is pink of face, stocky, weather-beaten, shrewd, and plump of stomach, the Argentine rather like a Spanish bull-fighter, the North American yellow as parchment, with a merry twinkle in his eye. At a pedigree show one's thoughts naturally run on purity of stock and good breeding, and I could not help thinking how much purer in breed these bull-lovers looked than those strange young men and women who drift from one Society function to another through the London season.

75

These men were present for a purpose. They knew the points of a bull. They were, as I was, filled with admiration for the perfection of the beasts. They were, so far as I could gather, pretty well to a man potential buyers and sellers of bulls. Indeed, as there were 400 beasts and each of them seemed to have three or four attendants, there wasn't much room for the casual looker-on, and, anyway, the ordinary man neither knows the points of a bull nor its monetary value. He is, indeed, inclined to give a bull a wide berth, while we were surrounded by bulls, stroking them and leaning up against them. One tired drover I saw lying dead asleep between two animals who seemed delighted to share their straw with him. But serious as the business in hand was, it is worth remarking that a mighty cheer went up when the bidding for Pittodrie Upright soared to 10,000 guineas and an even mightier round of applause was given both for the bull, the buyer, the runner-up and its buyer as soon as the sale was over.

The average price fetched for this year's bulls was nearly £440, whereas for the last three years it has been less than £300, and for twenty-three years before that it never reached £200, so there must be a very considerable boom in the breeding of Shorthorn bulls. The average prices made by individual farmers showed an amazing increase in many instances on the previous year. The Millhills bulls, which averaged £623 last year, rose to £1,152 this year, while the Pittodrie herd, which averaged £675 last year, rose to £1,497 this year.

I suppose it is the stupendous prices that have brought these bulls into the news. They were filmed and photographed as well as judged from 9.30 a.m.

till dusk, and the crowds were always so enormous that I heard many people suggest that the venue should be changed from the public street to an enclosure with stands, but it would lose its character if this were to happen, and the fascination to me of this remarkable exhibition was its homogeneity. As it stands, it is all of a piece, appealing like markets to its own specialist clientèle.

The Perth Bull Show would lose something of its dignity and individuality if it were turned into a circus. The privilege of being able to walk unchallenged and without payment into the dressing-room of so great a celebrity as Pittodrie Upright, of being on nodding terms with so many handsome and aristocratic bulls, is one not lightly to be forgotten. It is certainly well worth coming north from Hereford or Caermarthen, or from Missouri or County Kildare, even if you aren't bringing a bull and can't afford to take one home.

CHAPTER SIX

Etive

ALL the steamer excursions from Oban are first-rate, full of variety, colour, and excitement.

One might well travel the world over without finding more beauty, strangeness, or wealth of historic association in a single day than in the circular tour round Mull that includes Tobermory, the rock caves of Fingal in Staffa, and the graves of the ancient Scottish kings in St. Columba's holy isle of Iona.

I once took an almost equally exciting circular tour which began by catching the ten o'clock train to Achnacloich where we boarded a small motor-boat for a two-hour sail up Loch Etive, which entailed calling at various tiny landing stages to leave mails that were eagerly awaited by bare-footed children, whose presence only served to accentuate the loneliness and desolation of the little glens from which they came.

We disembarked at Loch Etive head, boarded a waiting motor-coach, and drove up the rugged, awe-inspiring glen to Kingshouse Inn, and thence down the long, grim pass of Glencoe to Ballachulish where we took a train back to Oban, after as full a day as any sightseer could possibly desire.

The actual entrance to Loch Etive is at Connel

78

Ferry. The main road and railway run for several miles close to the south bank of the loch before turning into the Pass of Brander under the southern shoulder of mighty Ben Cruachan, the loch's grim sentinel.

Formerly the loch at Connel could only be crossed by ferry, but a bridge was erected to join the coast road to Ballachulish on the northern side, and the charges for crossing this bridge have now been reduced to reasonable proportions. It used to cost 10s. 4d.

The loch was once a submerged glen, and if its mouth were twenty feet higher it would be an inland loch.

At low tide the entrance is only six feet deep, so it is fascinating to watch the waters at every half-ebb and half-flow tide racing frantically seaward over the cataract known as the Falls of Lora. These were known to the old Gaels as the Clacharan of Caille Bheur, or the stepping-stones of the witch Eiteag.

Connel, too, takes its name from these falls, for its name, 'A' Chonghail', means the 'dog-fight'.

At Benderloch on the northern bank of the loch is a vitrified fort known as Beregonium, 'the Point of the Blacksmith'.

The name Etive is derived from Eiteag, the mischievous witch who, from her fastness in Glen Salach, near Ardchattan, released the sudden winds and storms that make the waters of Etive so hazardous. Not only is the loch subject to unexpected gales but there are many treacherous sandbanks.

Ardchattan is interesting not only for Eiteag, but for the ruins of the thirteenth-century priory of St. Modan that was burnt down in 1644 by Colketto, and also for the fact that in 1308 Robert the Bruce

79

held the last parliament there that was conducted in Gaelic.

But it is not so much of the witch Eiteag that we think as we sail on these waters as of the lovely, hapless Deirdre of the Sorrows whose tragic love story has attracted so many generations of poets and dramatists from the most ancient to our own contemporaries, W. B. Yeats and J. M. Synge. It was to Etive that Deirdre fled from the unwelcome attentions of Fergus, King of Ireland, with her lover, Naisi, the black-haired, fair-skinned hunter.

They built their bridal hold at the head of the loch and lived in complete happiness together with Naisi's faithful brothers, Ainle and Arden, until one day, as they were playing draughts in their hunting-booth, they heard the thrice-repeated shout of Fergus the Knight of the Red Branch who had tracked them to their bower. Fergus falsely promised the pair forgiveness if they would return with him to their native land, and Naisi, against Deirdre's better judgment, believed in the king's promise.

It was not difficult, as we sailed along the lovely loch, to fancy that we still heard the faint echoes of that lovely dirge of the ill-fated heroine, known as *Deirdre's Farewell.*

> Glen Etive!
> There I built my first house;
> Lovely its woods after rising.

She well knew that her lover was going to his death, and that she, too, was doomed to die of a broken heart.

You may read of their story in the Glen Masan manuscript and in Macpherson's *Ossian.* In whatever form you read the story, whether in modern play or ancient poem, you can scarcely fail to be moved by its poignancy.

All along the twenty miles of loch and sixteen miles of glen there are reminders of the ill-starred lovers.

At Taynuilt, the House beside the Burn, there is Naisi's Wood, 'Coille Naoise', and shortly afterwards the water sweeps suddenly northward to face the glen where the site of her sunny bower is still shown, even if their garden of the three apple trees can no longer be located.

On the north side of the loch stand the rather grim-looking granite quarries of Bonawe, and above on the south rises the immense bulk of Ben Cruachan rising from a base of twenty square miles to a height of 3,689 feet.

> Cruachan Ben, Cruachan Ben, Cruachan Ben,
> King o' Mountains,
> To the lift towers its head,
> Down its shoulders pour the fountains.
>
> Noblest hill e'er I saw!
> It is grander a hantle
> Than aught Europe can show,
> When it shows its snowy mantle.

From every aspect Ben Cruachan is imposing.

I first came under its spell as the train wound its way along the Pass of Brander, with the thunder of the frequent waterfalls racing down the mountain's steep sides completely drowning the noise of the train, and so close as to threaten to dash into the compartments.

So close indeed does the railway line hug the base of the mountain that I always expect boulders as well as the water to come crashing through the carriage windows.

In many ways Ben Cruachan is the most profitable of all Scottish mountains to climb. It is an easy climb from Bridge of Awe, and the vista from the summit is nowhere surpassed, even in Scotland.

Just below on one side is the narrow shining Loch of Etive winding its way north-east into the heart of the grim peaks of Glencoe, while on the other stretches the whole length of the equally narrow Loch Awe away to the south-east.

Westward lie the islands of Loch Linnhe and the mountains of Mull, and on the far horizon are the faint smears of Col and Tiree and Rum, and on a specially clear day even some of the isles of the Outer Hebrides are just visible.

From each of its seven or eight peaks Ben Cruachan provides a different, but almost equally wide, vista of snow-covered bens and shining lochs. A razor-edge leads to the Taynuilt peak which provides the finest views as it juts out towards Loch Etive in such a way as to make the whole of the loch visible.

One can see an occasionable house or settlement at Craig, Cudderlie, Dail, and Barrs on the northern shores, and at Glennoe, Inverliver, and Ardmaddy on the southern bank, but these are at the outlets of little rivers, and only to be approached by water, for there is no road on the north bank after you leave the Bonawe quarries until you reach the end of the loch at Gualachulain, and none at all on the south bank after the main Oban road branches off to the Pass of Brander.

This absence of any track heightens the desolate appearance of the loch and explains why it is known only to the yachtsman and climber.

But it was not always deserted.

The lovely little valley of Glennoe down which the river Noe flows was for centuries the home of the clan McIntyre who paid to the Earl of Breadalbane a token rent of a snowball from Ben Cruachan in summer and a fatted calf, until the Earl imposed a money rent which eventually became so excessive that the McIntyres left the land that they so much loved.

One of them, Patrick, composed the famous 'Cruachan Beann' from which I have just quoted:

> I nae mair shall behold
> Spot on earth half sae takin':
> But they've put it under deer,
> And my heart's nigh a-breakin'.

The grandeur of the loch increases as we get farther up and pass Inverliver where the Liver flows into the loch, and Glen Kinglass, the Glen of the Dog Stream, which winds for miles up into the lonely hills to embrace the base of Beinn nan Aighean in two burns which have their sources on the wild lonely heights of Ben Starav (3,541 feet) and Glas Bheinn Mor (3,258 feet).

Though the hills rise more steeply from the northern shores of the loch they do not rise to such great heights as these on the southern bank, which curve gracefully and gently enough at their foot to permit of easy walking.

As we approach the end of the loch two great peaks stand out as sentinels, Ben Starav on the south and Ben Trilleachan on the north.

The loch itself ends in a narrow defile with a road running along the right bank of the river past Guala-chulain, Glenetive House (the home of a famous publisher), and Invercharnan to Dalness.

At the entrance of the glen the river is wide enough

to hold little islands, and the strath is green and wide with trees.

A mile or so up the glen, standing at the foot of the Allt nan Caoirean, is surely the most isolated school in all Scotland.

When we passed, the whole school, consisting of five, were sitting on a heap of stones by the roadside eating their dinner.

There was also an eagle hovering high overhead, to us an object of great interest, but to these children so common a sight that they didn't even lift their eyes.

On the south side of the river in spite of the lack of roads there are farms at Kinlochetive, Coileitir, and Glenceitlein.

From every side burns come roaring down from the heights to swell the river.

The glen, which is most impressive in its sombre grandeur, continues to be wide and green until we reach Dalness, the Dale of the Waterfall, where we are once more reminded of Deirdre, for it was here that she lived so happily with Naisi in their sunny bower.

On the opposite side of the river a waterfall cascades from the heights with unceasing roar.

The dark hills rise abruptly on every side, and over the exquisite bowl of the Hinds' Pass that leads directly from the glen to Glencoe, Deirdre could watch the great herds of deer in what is now the Royal Forest, part of the National Trust of Scotland.

At Dalness is preserved the Black Gun of the Misfortune with which Colin Roy Campbell of Glenure, the Red Fox, was murdered.

It was in 1752 that James Stewart of the Glen was, as everybody believes, wrongly executed for firing two shots at Campbell as he was travelling along the old road over the hills between Ballachulish and Kentallen while on his way to evict Jacobite tenants from Ardsheal. He was tried and condemned at Inveraray, hanged on a gibbet on a knoll at South Ballachulish, and after his skeleton had been hanging for some years it was taken away secretly, but no one dared to touch the gibbet until a madman threw it into the loch.

It is said that the real murderer was known to a few who guarded the secret well, and the name, though handed down from one generation to another, and still known, has never been disclosed.

Readers of *Kidnapped* will recall the fact that David Balfour saw Campbell fall and caught a glimpse of the unknown murderer.

At Dalness, the home of the hereditary keepers of the Royal Forest, the glen turns suddenly north-east under the shadow of those massive, craggy heights that guard Glencoe, the two Shepherds of Etive, Buachaille Etive Beag and Buachaille Etive Mor, with the fine long hill of Beinn Fhada rising to 3,500 feet behind.

Just before the bend the glen is wide and green with a thick belt of trees almost surrounding the big shooting lodge, and where the glen narrows and turns to the right there is a cluster of white houses at the foot of the burn that comes down from the saddle-back between the hills, known as Lairig Gartain.

Dalness is an admirable centre for the lover of the hills, for he has the choice of taking the pass at Allt Fhaolain (Pass of the Seagulls) and coming out at Glean Leac-na-Muidhe (Glen of the Churning Slope), or of climbing Lairig Gartain (Gartain's Pass) between the two Shepherds which will take him to Altnafeadh

85

(Quagmire Burn) or through the Pass of the Hinds, Lairig Eilde, that runs below Stob Dubh and Beinn Fhada, and brings him out at the Study.

After Dalness the glen runs below the long shoulder of the Eastern Shepherd and alongside the red waters of the river that falls over huge boulders with frequent waterfalls that tumble noisily into deep salmon pools.

On the right rise four massive peaks, crowned by Clach Leathad (3,602 feet). The whole sixteen-mile stretch of the glen is magnificent in its wildness.

As we go on the track becomes rougher, and all signs of trees cease.

The road climbs eventually to the threshold of the glen with its grand portal Stob Dearg, the Red Peak, standing like a giant sentinel, 3,345 feet above the junction of this glen and Glencoe, while on the opposite side of Glencoe's entrance rises with almost equal majesty the rocky heights of Beinn a' Chrulaiste (2,805 feet).

In front lie the vast long dark wastes of Rannoch Moor with its myriad shining little lochs bounded in the distance by the grim chain of apparently impenetrable mountains that cut off the moor from Loch Rannoch and Glen Lyon.

But above this chain we see the sugar-loaf top of Schiehallion and Ben More, and peak after peak of the higher mountains of the Grampian range.

And so we come, past the lonely white Kingshouse Inn, the scene of a fine episode in Neil Munro's *John Splendid*, the only building visible in all that wild waste land, to the source of this magic river in Lochan Mathair Etive, Loch of the Mother of Etive, most appropriately set in the very wildest and most remote corner of the moor.

CHAPTER SEVEN

Mull

I HAVE been racking my brains for nearly a week trying to recall her name.

I'm like a man trying to remember the name of the girl who first turned his head when very young. He can remember the honey-coloured hair, the green of her eyes, her laugh, her slim figure, and odd phrases of speech, but her name, no. So has it been with me and that ship. I can see her lines, her beauty, her deck, stout funnels, her luxurious saloons, but her name, ever on the tip of my tongue, keeps on eluding me.

I've got it. It was *Loch Fyne*.

It cost a pound, it took a day, and the experience was unforgettable. For weeks we had looked out from Oban on the sun setting each night more majestically beyond Kerrera, behind the sugar loaf of Ben More, to leave the magic unexplored isle of Mull, shrouded deeper and deeper in mystery. Then at last we could bear it no longer. We started off to encircle the island in this most stately of ships and with deeper knowledge found the mystery become more mysterious.

In the first place Mull is far larger than most people imagine. It is thirty miles long and in one part

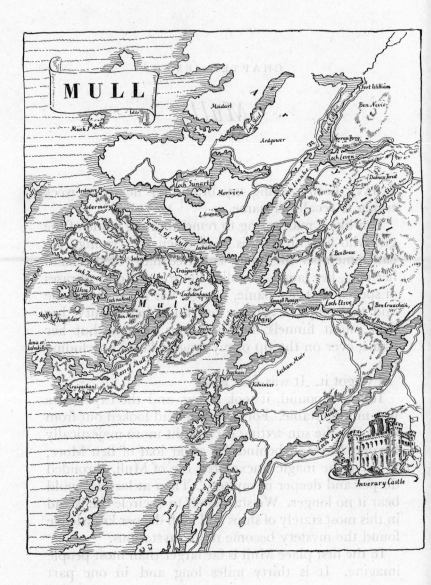

MULL

Muck I.   Isla
                                    Moidart
                    Ardmore Pt   Ardgower
Coll   Tobermory
                    Loch Sunart   Morvern
                        L Arienas
                    Sound of Mull
                                lochalina
                Salen
Loch Tuadh   L Ba   Craigure
    Ullva   Lochdonhead
            Loch naKeal
Staffa   Fingals cave   Mull
                Ben More
Iona or   Spelve
kolmkill
            Iridalın   Loch Buy
        Ross of Mull
                        L Teachan
    Craigachani   Kilninver

                Fort William
                Ben Nevis
            Corran Ferry
        Loch Leven
                Dalness forest
    Loch Linnhe   Glen Ettie
                Ben Breac
        Connell Passage   Loch Etive
                    Ben Cruachan
    Firth of Lorne   Oban   Pass of Brander
                Loch Awe
        Lechan Muir
            L Auch

                Inverary Castle

Colonsay
        Jura   Sound of Jura

twenty-five miles broad. It has not been exploited as Skye has. It remains aloof and in the main unvisited.

Boswell describes it as a hilly country, diversified with heathy grass. Johnson found it dreary, a most dolorous country, much worse than Skye. It took that doughty pair eight hours to ride the eight miles of road between Tobermory and the west coast.

As we cross the Firth of Lorne and make for the narrow entrance of the Sound of Mull Ben More recedes and other peaks come into the foreground, Sgurr Dearg, Beinn Talaidh, and Dun da Ghaoithe, all three round about 2,500 feet. But we forget these on approaching the rugged castle of Duart, seat of the MacLean, whose kinsmen have ruled this island uninterruptedly this last thousand years. The custody of the castle was given to a MacLean by a Lord of the Isles in 1390. The clan was dispossessed in 1691, but recently restored by a chief of the clan who lived to be a hundred.

The steamer here passes between the lighthouse and The Lady's Rock, which gets its name from one of those grim stories which we find everywhere in the Western Isles. One of the MacLeans of Duart, married to Elizabeth, daughter of the second Earl of Argyll, decided to avenge himself for her failure to bear him a son by taking her out to the rock at low tide and leaving her to her fate. Luckily some of the clansmen rescued her and took her over to Lorne, and the MacLean was later murdered in his bed by her brother. Another MacLean of Duart failed to send back a messenger sent to him by MacLaine of Lochbuie. A few years later the lady of Dochbuie paid a visit to Duart and at the end of her visit asked for an escort home. On reaching the head of Loch Spelve the lady's shoe-thongs became unfastened and she ordered the escort to tie her shoe up again. As he bent down to obey she stabbed him in the back and killed him. The islanders have long memories. They still show you the stone where her foot rested.

But I am anticipating. We have not yet set foot in the island. We are on the decks of *Loch Fyne* entering the calm waters of the Sound of Mull which is only two or three miles across with Ardtornish Castle, Loch Aline, and the hills of Morven away to the north.

Soon we draw near the green pleasance of Salen and see the one main road of Mull winding northward along the coast to Tobermory and south-westward towards Loch na Keal which so nearly divides the island into two parts.

At Tobermory we enter the one safe anchorage and bay in the island and can, if we so desire, land and split our journey by a short stay in the land of Mishnish. This is very well worth doing, for Tobermory has a strong character of its own. It afforded, you remember, much gaiety of spirit to Boswell after his long enforced sojourn in Coll. It is little more than a village in spite of its 'Western Isles Hotel'. The old part lies hidden among trees on the steep hillside, but there is a long row of houses, shops, hotels, and churches standing along the water front, and the bay onto which those buildings look is famous by reason of its submerged treasure. Much money and time have been spent in trying to recover from the depths the silver that is supposed to rest at the bottom with the wreck of Spanish Armada payship *Florida* that sank under strange conditions.

This is yet another MacLean story. In 1588 when the *Florida* sought sanctuary here after the defeat of Spain by England, it was readily granted by the MacLean, as Spain was not at war with Scotland. When eventually her commander thought it was safe enough to make for home he was provisioned by MacLean of Duart, but when he failed to pay for his stores MacLean sent his factor to collect the debt. He was seized as prisoner, the sails were hoisted, the anchor weighed and the ship set forth. Somehow the factor made his way to the powder magazine, set it alight, the ship blew up, spilt most of her cargo, and soon foundered. Cannon, swords, and plate were brought up, and not very long ago a hoard of silver coins, but it is believed that the great bulk of the treasure still awaits salvage.

I have never seen an anchorage that seemed more propitious for this sort of treasure-hunt. And how perfectly the calm harbour is protected by Calve Island. One realises that almost as soon as we set sail again into the open waters beyond Auliston Point. Here on the east is the wide mouth of Loch Sunart, a real fjord of the ocean, to the west Bloody Bay and Ardmore Point, to the north the rugged terrifying 'Height of the Great Headland', better known as Ardnamurchan, as desolate and savage a bit of coastline as any in Scotland, and then we need no reminding that we are in the Atlantic with only the rocky isle of Coll and low-lying Tiree standing between us and America. Even the sturdy *Loch Fyne* seems to diminish in size and importance as she plunges through these tremendous rolling waves.

I, at any rate, am relieved to be veering southward past Quinish Point and Caliach Point and not facing the journey that the intrepid Dr. Johnson and Boswell endured and partly enjoyed on that unpremeditated visit to Coll in a vastly less pleasant ship when the storm drove them off their course from Skye to Mull.

I had no ambition to be diverted from my course which was to hug the coastline of Mull, and as the waves grew angrier I recalled the story told by Seton Gordon of the women who embarked from Tobermory for Kilchoan, a ninepenny run of four miles across the sound, only to be carried to Tiree because it was too rough for the Kilchoan ferry boat to meet them, and at Tiree to put about and run for Coll as the ship couldn't even make Tiree pier.

"I think", said the captain to Seton Gordon as he watched them join the ferry at Coll, "they've had their ninepence worth." I was beginning, as we came southward past the scattered Treshnish Isles, to think that I too had had my sovereign's worth and looked longingly up Loch Tuath for a pier or harbour.

The rumour had got about that it would be too rough to land at Staffa. There were many travelled wise-acres at hand to tell me that they had often made this trip with the express intention of landing at Staffa but had never been lucky.

Rumour that day, as so often, was wrong. They and I were lucky. We were landed at Staffa. It was a wet and to my mind hazardous experience, but we got there, and I saw the sheep grazing on the un-expectedly rich grass of that rock islet and I explored Fingal's Cave.

Staffa is about one and a half miles round and stands less than 150 feet above the sea, but the cliffs rise to that height straight out of the water and the one landing beach is small and none too inviting.

There are four caves, Clam Shell, with queer-shaped columns bent over on one side, MacKinnon's, with an enormous mouth overhung with pillars, the Boat Cave, with penetrates the island to a depth of 150 feet, and Fingal's Cave which has been one of Britain's wonders ever since Sir Joseph Banks christened it by that name in 1772. It is said that its true name is the Melodious cave, but it is now finally associated with the great Gaelic hero of the third century whose exploits were sung by his no less famous son, the bard Ossian.

The cave is remarkable both for its volcanic geological formation, colonnades of basalt, erupted in ancient times from Ben More, and for the astonishing variety of colours in the rocks under the water. It is enormously high, about 230 feet long, but only about forty feet wide. What impressed me most of all about these columns was their mathematical symmetry, the fact that they are all perfect hexagons—or is it octagons?—and the fact that the great stalagmites were a brilliant yellow and red.

The high seas abated considerably as soon as we rejoined *Loch Fyne* and I lost my desire to land on the mainland of Mull, though Loch Scridain stretching right to the foot of Ben More looked inviting.

The Holy Island of Iona lay ahead, and after the geological glory of Staffa we now looked forward to the even more famous ecclesiastical and historical glory of Iona or Icolmkill as it was called in Boswell's day.

As we sailed along, I found myself thinking of his journey by boat coasting along from the island of InchKenneth by way of Gribon and MacKinnon's Cave where, according to tradition, a piper and twelve men once penetrated, never to return.

Boswell and Johnson explored about 500 feet of it by candlelight and then decided to return before their one candle burnt out. Unable to land at Staffa they passed by Nuns' Island to land in Iona which deeply impressed Johnson. 'That man', he wrote, 'is little to be envied, whose patriotism would not gain force upon the plain of Marathon, or whose piety would not grow warmer among the ruins of Iona.' Impressive indeed is the stalwart tower of the Cathedral rising above the white sands and green sea of the Sound of Iona.

It is curious that whereas Johnson was unimpressed by Mull and Boswell sang its praises, in Iona it was Johnson's turn to be impressed and Boswell to be left cold. Both apparently expected to see more dignified monuments to the forty-eight early kings of Scotland, four kings of Ireland, eight of Norway, and one of France, and deplored the fact that the grave stones were flat and without inscriptions. In addition, this burial ground of Oran contains the bodies of a vast number of great highland chiefs.

Most modern visitors find themselves sufficiently excited at standing above the grave of Macbeth not to worry about the absence of marble monuments which in any event would be anomalous.

There are many reasons for the great popularity of the sacred island, the main one being the fact that it was the Irish prince and saint, Columba, who landed on the 12th May 563 at Port a' Churaich, the Harbour of the Coracle, where you may still see the mound under which the coracle was buried lest the saint should ever be tempted to return home. He wrought many miracles in the island and had some difficulty before he finally dispelled the powers of darkness.

94

The legend goes that the walls of Oran's chapel (which stands above the burial ground) had a habit of falling to the ground by night. St. Columba decided that this called for human sacrifice, and Oran agreed to be buried alive with the result that the walls stood. But Oran disturbed his leader by coming back to announce that 'Heaven is not as has been written: neither is Hell as is commonly supposed'.

The landing-place is near Martyrs' Bay where Norse invaders murdered sixty-eight Iona monks in a raid in 806. There were at least five raids in the next century, and at Port a' Churaich there is a fifty-foot-long 'ship's barrow' or Viking's grave.

Always an island of pilgrims, the population has dwindled in the last hundred years from 500 to 100, and the Gaelic is no longer the spoken language. But there is activity, particularly the activity of the tourist and pilgrims come to worship in the great abbey originally built by Reginald, Lord of the Isles in 1203, though little of the original building now remains. Most of the present abbey dates from the sixteenth century and the nave is wholly modern.

The famous Black Stone on which oaths were sworn has disappeared, but the vast cross outside the abbey, known as St. Martin's Cross, with its heavily decorated spirals and bosses, has withstood the gales of a thousand years. The Nunnery, which is contemporary with the old abbey, is in ruins.

This would have pleased St. Columba who would allow no woman in the island, not even a female beast. "Where there is a cow", he said, "there is a woman, and where there is a woman there is mischief."

Very few visitors to the island leave without taking with them souvenirs, brooches designed, mainly in silver, by Alexander Ritchie, once guide to the Abbey, of Ancient Viking ships and early Celtic carvings of great beauty.

The sea-birds too are an outstanding feature of the island, particularly the ringed plover, terns, oyster-catchers and gannets, running on the white sands or diving into the clear green depths.

About the middle of the island stands the queer knoll known as the Large Fairy Knoll or Angels' Knoll. Here one of the monks saw angels in white garments flying to St. Columba and standing round him as he prayed.

Westward of this knoll is the Spouting Cave and beyond it a promontory where the people of Iona on a certain day in spring each year used to boil cauldrons of porridge which they poured into the sea as an offering to the god Shonny, who in return guaranteed a plentiful supply of seaweed, which was burned for kelp and is still used as a top-dressing for the fields.

About half a mile away to the east of the island lies the Ross of Mull and a little south the islet of Erraid and the dangerous Torran Rocks, on the reefs of which the brig *Covenant* foundered, leaving David Balfour marooned alone in the islet among a jumble of granite rocks and heather.

Here is Robert Louis Stevenson's description of Erraid: 'There was no one part of it better than another; it was all desolate and rocky; nothing living on it but game birds which I lacked the means to kill, and the gulls which haunted the outlying rocks in a prodigious number. But the creek, or straits, that cut off the isle from the mainland of the Ross, opened out on the north into a bay and the bay again

THE CUILLIN PEAKS, A PROSPECT FROM TARSCAVAIG OVER LOCH EISHORT, SKYE

STORNOWAY, ISLE OF LEWIS

opened into the Sound of Iona. Over the low country of the Ross, I saw smoke go up as if from a homestead in a hollow of the land.'

Sitting on a flat-topped high rock overlooking the sound David hailed a coble with a brown sail bound for Iona, but they turned a deaf ear to his cries and sailed on laughing. It was not until he had passed four days of thirst, hunger, and cold that he discovered from another passing boatload of fishermen that he needn't have been marooned at all. Twice a day at low water it is possible to wade across to the mainland of Mull.

But David has little to say in favour of Mull, describing it as rugged and trackless like Erraid, 'all bog and briar and big stones. There may be roads for them that know the country well; but for my part I had no better guide than my own nose, and no other landmark than Ben More.'

Even to-day there is but one main good road in the island, starting from Fionphort opposite Iona, clinging close to the south and east shores of Loch Scridain, winding round the foot of Ben More northward through Glen Seilisdair and then turning east again opposite the island of InchKenneth along the shore of Loch na Keal to make for the Sound of Mull at Salen. It then hugs the Sound northward to end at Tobermory.

There is a subsidiary road from Tobermory through Dervaig to Calgay Bay which then cuts south to Kilmintan, along the shore of Loch Tuath and north side of Loch na Keal to rejoin the main road near Gruline.

Another road follows the coast to connect Salen with Duart, continuing to Loch Spelve and up the valley of the Lussa river as far as Glen More where it fails by a mile or so to connect with another track coming up from the main road to Glen More by the side of the Coladoir river.

The only other tracks I know are one from Carsaig Bay down the Leidle river to Loch Scridain, one from Dervaig along the Bellart and Aros valleys to Salen, and one from Tobermory to Glengorm Castle, very few in view of the size of the island and in view of its fertility.

I can foresee a great opening up of Mull. Mull is not so austere as Skye, there are more crofters' gardens, there are hazel trees on the shores of Loch Scridain, birches and oaks in Glen Lussa, red deer and green hills in the Great Glen, and woods in Torosay.

Certainly the south coast of the Ross of Mull viewed from the decks of *Loch Fyne* after we passed the exciting reefs of the Torran Rocks struck me as rough and difficult to traverse. No road skirts this part of the island, and as we pass along eastward the hills seem to fall precipitously to the sea.

But Mull to me will always be associated with Doctor Johnson. It was while Boswell and he were waiting for the ship to take them there that Doctor Johnson administered his classic rebuke about the uselessness of bustling and walking impatiently up and down.

"It does not hasten us a bit," he said. "It is getting on horseback in a ship. All boys do it; and you are longer a boy than others."

CHAPTER EIGHT

Skye

To some people Skye is an island of mystery, to others an island of mists; to me it is both misty and mysterious, but it is also terrifying. I have been frightened climbing the bare rugged crags of the Cuillin, frightened on looking in to the sombre black waters of Loch Coruisk, and most of all frightened by the gaunt eeriness of the Quairaing where one's voice echoes back most hollowly from those pitiless savage rocks which stand in such utter desolation. There is, of course, a fascination in terror, but Skye has also other sorts of fascination that are softer and more pleasant.

Skye is so near the mainland that when you cross to it at Kyleakin you feel that you could easily put a washing-line across the narrow strait. When, however, you set sail to it from Mallaig you realise that even a narrow water can be as rough as the Atlantic.

At Kyleakin you get your first reminder that the island was for three hundred years a Norse island. The word Kyleakin means the Strait of Haakon, King of Norway, who in 1263 anchored here with his galleys before sailing south to be defeated on the Clyde. The queer distorted fragment of a castle on a rocky mound nearby remains to remind us that one of the

Butt of Lewis

Atlantic Ocean

Flannan I.

Loch Roag

Lewis

Scarp I.

Stornoway

Broad Bay

Tyne

The Minch

Harris

Taransay I.

Loch Resort

Lewis Forest

Pabbay I.

Scalpay

Shiant Isles

Sound of Harris

East Loch Tarbert

North Uist

Trotternish Pt.

Loch Snizort

Quiraing

Monach I.

Old Man of Storr

Sound of Raasay

Little Minch

Loch Maddy

Raasay

Benbecula

Vaternish

Inner Sound

Dunvegan Castle

Mt. Leon II
I. Tables

Bracadale

Portree

South Uist

Skye

M. Reckley I.

Broadford

SKYE and
The Long Island

Soay I.

Chuchulin Sound

Sound of Sleat

Eriskay Is.

Valla

Canna I.

Barra I.

Rum Is.

Eigg

Sound of Rum

99

Norwegian Princesses married a Chief of the MacKinnon and settled down here. She levied a toll on all vessels that tried to pass through the narrow strait, by stretching a chain across from Kyleakin to the Kyle of Lochalsh and lowering it only on payment.

The first port of call in the island, after leaving the Kyle of Lochalsh, is Broadford, which contains a jetty, a comfortable whitewashed inn, which is a favourite haunt of anglers and climbers, and a small village street.

After leaving Broadford we cross the water to Raasay, an island where few visitors ever disembark, except those bound for the big house, and then recross the Sound with the Cuillin, coming more and more into prominence if the mists have cleared, far behind the long Loch Sligachan whose shores are fringed with many white houses.

The main port and town of Skye is, of course, Portree, which is set steeply on a hill like Lynton and has just a small jetty and a row of houses at the edge of the sea. The hotel stands high up on the front of the terrace, which contains the main body of the town. There are high cliffs to the north of Portree and at the back a pleasant combination of moorland and woodland, with attractive burns cascading down deep ravines into the sea.

The town itself is a little chilly and bare, but the church is worth a visit because of the stained glass window put up in memory of Flora MacDonald. A brass bears this unusually informative inscription:

To the Glory of God and in memory of Flora MacDonald, daughter of Ronald, the son of Angus MacDonald the younger, Milton, South Uist. She was born in 1722 and was married 6th November, 1750 at Florigerry, Isle of Skye, to Allan VII in descent of the Kingsburgh MacDonald, Captain 34th Royal Highland Emigrant Regiment, who served with distinction through the American War of Independence. She died 5th March, 1790 and was buried at Kilmuir, Isle of Skye. She effected the escape of Prince Charles Edward from South Uist after the battle of Culloden in 1746: and in 1779 when returning from America on board a ship attacked by a French privateer, encouraged the sailors to make a spirited and successful resistance, thus risking her life for both the Houses of Stuart and Hanover.

As this is as much as, and perhaps even more than, the average Englishman knows of the part played in the Prince's life by this loyal and brave lady, it may be appropriate to amplify the story.

You remember that after an adventurous voyage in the course of which the Prince had a brush with an English frigate off The Lizard, he weighed anchor in the *Du Taillay* off Barra Head on the 22nd July 1745.

He disembarked at Eriskay and was carried ashore by a man whose great-great-granddaughter still lives there and displays with justifiable pride the rosy convolvulus, the seeds of which the Prince gathered while waiting on the coast of France. This convolvulus continues to flower here and nowhere else, either in Eriskay or any other place in the Hebrides. Alexander MacDonald of Boisdale did his utmost to persuade the Prince to go home.

"Home?" echoed the Prince, "I am come home." Boisdale then persuaded his brother Clanranald to forbid the MacDonalds to follow him, but Deness MacDonald went on ahead to Moidart and summoned the Clanranald chieftains to meet him. On the 25th July the *Du Taillay* sailed from Eriskay and anchored in an inlet of the sea between Moidart and Arisaig.

A contemporary describes the Prince as 'a tall youth of most agreeable aspect, in a plain black coat with a plain shirt, a plain hat and black stockings. I found my heart swell to my very throat; he saluted none of us, and we only made a bow at a distance.'

Of his triumphant progress through Scotland, his victories and march through England to Derby, his retreat and defeat at Culloden, most people know something. But ten months after his leaving, on the 27th April 1746, he was once again in the Outer Hebrides, with a price on his head. He arrived at Rossinigh in Benbecula in a fierce storm, but could not stay there owing to the efforts of the MacAulay to betray him. So he sailed to the island of Scalpay off Harris, where Donald MacLeod went on to hire a ship in Stornoway. The Prince sailed up Loch Seaforth and then walked thirty-eight miles through a dark and stormy night to the house of MacKenzie of Kilvern, just outside Stornoway. But the people of Stornoway refused to let him reach his ship, so he had to go back to South Uist where he remained in hiding for eighteen days. As the troops were then closing in on him, he had to run the gauntlet up and down the coast for ten days and when he reached Benbecula found that his friends had been arrested on suspicion of harbouring him. It was at this stage that Flora MacDonald, a girl of twenty-four, came into the picture.

She was staying with her brother in South Uist, and was brought into the Prince's presence in a boat on the 21st June 1746. She carried a letter from her stepfather to his wife at Armadale stating that Flora was bringing back an Irish servant, Betty Burke, under the care of Neil from Eacham.

Flora then disguised the Prince as Betty in a flowered linen gown, quilted petticoat, white apron and hooded mantle, and took him with her in a six-oared boat from Rossinigh on the night of the 28th June. The crossing was stormy and on reaching Vaternish they could not land as the soldiers fired on them. They crossed Loch Snizort and landed at Markstadt, the seat of Sir Alexander MacDonald, where they were joined by Kingsburgh, and went on to Uig and Kingsburgh, where the Prince rewarded Flora by letting her cut off a lock of his yellow hair. He then changed his disguise and went on towards Portree. He dared not, of course, ask for a boat there, so a small boat was carried from Loch Fada two miles to the cliff-face, lowered into the sea and rowed to Portree where the Prince was waiting, a little disgruntled because he had only been able to get thirteen shillings in exchange for a guinea. After taking his leave of Flora MacDonald ("I trust to see you in St. James's yet") he was rowed over to Raasay and then returned after two nights in a violent storm to Skye, taking refuge in a byre near the house of Skorrybreck on the moor above Portree.

He is said to have been so troubled as to have called out in his sleep, "Oh God! Poor Scotland!" He then walked thirty miles across the wildest part of the island up Glen Sligachan, over the ridge at Glamaig to Marsee, down to Loch Eynort, thence to Elgol by way of Strathmore, with only a bottle of brandy to keep the whole party going. At Elgol Mrs. Mac-Kinnon gave them breakfast and a bed, and the Prince then hid in a cave at the end of Loch Scavaig and left it on the 4th July to make another desperate thirty-mile journey to try to reach the mainland at Mallaig.

It speaks volumes for the loyalty of his followers that, in spite of a price of £30,000 on his head, only John MacAulay, Minister of Barra and South Uist, Lord MacAulay's grandfather, should have tried to arrange for the capture of the Prince.

Twenty years after the Prince escaped, Johnson and Boswell followed very closely in his tracks on their journey through Skye. They visited Flora Mac-Donald and her husband, of whom Boswell says that he was a large stately man with a steady, sensible face, the very picture of a gallant Highlander.

Johnson wrote of Flora: 'A name that will be mentioned in history, and if courage and fidelity be virtues, mentioned with honour.' These words are carved on her tombstone at Kilmuir. It was in the year following Johnson's visit that Flora and her husband sailed with her three sons and two daughters for North Carolina in a ship, the *Baliol*, that was attacked by a French privateer. During the fight Flora's arm was broken. They arrived in America just in time for her husband to fight in the War of Independence, in which he was taken prisoner and later given a lease of 5,000 acres of land.

Flora and her daughters came back to Scotland in 1779, leaving her husband to see the war through before returning to Kingsburgh to rejoin her in 1784.

Portree is the obvious centre for exploring the North and West of the island, but for climbers, who will find quite enough to occupy their energies on the Cuillin, the obvious place to stay is the famous and most comfortable Sligachan Inn, which stands in solitary white splendour at the very foot of the mountain, with the blood-red Cuillin standing away to the east above the sea-loch, and the savage jagged crags of the sombre black Cuillin pointing their gnarled fingers to the sky immediately behind and above the white inn. The entrance hall to this hotel is filled with a vast array of climbing ropes, crampons, stoutly nailed boots, and all the other accoutrements of the rock climber. There are peaks up which you can scramble, but there are also peaks as difficult of access as many of the famous Alpine peaks. The crags are of a hard black volcanic substance which is both rough and firm, giving a good foothold, and their height, in view of their capacity to intimidate, is quite inconsiderable. There are a dozen peaks in all, some over 2,000 feet high, more over 3,000, but the highest is only 3,308 ft.

The man who tries to tackle them casually or with contempt soon learns an invaluable lesson. The difficulty of scaling a hill is not to be assessed in terms of height. Man's most formidable enemy on these wild crags is not the rocks but the mist that suddenly descends from nowhere and envelops every corrie and crevice in its swirling embrace.

There is a rich reward for climbing these peaks on a clear day, for you not only get a superb view over the sea towards the Western Isles, but immediately at your feet, 3,000 below, you see the almost land-locked Loch Coruisk, the most sinister-looking of all waters that I have ever seen. The loch is associated with a number of legends, one of which tells of a mortal falling in love with the mermaid of the loch. Her fascination must have been as strong as that of the syrens if she was to constrain him to live with her in these imprisoned black waters. Coruisk is known as the loch that never smiles. That is an understatement. It is a loch that always frowns, and you feel the frown of disapproval more and more

as you get nearer to it. I have crossed the Bad Step
that brings you to its shores, but I have never made a
complete circuit of its shores; nor do I ever propose
to do so.

When you are climbing the Cuillin or encircling
Coruisk, you sigh for a touch of colour, some sign of
grass or a flower, but all is arid, grim, dour, black,
inimical.

Yet just over the other side of the hills I found
primroses and kingcups growing in wild profusion
near the Youth Hostel in Glen Brittle. This glen
is so remote that the postbox is only cleared twice a
week.

Beyond Glen Brittle lies Loch Harport, on the shores
of which stands Tallisker, the only legalised whisky
distillery in Skye. I always thought Skye to be the
home of Drambuie, that honeyed whisky liqueur, the
secret of which has been closely preserved ever since
Prince Prince Charles Edward first tasted it, or was it
his invention? But the whisky of Tallisker has its own
peculiar virtues too, and fortified by that I found
myself stepping out the eighteen miles to Dunvegan
as if on air. There can scarcely be any question that
Dunvegan is the most romantic castle in the British
Isles.

It stands superbly on a rocky promontory overlooking a sea-loch, with a water-gate cut into the rock.
The front has been badly restored, but nothing can
destroy the atmosphere of its interior. It dates from
the middle of the thirteenth century and is the most
ancient inhabited house in Scotland. The MacLeods,
who have always owned it, claim to be descended
from Olaf the Black, King of Man, whose son Leod
became the adopted son of the Sheriff of Skye for

the Norsemen, and married the daughter of the Lord of Dunvegan. The Fairy Tower was added by the hunchback, Alastair Crotach, in the sixteenth century, and later MacLeods changed the back of the castle to the front by adding a high wall and throwing a hedge across the moat. There is an oubliette some twenty feet deep below the floor of the main rooms, where the twenty-second MacLeod imprisoned his first wife in a dark hole six feet wide without light, air, food or water. One scarcely needs the reminder, that grim deeds were not uncommon in the earlier days of this castle.

Here is a typical example.

When the ninth MacLeod died in 1552, his two brothers were away, and Ian the Fairhaired, a descendant of the sixth MacLeod, was hailed as Chief. He had married a MacDonald of Knock, by whom he had a son, Ian Dubh, who invited the two brothers to a meeting to hear their claims. They foolishly fell into this trap, were murdered by Ian, whose father, rather surprisingly, ordered his arrest. Ian, of course, escaped and on his father's death seized Dunvegan and his brother's widow. When his brother's three sons returned from their father's funeral they found Dunvegan closed against them and Ian in full armour waiting for them at the head of the stairway. There was, of course, a fight, in which Ian killed all his three nephews, seized the wives and children of the clan and shut up his other brothers in the dungeon.

At this stage the Campbells of Argyll intervened. Ian agreed to meet the Campbells in Kilmuir church, where terms were agreed upon, and he invited eleven Campbell chieftains to a great feast. They foolishly

accepted, and each Campbell found himself sitting
between two MacLeods. When the feast was over a
cup of blood was placed before each guest and at
this signal each Campbell was stabbed to death by
his host. This scene took place in the drawing-room.

Villainy, however, received its just reward in the
end, for Ian Dubh had a red-hot iron pushed through
his bowels in Ireland. The main object in visiting
Dunvegan is, of course, to see the Fairy Flag, the
gossamer-like fragments of which still hang on the wall
in the drawing-room under glass. It is very light khaki
or biscuit in colour, and has been mended with blood-
red thread. It is a thing of shreds and patches.

It was originally found wrapped round the baby
Ian, the fourth Chief, in 1380, by fairies who were
singing a peculiar lullaby which has been sung ever
since over each new baby MacLeod. It has the
property of giving succour when waved in time of
dire need, but it can only be waved three times.

It was first waved in 1490 at the battle of Glendale
and again in 1580 at the battle of the Spoiled Dykes
at Trumpan.

There is a legend that it was also once waved to
save the life of a MacLeod before he was born. Sir
Walter Scott tells us that it brought herrings to the
loch and ensured fertility to the MacLeod women.

A curious prophecy was made about its final
waving by Corinneach Odal:

'When Norman, the fourth Norman, Tormod Ian
Breac, the son of the slender, bony English lady,
should perish by accidental death; when MacLeod's
Maidens should become the property of a Campbell;
when a fox should have young ones in one of the turrets
of the Castle; and when the Faery Flag should *for*

the last time be taken out of its box and unfurled, then the glory of the MacLeods would depart, a great part of their lands be sold, and a coracle would be sufficiently large to carry all the gentleman tacksmen of the name of MacLeod on the estate across Loch an Duin; but in times far distant another Ian Breac will arise who will recover the estates, and raise the power and honour of the House of MacLeod to a higher glory than ever.'

That is the prophecy. Here are the facts about its partial fulfilment:

(1) In 1799 an English blacksmith working at Dunvegan broke open the iron chest in which the flag was hidden in a box of scented wood;

(2) The fourth Norman was blown up in H.M.S. *Queen Charlotte*;

(3) Campbell of Kriskay bought the rocky pinnacles rising out of the sea, known as MacLeod's Maidens;

(4) A tame fox had a litter in the West turret;

(5) No tacksman of the name of MacLeod, it is said, remained on the estate and the last male heir Ian Breac was killed in the 1914–18 war.

The fairy flag is not the only MacLeod relic of great antiquity. Close by stand Rory Mor's drinking-horn, and the Dunvegan Cup. The horn is a huge ox-horn with a silver band and each Chief had to drain its contents at one draught on attaining his majority. The cup is a very ancient Irish chalice with silver filigree work and settings of gems that have been removed. The wooden bowl is said to have been the property of Neil Glendubh, King of Ulster in 900. You may also see the lock of hair which Flora Mac-

Donald cut from Prince Charles Edward's head, and the portrait of the MacLeod who refused to give him help.

At Trumpan, twelve miles north of Dunvegan, you can see the place where the Clan used to worship

One Sunday morning their enemies, the Mac-Donalds, sailed over from South Uist, surrounded the church and burnt up all the worshipping Mac-Leods, except one woman who managed to squeeze out of a window and escape to arouse the rest of the Clan. Then began the Battle of the Spoiled Dykes, the occasion of the second waving of the flag, as a result of which the raiders were beaten back to their boats, but as the tide had ebbed leaving their vessels high and dry on the beach, they were unable to escape and were all killed. This raid, by the way, was in revenge for a raid of the MacLeods in 1577 when they burnt 395 MacDonalds in a cave in Eigg. The burning was to avenge a still earlier episode when a band of MacLeods landing in Eigg made love to some of the MacDonald girls against their will and were, in consequence, tied up and set adrift in their boats.

In spite of their turbulent history, the MacLeods found time to develop their taste for music. The MacLeod hereditary pipers, the MacCrimmons, who had their college at Bouveraig for many hundreds of years, composed the classic pipe-music known as Piobaireachd or Leol Mor, and became famous as the outstanding bagpipe players of the world.

I said that Dunvegan was the most romantic castle in these islands, and even from the little bits of history that I have had space to record, you get some idea of the wealth of its history.

But there is another castle at the north end of the island which has an even wilder and more romantic setting. But whereas Dunvegan is inhabited and always thronged with visitors, Duntulm is a rugged ruin, desolate and isolated, perched on the very edge of a high sea-loch, the haunt of gannets, red sea-anemones and pink sea-thrift.

From its walls you look out over the sea to low-lying Lewis and high Harris in the north, and Uist and Benbecula lying low in the south.

Duntulm was the ancient seat of the MacDonalds, Lords of the Isles, who now live at Arundale Castle, in the extreme south of the island. Duntulm was abandoned when, 200 years ago, a nurse let the MacDonald baby heir fall out of the window over the cliffs into the sea below.

The castle is supposed to be haunted by Donald Gorm, who put his next-of-kin, Hugh, to death in a dungeon here by particularly foul means.

Hugh lived at Castle Uisdean, a tower without windows. The castle could only be entered by means of a ladder which reached to a little door high up in the wall. Hugh always took the precaution of pulling the ladder up after him. There was a reason for that, because he had arranged to murder his kinsman Donald.

Unluckily, when his plot was discovered, he expressed his sorrow to Donald in a letter which he sent by mistake to a fellow-conspirator and despatched to Donald the letter that ought to have gone to the conspirator arranging for his murder.

So Donald, not unnaturally, sent an invitation to the unsuspecting 'penitent' Hugh to come over to Duntulm. He rashly accepted, was thrown into the dungeon, and given salt meat which gave him such a thirst that he gnawed a pewter dish to pieces before he died.

Donald had a macabre taste. He took a violent and sudden dislike to his wife, who was a MacLeod of Dunvegan, the sister of Rory Mor, and an equally violent and sudden liking for a daughter of MacKenzie of Kintaire. His wife had lost an eye—one wonders how—so Donald mounted her on a one-eyed grey horse, led by a one-eyed boy, followed by a one-eyed dog, and drove them out.

One scents a *King Lear* atmosphere in this scene. The coincidence of so many one-eyed creatures at once is too great for them all to have been natural. I suspect Donald of doing a bit of malicious 'gouging' on his own. The arrival of this one-eyed troop at Dunvegan naturally gave Rory Mor an excuse for a raid, so he first killed as many MacDonalds as he could find and then Donald raided MacLeod's lands in Uist, and in his turn Rory Mor attacked the Mac-Donalds in Uist. And so the feuds went on.

In view of all these tales and legends, it is not surprising that I kept on imagining that I saw fierce kilted figures stealing furtively through the heather and boghead of the open moor. But when I got nearer these figures usually turned out to be just bush and shrub shaking in the wind, for I seemed to meet very few living people, either on the rough hedgeless roads or on the moors. The gayest collection of folk that I ran into in the island were the cattle-dealers in bowler hats or caps and knickerbockers in a tiny village market near Glen Brittle, and a mass of tinkers feasting and dancing round peat fires outside their tents near Loch Snizort, to celebrate a wedding.

There are gentle, genial pleasances in the island, where you will find a gentle, if reserved, population of crofters at Uig, a village in a deep, green hollow with neat cottages, colourful gardens, an hotel and numerous crofts dotted about round Uig Bay, but the impression I carry away of Skye is not of gentleness but weirdness, of miles and miles and miles of black, wet, open moorland and unforgettably impressive lonely peaks and crags.

One of the most formidable and isolated of these is the Old Man of Storr, an isolated black rock standing 160 feet up, rather like a giant cypress tree turned into stone, in the hollow of a black mountain covered with loose black volcanic cinders.

This crater-like chasm is eerie and sinister enough, but the Quirang, which means the pit of the Men of Fingal, is even more eerie and sinister. The Quirang is a hill rising 1,800 feet out of the sea, on every side steep, but almost a precipice on the right. At the top is a crater, walled round with rocks, and out of the middle of the crater there rises 'The Table', a flat mass of rock about 300 feet long with a cloth of brilliantly green grass. All round are rocks torn and twisted and tormented by earthquake and volcanic eruption, one of them, 'The Needle', standing up 120 feet and overhanging one of the ways down to 'The Table'.

The Quirang remains to me the most intimidating place I have ever visited. As you stand on 'The Table' and cry out, your voice reverberates all round the threatening crags and comes back again and again hollowly and ghostly. Whenever I go back to Skye I always feel an urgent desire to visit it again to see if its malign influence still persists. And whenever I

do penetrate its centre, I find that this influence is
stronger than ever I imagined and my one desire is
to escape from it while I can.

I have met people who are insensitive to the influence of hills and their shapes, but I have yet to
meet anybody who has spent a day scrambling about
in the crater of the Quirang without being deeply
affected. It is easy enough to laugh at the Quirang
when you're safely at home. When you are in its
shadow you do not laugh. You tremble.

CHAPTER NINE

The Outer Hebrides

LEWIS AND HARRIS

THE *Lochinvar* is a tough enough looking steamer to cross the Atlantic, but long before we reached Stornoway she had used up all her toughness.

The Minch looks an inconsiderable water on the map. It can be very formidable in reality.

Stornoway is a clean, compact little port, of clearcut grey houses with a long brown moorland behind, and one large park of trees (one notices those trees because they are almost the only ones in the island) surrounding the tall towers of Stornoway Castle, bequeathed to the town by the late Lord Leverhulme. About forty yards out from the shore we passed the place where the troopship *Yolaire* went down on New Year's Day 1919 taking with her 200 men of the island just home from the war. It was not, I think, however, the memory of them that made the blue-eyed and red-haired boys and girls who crowded on the pier, so silent. They whispered to each other in muffled Gaelic as we passed and then melted away into the shadows, some into the shadows of the fishermen's cottages, others into the shadows of very ramshackle old-fashioned 'buses that were bound for Tolsta, Shawbost, Islivig, Barvas, and other moorland hamlets.

The harbour was full of newly painted steam-drifters, but the fishermen were oddly at variance in their information about them. Each man spoke with great assurance, but as no two of them agreed as to the number of drifters that would be going out, I wasn't much wiser. One man was positive that sixty drifters would be setting sail each night, a second that ten would be, a third that none would be going out, because it would be too cold. "Herrings", he said, "like warm water." One of those who said that they would go out said that they would go because it was so rough. Herrings in his view prefer rough seas. I came to the conclusion, which was afterwards fully justified, that the Gael will provide any answer that he thinks will please the listener, purely out of politeness.

Even in June I found Stornoway a chilly, colourless town. Sunday is an unbelievably dead day. Not only are the pubs and shops all shut, but the streets are completely deserted except for the sheep who come off the moor to escape from the cold. No one will drive a car on Sunday, and if anybody pokes his nose beyond his or her doorstep, it is only to proceed in solemn black to the church or chapel service. There is, unexpectedly, a cinema in Stornoway, and its effect on the style of hairdress worn by the girls was obvious. Their speech, however, is less Americanised. They prefer to keep their Gaelic pure.

Intending visitors may like to be reminded that there is no hotel in Lewis outside Stornoway. On the other hand, it is easy to find accommodation in most of the villages either at the post-office, general stores, or in a croft.

There are no mountains in Lewis. It is mainly comprised of bleak, very wet moorland with a large number of little fresh-water lochs that provide excellent fishing.

The roads are few, hedgeless, narrow and full of potholes, good neither for cars nor bicycles. If you turn aside from the road on foot your chances of falling into a bog are considerable. Man's fight in the Outer Hebrides is not for comfort or luxury, but for bare existence. The majority of the islanders live in what are known as 'black houses'. They are not black, but are long and low, built by themselves from the loose granite boulders that strew the moor. The walls rise to a height of about six feet and are sur-mounted by a grassy turf ledge on the top of which the sheep and hens feed. Above that is a wagon roof of thatch tied down with ropes weighted with stones to prevent it from being blown off by the gales. There are no chimneys. The smoke from the peat fire in the centre of the living-room escapes through a central hole in the roof. Beds are built into the wall of the living-room which also contains a spinning-wheel and handloom for weaving the wool that they themselves shear, spin, and dye. The living-room is very smoky and dark owing to the smallness of the windows which are little more than loopholes.

The living-room lies to the right of the one door. The larger and more airy room on the left is for the beasts, but you will see calves, sheep, hens, and sheep-dogs also at large in the living-room.

Each cottage has a black stack of peat piled up against the wall, and a small plot of black reclaimed land raised high above a deep ditch, fertilised with seaweed, on which with great difficulty they raise a meagre crop of potatoes, cabbages, turnips, and corn.

They are as nearly self-supporting as any native of these islands can be. They build their own houses, live entirely on their own produce, burn their own fuel, and wear clothes of their own weaving. They presumably have to buy boots if they ever wear any. They go barefoot over the moor to cut the peat or to fetch in their beasts, so even shoes seem to be superfluous.

The first obvious excursion from Stornoway is across the island to the shores of the Atlantic above which stand the famous prehistoric stones of Callernish.

There are eleven stone circles in Lewis, seven of them within four miles of this most famous circle.

Callernish is a small bleak hamlet consisting of one street of black houses standing above a sea-loch, open to all the winds that blow. Just beyond the last cottage stand four avenues leading from north, south, east, and west to the circle of thirteen stones, each standing about thirteen feet high with one tremendous stone in the middle standing about fifteen or sixteen feet up, weighing about six tons. This is covered with lichen and faces a small grassy mound with four more stones in the middle The influence of these stones on the villages is obvious. I watched a girl come towards the village from the farther side of the circle. In spite of the fact that the rain was beating down and her direct route lay through the circle, she swerved like a shying horse and made a complete detour round it. It is said that lovers who make the stones their trysting place will be accursed. The local people call them 'The False Men', and it is said that no two people counting them ever arrive at the same total. The same is said of the Rollright Stones above Long Compton.

The age of Callernish and its purpose are both unknown. Its elliptical shape is very odd for a pre-Christian period, but it has been proved from the rate of growth of the peat-moss in which the stones stood that they are over three thousand years old. The circle itself is forty feet in diameter and the north avenue leading to it is 270 feet long, with its rows of slanting stones standing twenty-seven feet apart. The northern avenue is orientated to the star Capella just before sunrise on the day of the Winter Solstice 1800 B.C., and the eastern avenue points to the rising of the Pleiades at the Spring equinox of 1750 B.C. I leave the deduction to you.

Almost as exciting as, but quite different from, these stones is the ruined fortress or Dun of Carloway, a few miles to the north. This is a tall coneshaped Pictish broch standing high on a knoll overlooking a sea-loch. It has four layers of intermural galleries with loopholes. The entrance is only three feet six inches high and the guardroom, which is nine feet long, is only four feet high. Legend has it that it was built in the fourth century by a giant, Darg MacNurren. He must have been a very small giant, or else have had Alice's capacity for shrinking.

The people of Callernish keep well clear of their stones. The people of Carloway use their dun as their main meeting-place. I found about a dozen village boys in blue jerseys gossiping under its walls, but as soon as I began to speak they were all struck dumb. They avoided my gaze, looked sheepishly down on the ground and replied to none of my questions. It may have been shyness. It may have been that they were not bilingual. But as soon as I began to crawl along the passages that led me from one height to another of the dun, I could always see them below me peering furtively up at me from behind corners and then running away like frightened deer, completely silent. It gave me a far more eerie feeling than I got among the Callernish stones. It was strange too to find that my driver neither greeted any passer-by on the roads nor was greeted by them, though he must certainly have known many of them, because many of them were 'bus-drivers. Almost every village in the island has its own 'bus which goes into Stornoway every morning of the week except Wednesday, and returns every night after the mail-boat has come in. Communications, in spite of the bad state of the roads, are good. I counted over thirty telegraph offices during my tour of the island, though it is difficult to believe that the crofters ever have need to send a telegram or even to receive one, except in war-time.

The population is oddly dispersed. For some sixteen miles after leaving Stornoway on my second trip to explore the north-west coast, we passed no village at all, no sign of any habitation except the small thatched sheilings which the townspeople stay in while their beasts are grazing on the open moor.

But after Barvas the villages all along the coast crowd so closely together that there is hardly any gap between them. It was near Barvas that my driver broke his rule of silence. He had sternly obstructed all my attempts to get into conversation with the many tinkers who wandered by hawking crockery and tins from their blue-and-yellow carts, but on this occasion we first passed a stray horse with a halter but no attendant, and four miles farther on a tinker with a rope obviously in search of the horse. This gave my driver a chance to indulge in a conversation (in Gaelic of course) which was remarkably long and accompanied by a great deal of gesticulation. The tinker was in a great state of agitation, but he must have lost at least a quarter of an hour discussing, I suppose, the vices of his lost animal because they could scarcely have discussed the direction in which he had gone, as there was only one road.

Yet when we met the tinker returning much later in the day he was even more agitated and cursing loudly. He had not found his horse. This slight incident had the fortunate result, for me, of loosening my driver's tongue. Up to that moment he had either refused to answer my questions or just said "Yes" or "No" quite indiscriminately and often, I guessed, inaccurately. His object was to please me rather than to inform me. But after the tinker had passed, to my surprise he became not only voluble but informative.

"Barvas", he said, "is a sad village. A young girl was taking her cow to graze when she saw a body washed up on the shore and on one finger of the body a gold ring. As she couldn't get the ring off, she bit off the finger and the plague caught her and spread to the whole of the village."

He showed me a church in Barvas that had been converted into a private house, which reminded me of a church in Stornoway that had been turned into a warehouse. But he also showed me in Barvas parish the splendid church called Eorapidh or the Great Temple, which has been lavishly restored. I was surprised to find in these coastal villages quite a number of detached grey stone modern houses, standing in front of the older black houses. Some of the houses were in a state of transition, black houses with modern, usually corrugated, additions. The old black houses suit the scenery. The modern ones look very much out of place, but they are undoubtedly more convenient and comfortable, so that in a few years the black house as I saw it may well become a museum piece.

I passed through Shader, Borve, Dell, Suainabost, Habost, and Lionel and so came to Port of Ness and the Butt of Lewis. Port of Ness is a sad, derelict place with its harbour all going to pieces because the natives have no money to repair it. The Butt is rather like Land's End. I went beyond the lighthouse and saw the Pigmies' Isle, where there are the ruins of an anchorite's cell and an oratory.

The land hereabouts is (for Lewis) quite fertile, consisting of close-cropped downland tilled into strips. I saw great activity in the fields. In the middle of one of these fields, quite close to the Butt of Lewis, I came upon an ancient sun-temple. As I was watching a flock of gannets flying over the Butt, my driver said: "They remind me of a queer story. About twenty years ago a boatload of men went out from the harbour here in search of gannets, but stayed away so long that they were given up for dead and then, when their wives were either mourning as widows or thinking of re-marrying, the boat reappeared round the Butt and they all arrived safe and sound. They had been marooned in the Flannan Islands and lived there on the gannets they caught."

To my surprise, he didn't appear to know the well-known story of the three lighthouse-keepers in the Flannan Islands whose empty chairs, drawn up to the table where everything was ready for a meal that had never been eaten, were discovered by the relief men. So I told him the tale in full detail. "The fate of the keepers or what disturbed them remains a mystery," I said. "There's a fine poem about it by W. W. Gibson." From the way he nodded his head I began to have a suspicion that out of politeness he had encouraged me to tell a story which he knew far better than I did.

At any rate he made no comment, but said:

"The people of Berneray have the right to graze sheep and beasts in the Flannan Isles. The cows swim across the Sound from Blavvaglom to Earshadir and the young calves go by boat. When the summer is over the women on the Berneray shore call out to their cows on the Earshadir shore by their names and they swim home again."

He also told me that in olden days a Norse princess suspended a great chain between Lundale and Berneray in order to collect her toll from ships that passed through the straits, and that she would let no man land at Berneray unless he proved his strength by swinging this chain.

By far the most interesting experience I had in the island happened the next day when my driver drove me across the island in a howling blizzard to Uig, the ancient home of the MacAulays, where I found once more an unexpected number of tiny hamlets. At Islivig, right on the Atlantic Coast, I watched the veil of snow and sleet lift off the ocean long enough for me to see far out a slow and stately procession, a huge white-tip father in front, followed by mother at a discreet distance. The rear was brought up by three little ones. I lay flat on my stomach and picked out a point to make quite sure that they were moving, and having satisfied myself what they were I turned to the driver for corroboration. "Icebergs?" I queried excitedly. "Yes," he said, "Icebergs."

I gazed at them in rapture for a long time. They appeared to move even more quickly towards the north.

Then I pointed them out to a passing crofter. "Icebergs," I said.

His voice was soft, and full of pity for the too credulous.

"No," he said. "The Flannan Isles."

He was almost the only man in the island who ever said "No" to me.

I continued to watch them. They stopped moving. They were indeed the Flannan Isles.

But I was to be richly rewarded for my disappointment. I drove on to the farthest point of Uig above the ocean, a lovely place of huge grey boulders with a light green sea breaking over low rocks, when I heard for the first time in my life a low, very happy sound of bells ringing most tunefully. Quite instinctively I said: "Fairy bells."

It was not a question this time. I was stating a fact. I ran quickly along the boulders searching for more of this all too brief music, but now there was nothing to be heard but the roar of the breakers. There was a shaggy black calf nearby and a few sheep, but no bell-wether. The spot where I heard this fairy music lies between Breidhnis and Mealastadh.

When I mentioned this experience to Dr. Thomas Wood the composer, he asked me if I should remember the tune if I heard it, and went over to the piano and played exactly the notes that I had heard on that memorable day. I know that I am not alone in having heard fairy music, but I do regard myself as unusually fortunate, for I am neither a Gael nor a man of undue imagination.

Lewis and Harris are, of course, part of the same island, but whereas Lewis is flat, Harris is mountainous. I was surprised on my journey southward towards Harris to find how busy all the islanders are. I passed very old women carrying loads of peat over the moor, girls carrying buckets of water, suspended on either side of a wide hoop, more girls harrowing the rough soil, old men feeding hens, old women broadcasting seed, and a Seaforth Highlander in full uniform leading a cow on a rope.

We passed the usual ramshackle 'buses on their way to Stornoway and occasional roadmenders, who cautiously and wisely got off their bicycles on our approach and left the road altogether, much as the Mexican Indians drive their wagons off the road whenever they see a car. There were a few villagers, an occasional fishing-lodge, and once I passed two churches and two manses within a hundred yards. At Loch Seaforth we passed out of Lewis into Harris and climbed over the shoulder of that most impressive and steep mountain, Clisham, which overlooks Loch Tarbert, where my driver told me that the speck that I saw far out to sea, forty-five miles away, was St. Kilda. It may well have been St. Kilda. It certainly wasn't an iceberg.

Tarbert is to Harris what Stornoway is to Lewis. It boasts the only inn in the island and the Tarbert Harris Hotel caters for anglers, which is another way of saying that it is warm, feeds its guests well, and makes them welcome. There are two other houses in the island marked as inns, but as they both refused me food and drink, I think the title to be misleading. The castle in which Sir James Barrie wrote *Mary Rose*, and the island that likes to be visited but has a habit of disappearing, are both near here. The island is in Loch Voshimid, but I was much too preoccupied watching the twists in the narrow, appallingly rough road to remember to look out for them. The country after Tarbert is so barren that the sheep seem to have no alternative diet to seaweed and bare boulders, of which there are plenty. The black houses on this coast are built right into the sides of sea-cliffs just above the creeks. How they escape being washed away by the rough seas I don't know. The main product of this part of the island is a succession of cairns of loose stones. My driver volunteered many reasons for their presence. First he said that they were piled up by boys while they were looking after their cattle. Then he remembered that a motor-cyclist had been killed on this road the week before and suggested that they marked the scenes of fatal accidents, which I was well prepared to believe. Then he changed his mind again and said that they marked the places where the biers rested on the way to funerals. That seemed to be the most feasible explanation.

And then I saw rising out of the midst of the barren wilderness the imposing tower and church of St. Clement's Rodel, the burial place of the great Mac-Leods. It seems a far cry from here to Dunvegan, but here I found further links with the Lords of Skye.

One of the chiefs, who is supposed to have fought in the '45 (why did he then deny help to the fugitive Prince in '46?), married in his seventy-fifth year his third wife by whom he had nine children before dying at ninety. The inscription tells us nothing about his other wives, but I discovered (I don't know where) that his first wife bore him twenty children and his second none.

There is the very elaborate Tomb of Alasdair Crotach of whom we heard such unpleasant things at Dunvegan. He prepared this tomb for himself in 1528, nineteen years before he died. It contains some finely sculptured panels, and the effigy of a warrior in armour with his feet resting on a large lizard. It was Alasdair Crotach who was responsible for the burning of 395 MacDonalds in the great cave of Eigg. Being a devoutly religious man, he prayed for six hours before the massacre, and declared that if the wind was blowing off the mouth of the cave at the end of six hours, the MacDonalds should be spared. The wind blew strongly on the mouth of the cave, so he took this to be a sign from Heaven, and sailed away, leaving his son to burn his enemies.

Yet even Alasdair Crotach had his good points. When sneered at by a Lowland noble at Holyrood with the words, "You have no such hall, no such table and no such candlesticks in Skye," he replied, "Sir, if the King and you come to Dunvegan I will show you a nobler hall, a finer table, and more precious candlesticks than any you have here."

The King overheard, and leaning forward said: "We will come, Alasdair, next summer."

When the King arrived in Loch Dunvegan the following year with his fleet, Alasdair went aboard and pointing to Healaval Mor, the greater of the hilltops known as MacLeod's Tables, said:

"Yonder is my table, and horses are waiting to take us to the top where your Majesty's banquet is spread."

THE VILLAGE, SCARPA, WEST HARRIS

OUTER HEBRIDES, LOCH SEAFORTH, ON THE BOUNDARY BETWEEN HARRIS AND LEWIS

When they reached the summit, hundreds of clans-men lit their way holding flaming torches of pine in their hands.

"Here, Sire," said Alasdair, "is my hall. Its walls are great mountains: its floor is the sea: its roof is the canopy of heaven. Here is my table, a great hill two thousand feet high. Here are my candlesticks, your Majesty's faithful servants. I ask you to partake of the banquet which is spread on my table by the light of my torches which my sconces hold."

"I can show nothing like this in Holyrood," said the King.

Much may be forgiven the hunchback for that magnificent gesture.

From Rodel you look across the watery wastes to the fjords of North and South Uist, but the boat runs rarely, so I turned north again by way of the derelict fishing-sheds of Leverburgh, where Lord Leverhulme tried in vain to provide an industry for the islanders. There are unexpected golden stretches of sand on the coast just here opposite the very attractive-looking island of Taransay.

At the post office at Leverburgh I asked if there was any cottage where I could see the home-weaving of Harris tweed done and I was recommended to call at a certain cottage. The woman of the house made it immediately clear that I was unwelcome, and shooed me down the garden as if I were a neighbour's hen. Luckily I received more courteous treatment at Ballalan, where the MacDonald family, who live in a black house overlooking Loch Erisort, devoted a couple of hours to showing me their treasures. I remember best the natural dyes they used for their Harris tweeds. The crottle off the rocks gives a brownish-gold colour,

heather gives a yellowish green, iris a lighter green,
and the water-lily jet-black. Mrs. MacDonald baked
a bannock for me on a grid over the peat-fire in the
middle of the floor. MacDonald was wearing a roll
of bracken-brown tweed flecked with the blue of the
Atlantic. A shy boy sat on a sofa in silence. This black
house had three rooms, one for the cattle, one for the
family to live in, and the third held two enormous
beds let into the wall and also contained two spinning-
wheels.

The mill-owners in Stornoway encourage the crofters
to do as much of the spinning and weaving as possible
in their homes and then buy the cloth from them. It
costs about four shillings a yard in the village stores.

On my way home my driver told me of the mysterious light of Tolmachan.

Tolmachan lies on the Atlantic side of Tarbert, and
on the hillside a strange light has been seen flashing
at irregular intervals for the last forty years. It is no
will o' the wisp. It is visible only to those who approach the hill from the east, and as soon as you get
near it disappears. No one has found any explanation
of this phenomenon which seriously disturbed the
Naval Commander in charge of this area in the 1914–
1918 war. One feature of this Outer Hebridean life
that gave me particular pleasure was the Nicolson
Institute at Stornoway, a co-educational school of
very high standard, which draws boys and girls
from all over the islands and equips them admirably
to proceed to the Scottish Universities. The crofters
themselves may find their time so fully occupied as
to leave little leisure for reading, though they do
manage to relax a little at the ceilidh, but they are
very anxious to give their sons and daughters a

chance to make good, and the MacAulays are not the only family to have made a big name for themselves. There are Nicolsons, Mackenzies, and MacLeods, all sprung from Lewis and Harris stock, who have held responsible positions in many diverse professions the world over.

chance to make good, and the MacAulays are not

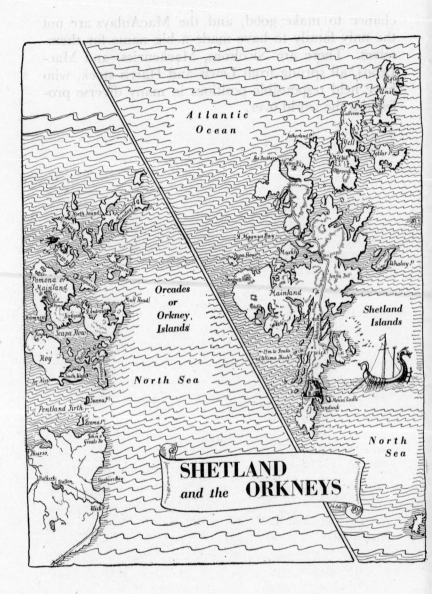

Atlantic
Ocean

North Sound

Orcades
or
Orkney,
Islands

Pomona or
Mainland

Kirkwall

St Andrews

Mull Head

Kromney

Scapa Flow

Hoy

Hoy

Joy Ness

South Walls

Swena Id

Pentland Firth

Stroma Id

John o
Groats Ho

Thurso

Halkirk   Watten

Sinclairs Bay

Wick

North Sea

St Magnus Bay

Papa Stour

Sandness

Muckle

Mainland

Meal

25 m to Foula
(Ultima Thule)

Lerwick

Sandwick

Unst

Cullivoe

Fetherland

The Faithers

Roeness Hl

Yell

Mid Yell

Otterswick

Scalla Fell

Fair Is Cld

Fetlar

Whalsey Id

Shetland
Islands

North
Sea

Mousa Castle

SHETLAND
and the **ORKNEYS**

CHAPTER TEN

Orkney

ORKNEY always seems near to me because I went to the islands first by air and the journey took less than two hours from Aberdeen. To see Aberdeen at its best, you should certainly look down on it from the air, because only then do you get the chance of realising its complete homogeneity. The granite sparkles in the sun and the whole city is of granite. After clearing the Buchan fields and the woods of Banff we crossed sixty miles of sea over the Moray Firth with only an occasional drifter to be seen in all that wild waste of waters. We came down at Wick, only to climb up again over John o' Groat's to see below us on the farther side of the Pentland Firth the low-lying southern islands of Orkney. Scapa Flow was as usual full of battleships, and we could see the hulks of battle-ships that had been sunk in this wide harbour. We skimmed over the green fields of South Ronaldshay with their fine herds of black cattle, and then saw the grey roofs of Kirkwall and its impressive red sandstone cathedral in the very centre of the town. We landed in a small rough field just outside the town. It was the first official landing of the new air route, and we were met by the civic authorities. The first feeling I got in the Orkney was that I had landed in an island of great prosperity and unremitting industry. The farms are all trim and neat, the fields filled with sleek black cattle and rich fleecy sheep, and the poultry were not only more numerous than I have ever seen anywhere else, but about twice or three times the size of ours.

Orkney is, of course, famous for its export of eggs and professors, but I had not realised either the plumpness of the hens or the humour of its professors, or for that matter the wealth of its farmers. I remembered the old saying that an Orcadian is a farmer with a boat, while the Shetlander is a fisherman with a croft, but the contrast between the conditions of living in the Hebrides and those in the Orkney is as different as those between Park Lane and the Mile End Road.

Kirkwall is like its people, a well-groomed, cheerful opulent town. Its shops are modern and attractive, though its streets are oddly narrow. There is no road in the ordinary sense. The main street in Kirkwall, as in Stromness and Lerwick, is little more than a pavement on which carts, bicycles, cars, and pedestrians get hopelessly entangled. There are no accidents because no one is ever in a hurry. The cathedral of St. Magnus dates from the thirteenth century and the spire surmounting its sixteenth-century tower rises to a height of 165 feet. It has an unusually interesting series of memorials including one to Rognvald Kolsen, Earl of Orkney—'Warrior, Navigator, and skeld, who founded this cathedral 1137 in memory of his uncle St. Magnus, assassinated at Calder 1511'.

There is a memorial to Lord Adam Stewart, son of James V, who died in 1575, and another to John Rae,

'Arctic explorer, Discoverer of the fate of Sir John Franklin's last expedition'. There is fine vaulting in the roof of the cathedral and a superb view from the top of the tower.

You cannot, of course, see all the sixty-eight islands that form the Orkney archipelago, but you get a faint idea of their number, size, and variety. Below the cathedral and surrounding three of its sides is the Kirk Green with its seventeenth-century Market Cross, where every Christmas and New Year's Day the lower and upper halves of the city play their famous Ba' game of football to commemorate the fact that when Kirkwall became part of the diocese of Trondheim in Norway the town was split into the Earl's Town and the Bishop's Town. One of the more memorable relics kept in the cathedral is the double ladder used by the hangman and criminal going up the scaffold, but only by the hangman coming down.

Quite close to the cathedral are the lovely ruins of the Earl's Palace, built after the French fashion by the tyrannical Earl Patrick Stewart whose execution was deferred in order that he might learn the Lord's Prayer. In his heyday he kept a seraglio in very ornate apartments that lay just below his own rooms on the way to the Banqueting Hall.

The Duke of Montrose was entertained here in 1647, and again in 1650 when he was raising troops for the King. Cromwell's soldiers, after their usual custom, stabled their horses in the Palace and stole the nameplates from the tombs. King Haakon, after his defeat at Largs, retreated to this Palace and died in it.

Its most famous owner was Bishop Reid, who was sent to France to attend the wedding of Mary Queen of Scots. He was poisoned on his way home and died in Dieppe.

Robert the Bruce is also supposed to have taken sanctuary here in 1106 after his defeat at Methren.

In the treaty signed between Bruce and Earl Magnus, Orkney was to be retained by Norway and the Western Isles returned to Scotland, on a payment of 100 marks a year to the Bishop of Orkney. Magnus brought a Norse contingent from Orkney to fight on Bruce's side at Bannockburn, but on the day of the battle a shining figure on horseback appeared in Orkney announcing the victory over the English.

James V, accompanied by twelve ships of war and a thousand men, put into Orkney in 1539, and was royally entertained in the Palace.

The Deanery, which stands behind a high wall in the main street and occupies three sides of a square, is rather like an Oxford College Deanery, with fine panelled rooms overlooking a particularly delightful garden. It is the home of the Lord Lieutenant of the county.

I was surprised to find that, in spite of the fact that Orkney is nearer to the Arctic Circle than it is to London and that it is within twenty-five miles of the latitude of Greenland, the winter temperature is the same as that of the Isle of Wight and warmer than the Thames Valley. The Orcadians practically never see ice or snow, and the average annual rainfall is only about thirty inches. They never suffer from either flood or drought. There are no mountains and no deer forests. The Orcadians bear no resemblance to the Highlanders and do not speak Gaelic. The stock is mainly Norse, the same stock that conquered Normandy and England.

The Scots element, which is not predominant, comes from east and lowland Scotland, so you see no kilts and hear no Scots talk.

The modern Orcadian is cosmopolitan in outlook, well-read and usually widely travelled. He is a genial, humorous companion, and judging from the ages on the tombstones and the number of hale and hearty octogenarians whom I met, exceptionally long-lived. In one morning I met four craftsmen in Kirkwall, all over eighty, and all at work. These were Mr. Kirkness, who was making a straw-backed Orcadian chair, Mr. Kent, a photographer of rare birds, Mr. Bertram, at work on a saddle, and Mr. Maxwell constructing a model Orkney yawl on the scale of one inch to a foot.

From my hotel window I looked down on a harbour which, unlike that at Stornoway, contained no drifters, but a large fleet of cattle-boats, yawls, dinghies, and private yachts. I watched the passengers disembarking from the steamers *Earl Sigurd* and *Earl Thorfinn*, villagers from the surrounding islands, Shapinsay, Garisay, Wyne, and Egilsay come into market.

My first excursion from Kirkwall was the sixteen-mile drive along the north shores of Scapa Flow to Stromness.

I stopped on the way at Smoogro, a charming grey house on a sandy beach overlooking 'the Barrel of Butter Beacon' in Scapa, to call on the Convenor of Orkney, Storer Clouston, the author of *The Lunatic at Large* and *The Man from the Clouds*. He showed me the bluebells in his woods and the rich tulips in his garden before setting me on my way to the picturesque ancient port of Stromness, which was famous in the days of the whalers and Arctic explorers.

I passed a sealed-up wall bearing the words: 'There

watered here The Hudson Bay Company's ships from 1670 to 1871: Captain Cook's vessels *Resolution* and *Discovery*, 1780, and Sir John Franklin's *Erebus* and *Terror* 1845'.

Stromness is certainly a port with an atmosphere. Its glory has faded. It has none of the liveliness of Kirkwall. It dreams of its past when a hundred ships at a time would collect in the harbour during the Napoleonic wars waiting for protection from the Navy. The whalers called every summer to make up their crews. About seventy-five per cent of the Hudson Bay Company men came from Orkney. They ordered their year's supplies from Stromness.

Captain Cook made Stromness his first port of call after going round the world, and it was the last port of call of Sir John Franklin.

I didn't hear as many grim stories of feuds and raids and inhuman cruelty as I had heard in the Hebrides, but one stands out in my memory. In 1527 the Earl of Caithness sailed over to Orkney to help one of his Sinclair kinsfolk to recover lands of which he had been robbed by another Sinclair. When he landed on the Orkney shore he met a "spae" wife and asked how his fortune would turn out. She gave him two balls of wool, one to choose for himself, and the other for the Orkney Sinclair, the longer thread to show the winner. He drew the shorter. She then told him that the one whose side lost first blood would be the loser. A herd boy was standing by, so one of the Earl's men killed him to make sure that his should be the winning side, only to find that the boy came from Caithness. So the Earl was defeated and his army annihilated at the Battle of Summervale when the Orcadians fell upon them in a fog.

Within a few miles of Stromness I found two of the strangest ancient monuments I have ever seen. They are close to the shores of two fresh-water lochs, Stenness and Harray. The first of these ancient monuments is Maeshowe, a green mound surrounded by a wide moat, a four-thousand-year-old burial-ground that had been rifled by Earl Rognvald IV in 1151 before setting out on a pilgrimage to Jerusalem.

My guide took me inside and lit thirteen candles, running one up and down the stones showing me the Norse names and translating them. One ran: 'Ingiborg is the fairest of women', another, 'Jerusalem forces broke into Orke-howe', and a third, 'Harmunde of the hard axe carved these runes'.

These child-like scratchings had a greater power than anything else I saw to bridge the gulf of time.

I could almost see the shadowy Viking vandals at work. I was told by one of the professors that these superstitious warriors violated the old burial-grounds as a sort of nerve test, and as there are in Orkney almost as many of these green mounds or barrows as there are puffins, plover, and poultry, they certainly lacked no opportunity to test their valour.

The farmer who showed me over Maeshowe pointed to a standing stone away over in the distant fields. "That's exactly forty-two chains away from this entrance, and when you get there you'll find it is exactly forty-two chains from the Sentinel Stone, and that in its turn is precisely sixty-three chains away from the Standing Stones of Stenness." So I paced it out to see for myself. There used to be a Stone of Odin near the Stones of Stenness with a hole pierced through it for men and women to plight their troth by joining hands through it. They were then regarded as married. But if they found that they were not suited to each other and wished to break their vows, all they had to do was to go to church together and leave separately, one by the north door and the other by the south. There must have been many an occasion when only one wanted to break the vow, leaving the still loving but unloved partner most reluctant to leave by a different door. The Standing Stones of Stenness are far taller and heavier than the Stones of Callernish and have a remarkably fine Table Stone or sacrificial altar standing on three irregular mega-liths in the centre. These Stones of Stenness are also known as the Ring of Brogar and the Temple of the Sun. There is also another Ring close by called the Ring of Bookan.

The Stenness Stones stand on a flat low-lying land between two vast lochs where you may fish for trout without fee. All round are rich green fields and prosperous-looking ferns, the haunt of golden plover.

The most interesting relic of the past on the main-land is Skara Brae, a village of the Stone Age lying among the sand-dunes on the Bay of Skaill, quite close to Marwick Head where Lord Kitchener was drowned in 1917.

The huts are in a perfect state of preservation, because they have been buried under the sands for centuries. There are seven of them in all connected by covered galleries. They are buried to the tops of the walls in heaps of peat-ash and broken bones mixed with sand. These huts in their turn were built on the tops of others left by still earlier races. They are rectangular with rounded corners, and each measures about twenty feet by thirteen feet. The smoke came out through a central hole and the way

in was by a narrow tunnel about four feet high. The
Stone Age men must have been dwarfs, because the
doorways were only one foot ten inches wide and three
feet nine inches high. The surprising thing was their
compactness inside. Against each wall was a pen
formed by stone slabs set on end, usually about six
feet six inches by three feet six inches. These beds
may have been lined with heather. The inhabitants
would obviously sit on the edge of the bed-slabs to
work, and warm themselves by the central fire. A
two-storeyed stone cupboard with three legs acted as
a dresser, and in one corner I saw boxes of slate slabs
let into the floor and tightly joined on the edges to
keep them watertight. These are called tanks. There
were cells built in the thickness of the walls opening
off the huts and stone-lined divisions roofed with
flagstones.

Apparently the inhabitants buried the huts as soon
as they were built in order to avoid attracting the
notice of other would-be settlers as well as to avoid
the winds and storms.

They lived, both for food and clothes, on their herds
and flocks. Beads made from walrus and whale tooth
have been excavated, and red, blue, and yellow
pigments found in stone cups lend colour to the theory
that they painted their bodies. I have seen examples
of their pottery which is crude, but I possess a number
of their shaped stone pot-lids which show a much
higher sense of craftsmanship. Owing to the kindness
of Mr. Grant, the owner of the island of Rousay, I was
privileged to watch the excavators at work on another
broch where I saw a professor digging out human skulls.

I have good reason to remember those skulls because on my flight back to Aberdeen we ran into bad

weather and as the professor was a fellow-passenger, I spent an uneasy time watching his skulls tossing across the deck in competition with a number of loose live lobsters.

To reach Mr. Grant's house in Rousay, I had to be rowed across Eynhallow Sound, and while I was admiring the eider-duck and other sea-birds all round me, I suddenly saw the fins of two basking sharks quite close to the boat side. My guide was unconcerned, but I couldn't have got a greater thrill if they had been icebergs.

These sharks are not uncommon in Orkney waters, and they do occasionally overset small rowing boats, but the Orcadians don't seem to worry about them.

Most men who live in islands are knowledgeable about birds, but Mr. Grant has an unusual enthusiasm for and knowledge of Orcadian bids. He showed me a white starling, and three hen-harriers, which so far from being a rare bird in Rousay are, in his view, far too common.

He took me over the wild cliffs of Scabra Head where I saw vast colonies of razor-bills, puffins, and every species of gull and diving bird. They were chattering as noisily as women in a bargain basement.

Mr. Grant told me that there are about 250 different kinds of birds in the islands. There is a colony of herons in the cliffs at Lyra Ged, peregrines on Black Craig, fulmar petrels in North Gaulton Castle, and even the great skua has now come down from Shetland to nest in Orkney.

There are no deer, partridges, pheasants, or ptarmigan, and wood pigeon are rare, but there are large numbers of red grouse, snipe, and hares.

I had, of course, expected to find a very rich bird life in Orkney, but I was totally unprepared for the wealth of wild flowers, particularly the wild blue lupin which grows profusely all over the moors and fertilises the soil with nitrogen. The primula scotica, also a rich blue, is to be found, but I didn't see any.

Blue seems to be the predominant colour for wild flowers in Orkney, for bluebells too grow very plentifully everywhere.

A very pleasant holiday might be spent in visiting all the Orcadian isles. One of the most charming is Eynhallow, a small, smooth, rounded knoll of about 200 acres, known as Holy Island. It was at one time a priests' sanctuary and contained a monastery. It is now a bird sanctuary. It is known as the vanishing island, the island that could often be seen but never reached. The only way for the boatman to be sure of reaching the island is to keep his knife firmly clasped in one hand and his eyes fixed on the island. How you row with a knife in one hand facing your objective I don't pretend to know. The earth from Eynhallow is supposed to have the power always to keep rats away, so it is in great demand on the mainland.

Stronsay has the largest farms and a very active herring fishery. Sanday, which is twelve miles long, is submerged for a quarter of its area at every high water. Eday, once the seat of John Stewart, Earl of Carrick, is famous for its peat, and off it stands Calf Sound where the notorious pirate John Gow ran aground and was taken prisoner by James Fea while drinking in the local ale-house. Westray contains the ruins of Noltland Castle, the fifteenth-century home of the Orcadian Bishops where Bothwell, after his defeat at Carbery Hill, sought sanctuary which was

I RETURN TO SCOTLAND

denied him in spite of the fact that he was Duke of Orkney. He went on to Shetland where he only escaped capture by the skin of his teeth and had to go on to Norway where he was imprisoned as a pirate and died there in Norwegian hands in 1576.

The best way to see the western group of the South Isles, Hoy, Graemsay, Cava, Risa, Fara and Flotta, is to take the local mail steamer, the *Hoy Head*, which makes the round trip from Stromness three or four times a week. There are piers at Lyness and Long-hope. Everywhere else you land by boat. Bullocks are swung up and lowered into the hold on cranes.

Hoy is perhaps the most worthwhile of this group of islands because of the amazing sea-cliff of St. John's Head that rises straight out of the sea to a height of 1,140 feet, and two miles south of the Head is the Old Man of Hoy, a rock-pillar or stack that stands 450 feet out of the sea and some distance away from the main cliffs. The Dwarfie Stone, which has been hollowed out into a sort of hermit's cell, with enough space to bed two dwarfs, is also in Hoy. It looks exactly like the fallen trunk of a giant tree that has been hollowed out and petrified.

Before I left I picked up a few Orcadian words. They call the language Norn. 'Grullion' means ogre, 'peerie' means little, wheat-ears are known as 'stinkie bruie' and daddy long legs are called 'krissy-kringlo', which shows you how little connection the Orcadians have with the Gael.

The most famous Orcadian surnames are nearly all Norse: Fulett, Linklater, Kirkness, Clouston, Paplay, Dyrland, and Hacro. There are of course some Scots families in Orkney, Sinclairs, Irvings, Tullochs, and Craigies, but they are in the minority.

Just before I left Orkney I asked one of the professors to explain why the Orcadians are so rich and the Hebrideans so poor. He replied: "It's the nature of the people. If you put the Orkney man in the Hebrides he would turn it into another Orkney, and if you put the Hebridean into Orkney he would make it another Hebrides."

I cannot believe it to be as simple as that. The Orcadian's lot has fallen to him in a very fair ground. The climate is agreeable, the soil fertile. Cattle thrive, poultry thrive, birds thrive, plants and grain thrive, man thrives. And if you transplanted the Hebridean to Orkney, he would thrive. Climate plays a predominant part in shaping man's destiny.

CHAPTER ELEVEN

Shetland

ALL that most English people know about Shetland is that its ponies are small and shaggy, its sheep-dogs small and shaggy, and its wool particularly soft.

They picture it as a land of ice and snow and fierce Atlantic storms, where the islanders live a primitive and very hard life.

Outwardly they do appear to be destitute of all amenities, but if you are privileged to be entertained in one of the crofts you will be startled by the comfort and the richness of their social life. It is no more easy to get past the barrier of secretiveness that bars the way to intimacy than it is in the Hebrides, so the average visitor has to be content with the outward superficial view and not try to penetrate beneath the surface.

Hugh MacDiarmid lives among them, and to him is revealed a quite different picture from that which we form. They have, according to him, an unnatural fear of catching diseases. Their code of morality too differs from that of Scotland and England. Young betrothed couples live with one another before marriage with the full approval of their parents, but once an islander goes with a girl he is hers for the rest of their lives.

You may find facts of this nature, which you could scarcely expect to find out for yourself, from Mac-Diarmid's admirable book, *The Islands of Scotland*.

I did not find the Shetlander anything like as reticent and shy as the Hebridean.

I did feel (probably because I made the journey by steamer instead of by air) that whereas Orkney was near the mainland, Shetland was very remote.

Long before I sighted Lerwick, I had good reason to know that we were as far north as Greenland and as near to Bergen as to Aberdeen. On our way we passed Fair Isle, which is the same size as Lundy, three miles long and a mile broad, past which the roost of tidal waters makes the sea rough on the stillest day.

We seemed to spend our voyage going into and out of roosts which tossed our little ship about like a cork.

There are over a hundred islands in Shetland, but only twenty of them are inhabited, and there are only about 20,000 inhabitants in all. The mainland is a long narrow neck about seventy miles from north to south, but the Atlantic and the North Sea cut into it on both sides so severely that it is mainly made up of fiords, which they call 'voes'. As we sailed up past Sumburgh Head I felt as if I were nearing Stornoway. There were no trees to be seen, only bare brown moorland and 'black houses' of one storey with rounded roofs of thatch, outside which I saw the crofters working on their tiny strips of green.

I also saw a prehistoric 'broch' standing just above the beach on the rocky island of Mousa near the spot where the *St. Sunniva* was wrecked. It took us just twenty-four hours by sea to sail the 187 miles from

Aberdeen and I was extremely glad to reach the quiet waters of Lerwick.

Lerwick has a spacious harbour which is protected from the south and east by the island of Bressay. It is a grey town, not unlike Stornoway, with narrow alleyways and stone steps leading from the hill on which the town is built to the sea. There were hundreds of dinghies tied up to the wharfside, some Norwegian lumber-boats, Dutch naval patrols, and British destroyers and mine-sweepers.

I was again reminded of Stornoway by the crowds who came down to the quayside to watch us disembark. It was unlike Stornoway in that I could get nothing to drink. Lerwick is a 'dry' town. You can buy cases of twelve bottles of whisky in the shops. You have to go to Hillswick if you want a drink, and Hillswick is thirty-five miles away. But I went there all the same.

First, however, a word or two about Lerwick. There are enclosed spaces at the backs of the houses called 'lodberries' where the smuggled tobacco, gin, and other contraband used to be stored. I imagine that much of Lerwick's history is bound up with this question of contraband, but it doesn't explain why it is a 'dry' town.

There is a cannon on the Esplanade to remind us that the Dutch and Spanish fought a sea battle in Lerwick Bay in 1640.

There are stained-glass windows in the Town Hall showing how completely Norwegian have been the influences on the island ever since its subjection to that country in A.D. 870. Even now I imagine that the Shetlander would more naturally gravitate to Norway for his holidays than to England.

148

The road from Lerwick to Hillswick runs right along the spine of the mainland. It is a hedgeless road and a rough one, going straight out onto the barren moors on which the shaggy ponies and speckled sheep graze. Occasionally I caught a glimpse of a queer fertile valley like that of Tingwall, which has a loch in the middle of it. Tingwall was the meeting-place of the Althing of the Norsemen, where the Great Fowd judged the people and the laws were proclaimed from a circle of stones. When judgment was pronounced on a murderer, the people stood ready armed with sticks and stones and the culprit had to run the gauntlet.

Long narrow tongue-like fiords or 'voes' come running in from the east, and we passed the large inland loch of Girlsta, and at Voe I saw the derelict sheds of the once famous whaling-station. The Shetland whalers have now all gone to South Georgia. When my guide told me that the flesh of whale was sold as beef I was sceptical. I did not visualise that the time would come when I and my fellow countrymen would be prepared to queue for hours to procure it and then only be allowed a few ounces every week. "Cows love eating whale," said my guide. And so do men when they can get it.

He pointed across St. Magnus Bay to the island of Papa Stour where an earl's son was once imprisoned by his father for twenty-six years for refusing to fight a duel and was only rescued by the efforts of a lady missionary.

Beyond Papa Stour lie the dreaded rocks of the Vee Skerries. "No ship", said my guide, "that hits the Vee Skerries has ever got off. There's a whistling buoy there now, with a light. It's about time."

149

Thirty miles to the west stands Foula, where one of the best of our modern documentary films was made. It is commonly accepted that this was the Ultima Thule of Agricola. Its sea-cliffs are the highest in our islands, rising to nearly 1,300 feet out of the sea.

Hillswick has an unexpectedly large hotel, which I found to be, not so unexpectedly, full. I had met only one person on the road in all the thirty-five miles, an old woman driving a sheep and a lamb.

But at least a dozen people passed below the hotel window coming out of church, and at two o'clock I attended the roll-call in the post-office for all those for whom there were letters and Sunday papers a week old. These Andersons, Jamiesons, Hendersons, Sandersons, and the rest were mainly young crofters in blue suits and caps and there were many letters from all over the world. The Shetlander is a widely travelled man. Most of the men I talked to had sailed the seven seas. Very few of the women had ever left the croft or the children. They are indeed, according to Hugh MacDiarmid, extremely bad sailors.

I left the crowd reading their letters by the quay-side and walked to the top of the Ness of Hillswick and looked out over the magnificent sea-cliffs to the wild rocks of the Drongs and Dore Holm off Esha Ness.

Curiously enough the island seems to wake up in the evening. On my way home I passed quite a number of boys in Fair Isle jerseys walking along arm in arm with girls in coats of vivid red and blue. There seemed to be more colour everywhere; I saw some yellow marsh-marigolds, and one field looked as green as if it had been planted with alfalfa. There were quite a number of cyclists and motor-cyclists to be seen on the roads that run along the shores of the various voes.

The Shetlander obviously goes out visiting on Sunday evenings. But I did miss the absence of trees, of rivers, and of all inland birds. I saw no plover (Orkney abounds in them), no swallows, and no cuckoos. The bird life of Shetland is confined to the sea-cliffs, just as the cream of the scenery is cliff scenery.

I spent most of my time in the island of Bressay, which is probably the richest of all the islands in bird life and shares the honours in cliff scenery.

I had been invited to stay in the island by Captain Cameron, a most intrepid sailor, whose house, built in 1724, looks out over the great bay in which the Dutch and Spanish fleet fought.

I got some idea of the way of life of the Shetlander in a cottage on the Bressay moors, where I was struck by the beauty of the pink flowers that grew all round the croft. The woman of the house was knitting a white Shetland shawl, which had taken her a year to make, and for which she would get ten shillings. She told me that two of her three boys were away at sea, one whaling in South Georgia. While we were talking, her third, aged fourteen came in. "He'll have to go to sea too," she said. "I can't afford to give him the extra schooling or to apprentice him to a trade."

Her sixty-year-old husband joined us and showed me pictures of ships in which he had sailed. The walls were crowded with them. "I'm always restless to be away again," he said. "New Zealand's the place to live." He disclosed the fact later that he hadn't been off his own tiny island of Bressay for nearly two years. No wonder he was restless. After walking for some time over the bare moor I came to Noss Sound, and had to shout across the water for the shepherd to ferry me over. I was now on the lookout for rare sea-birds, but they were already on the lookout for me. The great skuas, who allow only the eider-duck to nest near them, intensely resent the presence of strangers, and I had to ward off attacks with my stick as they dived down perilously close to my head and tried to frighten me away. I watched a number of these great speckled birds wait for the gulls to come home with their prey and then swoop down on them out of the sky and force them to disgorge their food, which the skuas were able to catch in mid air before it fell again into the sea. It was exactly like watching an aerial battle, except that the gulls made no attempt to fight back. Their only object was to escape.

Long before I reached or saw the high cliff of the Noup of Noss I heard a wild chattering, very much like that of children coming out of school to play, and when I reached the great cliff-face I found that it was cut into narrow ledges, and that every inch of every ledge was packed with chirping, fluttering birds. There was one long patch of black where the guillemots (they call them 'tysties') stood each above its one egg, immovable as mussels. Another patch of white revealed the gulls' colony, and a patch of black and white the razorbills.

The sea below the vast cliff was even more crowded. The whole face of the water was pitted with tiny dots of birds which made the surface look as if it were being disturbed by a heavy shower of rain.

I peered over the edge of the cliff down into the inaccessible Holm of Noss and there saw a family of three grey seals, father, mother, and baby, basking on a rock close to the water, while by my side the red-beaked puffins kept on darting out of the rabbit-holes where they try to keep their eggs secure from the marauding birds. Overhead I watched the loveliest of all sea-birds, the delicate blue Arctic skuas, which are easily distinguishable because of their one tail feather, and the exquisite flight of the white swallow-tailed tern, who have black caps.

There were also flocks of gannets, cormorants, more razorbills, and a pair of jackdaws. As jackdaws are so common on the English cliffs, I took little notice of them, but Captain Cameron told me that no one had ever seen jackdaws there before. The Noup of Noss was the last place where the white eagle was seen, but I don't know how long ago that was. The peregrines who used to harass the puffins had also disappeared. The curious thing is that while I saw tens of thousands of birds on the Noup, I hardly saw ten birds on my way to it over the moors. I am told that there are exceptionally fierce ravens who drive half-starved ponies and sheep over the cliffs in Gunnista. I saw a few snipe, golden plover, heron, mallard, and teal; and the eider duck looked so plump that I longed to try one as a dish. They are not, I discovered, edible.

I saw also plenty of fulmar-petrels, stormy-petrels, and shearwaters, but the great skuas, because of their intimidating ferocity, and the Arctic tern stood out in my mind far beyond the other birds. When the Arctic tern settles on a rock it alights with its wings almost vertical like a butterfly. The great skua has a wing-span of four feet four inches and measures about two feet from the end of its beak to its tail-tip. It weighs about three pounds. I am told that in confinement it becomes quite tame almost at once, whereas the Richardson's skua, which is so ferocious that it is apt to kill itself by the force with which it swoops down on you, always pines away and dies in confinement.

The wildest cliff scenery on the mainland is at North Marine, which lies in an isthmus so narrow that you can throw a stone from the Atlantic into the North Sea. Almost everywhere in Shetland you get the feeling that the two oceans resent the presence of this slight intervening barrier, and may at any moment sink her with a single large tidal wave, and so become united.

The most northerly of the Shetland Isles is Uist, which is called 'the Garden of Shetland', has nearly two thousand inhabitants, and is the chief source of the famous Shetland shawl. Its lighthouse, Muckle Flugga, is the most northerly of all British lights. In Uist you will see the ruins of Muness Castle, built in 1598 by the Fowd of Shetland (half-brother of Mary Queen of Scots) who tampered with the weights and measures used to assess the taxes. The Great Fowd collected the revenues and presided over the Supreme Court called the Supreme Thing. There were local Things presided over by Under Fowds, and the rents were measured and delivered to him by Lawright men elected by the people. There were also Rauselmen who acted as police and guardians of ecclesiastical rights.

The Stewarts abolished the Norse regime, and the Great Fowd became a Steward, and the Under Fowds bailiffs. To-day there is one Lord-Lieutenant for Shetland and Orkney jointly.

It was the Stewarts who evicted the crofters to make room for sheep and so caused the islanders to emigrate in large numbers.

154

The southern part of the island is being rapidly developed. There is a good landing-ground for aeroplanes and a golf-course over the sand-dunes at Sumburgh Head, which has become a popular tourist centre, with a large hotel at Sumburgh House overlooking the fine bay.

There are many things to draw the visitor to Sumburgh Head. The archæologist will find newly revealed prehistoric huts and villages even more exciting than those at Skara Brae.

There is a ruin here at Earlshof that attracted the attention of Sir Walter Scott as there were many battles fought on this strip of sand-dune and cliff. The lighthouse was built by Stevenson, and beyond it is one of those fierce 'roosts' or races which churn up the sea on even the calmest day. Near Sumburgh is the house of Betty Morrat, who at the age of sixty and an invalid suffered an almost incredible experience. She set out from Jortness towards Lerwick in a sailing-smack and the skipper was knocked overboard by accident. The crew of two tried to rescue him in a small boat and the smack went adrift over the North Sea with only the old woman aboard her. Eventually she was cast up in the island of Lepsoe in Norway and rescued by climbing hand over hand through the surf on a rope.

Though I heard no such cruel stories of vendettas as I heard in the Hebrides I was told of the circle of stones at Housay called the Battle Pond that marked the scene of the Skerry Fight when the fishermen belonging to the Giffords of Bista came over to take possession of the boat they had put up the previous year. They were besieged by the fishermen of the Sinclairs, headed by the lady of the family. One of the Sinclairs forced an entrance and was shot dead, whereupon the Sinclair fishermen fled, leaving their lady prisoner in Gifford hands.

The fishing industry, on which the islanders depend so largely for a living, is in a bad way. There seems no reason, in a time of world-shortage of food, why it should not be in a good way, but I myself saw with horror a whole fleet of dinghies go out into the harbour and dump 1,200 crans of herrings back into the sea because the curers would not pay their price. In the old days they were practically the slaves of the laird and the minister, both of whom got the best share of all the fish caught, and in a bad season they often got into debt to their overlords. Their boats and tackle were inferior, and they certainly could not make a living out of crofting alone, the crops of which were also taxed. And yet in its heyday, when the Lerwick roadsteads were packed with Dutch vessels, the Dutch are said to have taken £300,000,000 as their share of the Shetland fishing, so obviously the industry is there waiting to be put on its proper footing again once the laws of supply and demand can be stabilised. But I saw no evidence, as I saw everywhere in Orkney, of prosperity, past or present. The most encouraging sight I saw was that of the shy boys and girls in the Anderson Institute at Lerwick who were developing a natural aptitude for engineering and chemistry, and obviously intending to turn their backs on the sea for some more congenial, secure, and profitable occupation. Shetland's main problem would appear to be that of re-establishing an adequate population on a depopulated land and providing them with a better chance both of cultivating the land and gaining the rich harvests that await them in the sea. There is, of course, a third way in which the Shetland could quickly become financially stable, and that is the Scots way of encouraging tourist traffic.

It is an easy journey by air and usually a pleasant journey by sea.

It has the great advantage of not being overcrowded or exploited.

But this entails the building of hotels and organised publicity. There is the attraction of a nightless summer, of fishing that is perilous and fishing that is easy, of lovely walks along deserted cliffs that are the highest and most magnificent in the British Isles, of watching more and rarer sea-birds than you will find anywhere else in Europe, in meeting a courteous and kindly, if rather reticent, people, of sailing between islands, of inspecting relics of a very ancient past like the Pictish castle of Mousa, which is even more impressive than that at Carloway, of getting tossed about in 'roosts' and exploring the quiet waters of a hundred 'voes', of riding Shetland ponies, and wearing Shetland jerseys; and of witnessing, if you choose the right time of year, the ceremonial Norse ritual of Up-Helly-Sa. This consists of a procession at the sight of which you may well rub your eyes, for on the poop of a Viking war galley you will see the Guizer-Jarl standing in full Norse mailcoat, raven-winged helmet, carrying battleaxe and shield. You will hear a bugle sounded and then watch three hundred torch-bearers hurl their flares into the galley, which is then burnt, after which the guizers dance and drink with the girls in all the various halls of the town.

Lerwick is not 'dry' all the year.

This exciting ceremony will remind you that even after a lapse of five hundred years since they belonged

157

to Norway, the Shetlanders' bonds are closer to the Norse than to the Gael.

It was in 1460 that Shetland changed hands. The suzerainty of the islands had been transferred to Denmark at a time when Princess Margaret of Denmark was about to marry James III of Scotland. The girl's dowry was fixed at 60,000 florins, but the King of Denmark could only raise 10,000, so Shetland was pledged as security for the remainder and never redeemed, with the result that Shetland became a dumping-ground for the worst sort of Scots adventurer, and when you are shown over the ruins of the castle of Scalloway your guide will most feelingly remind you that its builder, Earl Patrick Stewart, was a cruel tyrant who used forced labour.

Incidentally, you can make a round tour of your trip by returning home down the west coast by way of Scalloway, which was not only the ancient capital of Shetland but is a most attractive seaside resort with a fine bay facing south, lying under the lee of a very pleasant hill, and several little islets inviting inspection just off the mainland.

CHAPTER TWELVE

Edinburgh and East Lothian

OF all our large cities Edinburgh is by general consent easily the most fascinating, partly because of her outstanding architectural loveliness, partly because of her close proximity to the sea and the hills, partly because of her exhilarating air, partly because of her almost inexhaustible literary and historic associations. Incidentally, it is curious to note that Glasgow's literary and philosophic lectures draw larger audiences than Edinburgh. Glasgow is, of course, three times the size of Edinburgh.

The first thing that pleases the Englishman on arrival in Edinburgh is to find himself greeted with smiles and courtesy in the shops, restaurants, and hotels, a pleasant change after any English town, and the second thing that pleases him, perhaps equally, is that he gets much better fed. I have stayed in many Edinburgh hotels, from the vast, splendid and always busy Station hotels at either end of Princes Street, to the quiet, comfortable and extremely dignified Roxburghe, and everywhere I have been struck by the outstanding quality of the food and the attentiveness of the staff, who are prepared to go to any lengths to secure one's comfort.

The shops, particularly in Princes Street, are remarkable for their good taste, especially in clothes, jewellery, pictures, food, and books. The Scots are, of course, omnivorous readers, and I know of no other town, not even Oxford, where the bookshops are so numerous or so well stocked with the best literature of all nations of all time.

But one's first thought on stepping out of the station into Princes Street is not of the shops that line its Northern side, but of the stupendous rock that dominates the city, on the summit of which stands the great castle. Edinburgh's earlier name was Dunedin, which means 'Fort on the hill slope', and in old days the castle rock was islanded by a series of lakes and swamps and so cut off by water both from what is now the new town and the imposing peak of Arthur's Seat that rises above it, away to the east.

It was the Normans who first planned the connecting link, now known as the Royal Mile, that was to connect the castle with the Palace under the hill.

It is generally believed that Robert the Bruce granted the city its first charter, but it was not until after the '45 that the old town spread out northward, and the fair new town rose on the other side of the Nor' Loch, with its spacious and dignified squares and streets and succession of beautifully laid out gardens and parks. It was a stroke of genius to keep the southern side of Princes Street open so that the visitor should get an unbroken view of the glory of the castle across the open lawns and gardens. This also gives us a chance to get an uninterrupted view of the classic buildings on Calton Hill, the lofty ornate pinnacle of the Scott Memorial, and the dignified Royal Scottish Academy and National Gallery.

THE VILLAGE OF DEAN WATER OF LEITH, EDINBURGH

LOCH LOMOND, VIEW OF NORTHERN END, BEN LOMOND RISING IN BACKGROUND

There is much to tempt us to spend a whole day in Princes Street apart altogether from the appeal of the shops. You may be lucky enough to see a Highland regiment in kilts marching along to the music of the bagpipes, you may see crowds of people in an easterly gale holding on to the railings to prevent themselves from being swept under the wheels of the passing traffic. You will certainly be entertained by the motley crowds of all nationalities who throng the wide pavements.

But though Princes Street may fairly claim to be the most imposing street of any city in the British Isles, if not in the world, there lies above it and a few hundred yards to the north a parallel street that in its associations outrivals it. George Street is a very solid, handsome street of unusual breadth, and contains a number of dignified banks and offices, the Masonic Hall, the Old Assembly Rooms, St. Andrew's Church and, perhaps most impressive of all, the publishing house of Blackwood. As we walk down this spacious and quiet street, we can hardly fail to conjure up visions of the great host of notabilities who sojourned, stayed, or wrote here in the past. These include Sir Walter Scott, who had rooms at 108 immediately after his marriage in 1797, Robert Louis Stevenson, Carlyle, Shelley, Dickens, de Quincey, Burns, Mrs. Siddons, Raeburn, and Sidney Smith.

It was, however, at his later town house, 39 North Castle Street, which he occupied for twenty-eight years, that Scott wrote *Waverley*, and it was here that the young barrister Menzies used to see a shadowy hand and pen, silhouetted on the window-blind, working unceasingly hour after hour, night after night, in the composition of the immortal romances.

Robert Louis Stevenson was born at 8 Howard Place and spent his early childhood at 17 Heriot Row, which is just off George Street. Before, therefore, giving way to the obvious temptation to climb up to the Castle, the visitor who cares for literary associations would be well advised to explore the new town first.

The best way to reach the Castle is by way of the Manor and up the slopes past University Hall.

There is a large barrack-square just in front of the Castle gateway and immediately inside is the Half Moon Battery, built in the sixteenth century by the Earl of Morton after the Castle had been captured from Kirkcaldy of the Grange, who held it for Queen Mary. Inside the Battery are the buried remains of the David Tower, which once stood sixty feet high.

We pass under the Argyll Tower through an archway which was once barred by a portcullis and three gates. It was here that the Marquess of Argyll awaited his execution in 1661 and from which his son escaped death twenty-two years later. Montrose too was imprisoned here before his execution. On the summit of the rock is one of the smallest and oldest buildings in Edinburgh, Queen Margaret's Chapel, which measures $16\frac{1}{2}$ feet by $10\frac{1}{2}$ feet.

In front of the Chapel stands Mons Meg, a cannon forged in 1486, removed in 1745 to the Tower of London, and restored to her rightful place by the efforts of Sir Walter Scott.

The view from the Castle top extends over the sea beyond the Firth of Forth and as far north and west as the peaks of Ben Ledi and Ben Lomond.

Every step we take here is full of interest, for round the Crown Square are the Palace, the Great Hall, the Barracks, and the Scottish National War Memorial.

In a tiny room in the Palace, Mary Queen of Scots gave birth to the boy who grew up to be the King who was to unite the two kingdoms of England and Scotland. The Crown, Sceptre, Sword of State, and other regalia are also to be seen in the same building. The Great Hall, built in the early part of the fifteenth century, is now an armoury, but the memory that we are most likely to carry away is of the Black Dinner of 1440, when Sir William Crichton and Sir Alexander Livingstone invited the eighteen-year-old Earl of Douglas, his young brother and the young King James II to a feast, one course of which was the head of a black bull, a certain sign of death. The Douglases were seized and given a mock trial, over which the boy king was forced to preside, and then beheaded.

It is with a sigh of relief that we cross the quadrangle to enter Sir Robert Lorimer's Scottish National War Memorial. It is floored with polished granite, through which the top pinnacle of the rock emerges to hold a queer altar-stone. Above the stone is the figure of St Michael, and on it rests the Roll of Honour of a hundred thousand Scotsmen who fell in the war of 1914–18. There are records, all round the walls and in the stained-glass windows, of achievements in the war, and on stone tables lie scarlet folio volumes each containing the names of men, classified under their different regiments, who died.

It is time to take the journey down the Royal Mile. What immediately strikes the eye is the change in fortune that has overtaken vast houses that were once the town houses of the aristocracy and are now the drab tenements of the very poor. There are open stone staircases leading up to every house and a number of narrow wynds and closes that tell

163

their own tale of furtive murders and hide-outs for fugitives.

The villa with the octagonal tower to the east of the Castle was built by the wig-maker, Allan Ramsay, who is now better known to us as a poet. Later it became the home of John Galt. In Boswell's Court, the uncle of James Boswell once lived, and Dr. Johnson was taken there by his biographer to call on his uncle and inspect the motto on the lintel: 'O-LORD-IN-THE-IS-AL-MI-TRAEST.' All along the Royal Mile you will see strange inscriptions and coats of arms carved on the lintels of the once majestic doorways.

The building with the tall tower and spire is the Assembly Hall of the Church of Scotland. There is a flight of steps at the West Bow leading down to the Grassmarket, where the public executions used to take place.

Every visitor who has read *Dr. Jekyll and Mr. Hyde* makes a point of visiting Brodie's Close, for here lived that strange man whose double life was so fascinatingly described in that novel by Robert Louis Stevenson. Brodie was an excellent cabinet-maker and a Councillor held in the highest esteem. He was also a burglar and, like most burglars, he made a fatal mistake. After stealing a few guineas from the Excise Office, he lost his nerve, fled to Amsterdam, was caught there and brought back to Edinburgh to be hanged at the Tolbooth. The Royal Mile has harboured another pair of impious scoundrels, Burke and Hare, who committed at least sixteen murders in order to sell the bodies of their victims to an anatomist called Knox. They invited down-and-outs into their house, gave them food and drink and then suffocated them. Hare turned King's evidence and Burke was hanged in the Lawnmarket. Three cross-stones still mark the place where the gallows stood. The outstanding building hereabouts is the Cathedral of St. Giles, with its open arched corner steeple where John Knox was Minister from 1559 to 1572 and terrified his congregation by his virulent denunciations of their vices. We commonly regard him as a hair-shirted ascetic, so it is perhaps worth while remembering that in old age, as a widower, he married a girl of sixteen.

In Parliament Square there is a stone bearing the initials 'I.K.' which marks his burial-place. Here too stand the very imposing chapel of the Order of the Thistle, the Parliament House, the Court of Session, and the National Library of Scotland. So a whole day may profitably be spent in Parliament Square alone.

Beyond, we enter the High Street and pass on our way to John Knox's house, and the Market Cross where Royal Proclamations are made by the Lyon King at Arms. Then comes the Canongate, once the favourite resort of the nobility, with a projecting clock standing well out from the quaint sixteenth-century Tolbooth, which was built in a semi-French style as a Council Chamber and used for centuries as a prison. In the churchyard of the Canongate Church you will find the graves of Adam Smith, the publishing brothers Ballantyne, Burns, 'Clarinda', and David Riccio. Obelisk pillars mark the entrance of Moray House, built in the reign of Charles I, where on the 18th May 1650 Lord Lorne was celebrating his wedding to the Lady Mary Moray just when his enemy Montrose, roped to a cart, passed by on his way to his execution.

Close by is another dignified mansion with timber-breasted gables, Huntly House, now a City Museum.

And so we come to Holyrood, with its unforgettably poignant memories of the ill-starred Mary Queen of Scots. It was here that she came as a girl-widow of nineteen, and six years later went out for the last time as a prisoner. It was here that she lived with the husband, Henry Darnley, whom she learned so soon to hate and despise, here that she was compelled to watch the murder of her faithful henchman, David Riccio, while Darnley held her arms, and here that she married Bothwell.

Holyrood is full of tragic memories. They delight in showing you the marks of Riccio's bloodstains on the floor, and you can almost hear Mary's screams as she sees them, but there is anticlimax to be found as you leave Mary's bedroom and wander round the picture gallery to inspect the portraits of over a hundred kings of Scotland, all painted out of his own head by a Flemish artist who was paid £520 a year for the job. One feels that he was grossly overpaid, and that no King of Scotland ever looked quite so vapid or characterless as these dummies.

We are apt to be so obsessed by the omnipresent spirit of Mary as to forget that Holyrood has other claims to our notice. Charles I came in 1633 to be crowned in Holyrood. Cromwell quartered his troops there. Charles II added to it. The gateway put up by James IV was pulled down in 1753, and the Abbot's House, built in the sixteenth century, was removed in the nineteenth.

Prince Charles Edward held a Court there in 1745, and to-day Royal Dances are the occasion of colourful ceremony and lively entertainment.

166

The eight-hundred-foot climb to the summit of
Arthur's Seat is a natural corollary to a visit to Holyrood, and from it there is a grand view of the city.
At its foot lies the bird-sanctuary of Duddingston Loch
near the ruins of Craigsmillar Castle, where Bothwell,
Huntley, Maitland, and Argyll assembled to sign their
agreement to murder Darnley.

If you can possibly spare the time you should not
leave Edinburgh without a visit to its port of Leith,
where you may see ships of every type and every
nationality. You may sail from there to Incholm, the
Isle of St. Columba, where in 1123 Alexander I found
refuge in a storm and was given shelter by a hermit,
as a result of which he founded the Augustine Priory
which flourished for many centuries. You may also
visit the Bass Rock, that sinister island prison, which
rises out of the sea to a height of 313 feet. It is composed of volcanic lava, shaped like a crater, and contains thousands of gannets and a lighthouse. In 1691
four young Jacobite prisoners prevented the garrison
of fifty men, after they had been landing coal, from
re-entering the fort, and these four were mysteriously
joined by twelve others, and the sixteen prisoners
managed to hold the rock for three years and make
favourable terms before they gave themselves up.

The Bass Rock stands out about a mile from a lovely
strip of the East Lothian coast, which is the haunt of
all good golfers, for here stand the famous links of
North Berwick and close by are the ruins of the grim
castles of Tantallon and Dunbar.

It was at Dunbar in September 1650 that Cromwell
turned what looked like an inevitable rout into a
magnificent victory. With only 12,000 men, many of
whom were sick and all nearly starving, he retreated

from Edinburgh to find his path barred by General Leslie, who had an army more than twice as strong. Unluckily for the Scots, Leslie changed his formidable position at the mouth of Cockburns path on the advice of his ministers, and Cromwell caught him in a dangerously cramped corner, and after killing three thousand of the army, captured ten thousand more, losing only thirty of his men.

It was to Dunbar Castle that Mary came with Darnley after the murder of Riccio and later with Bothwell after the murder of Darnley. It was from here that she rode with her lover and parted from him for the last time at Carberry Hill.

Tantallon Castle was, according to legend, first owned and occupied by MacDuff, the Thane of Fife. It passed into the hands of the Douglases, and then to the Earls of Angus, one of whom was besieged there by his own stepson, James V, and starved into surrender.

Tantallon Castle was also the scene of the narrow escape of Marmion when the falling portcullis grazed the plume of his helmet as he was riding out of the gateway. Canty Bay, which lies under the shadow of the Castle, was the embarking-point for the prisoners bound for exile on the Bass Rock. In the same neighbourhood is the lovely village of Dirleton, with yet another castle (De Vaux) with gateway, moat and dungeon still standing, and yet more golf-courses at Gullane (pronounced Gillan) and Aberlady, where there is the country seat of the Hope family at Luffness.

The ancient town of Haddington, which lies a little inland, boasts an Abbey Church which was once called the Lamp of Lothian, but most of it was destroyed in the fourteenth century by Edward III.

168

There are two very old bridges spanning the Tyne, the Abbey Bridge and the Nungate Bridge, and in the High Street you may see the house where Thomas Carlyle wooed Jane Walsh, whose body lies in St. Mary's kirkyard.

CHAPTER THIRTEEN

Glasgow and the Clyde

In spite of the fact that I am no lover of towns, I like
Glasgow as I like Wigan. Both these towns have been
grotesquely and grossly maligned. Both are towns of
ancient and honourable tradition, and they are both
extraordinarily alive in spite of, or perhaps because of,
hard times endured with amazing fortitude in the past.

Even now I find it hard to believe that I once spent
the whole of a snowy New Year's Eve among the slagheaps of Clydebank, seeing huddled, threadbare
bodies of unemployed shipbuilders lying with one
half of their bodies burning on the hot slag and the
other half frozen with the icy wind. They kept on
turning over like grilled joints on a spit.

The men of Glasgow and Clydebank have the
reputation of being the finest shipbuilders and marine
engineers in the world, yet these superb craftsmen,
riveters, caulkers, and the rest were left in the years
of the depression to freeze to death or burn to death.

To see Clydebank in its heyday at the launching of
the *Queen Mary* or the *Queen Elizabeth* and then to
pass through it when the yards are silent and the
workmen are left to sit on their haunches on the kerb
or loll up against the lamp posts, is to realise how

incalculable and wayward are men's destinies in this vast city. When I set out on my expedition to see for myself the conditions of the unemployed I left at the next table to mine in the hotel a young Scots ship-owner sitting alone with a dozen oysters and a magnum of champagne. If I had known what I was going to see I should have compelled him to accompany me.

I have seen strange contrasts between millionaire and beggar in the United States, but I had never seen so striking a contrast between two different conditions of living as this, and whenever I think of Glasgow now, my mind flashes back to the Inferno of the slagheaps in the bad years.

But Glasgow can take it. It has endured semi-starvation and recovered. Even in the worst days Sauchiehall Street was merry and full of song.

The keynote to Glasgow is its friendliness. Edinburgh is slightly formal and conventional. But Glasgow, like Birmingham, greets the stranger with a real smile of welcome. Its behaviour is that of a country market-town rather than that of a huge metropolis. Its very distinctive trend of dialect is most misleading. It sounds harsh and is much less pleasant on the ear than any other Scottish dialect, but there is a warmth behind the harshness that in England is seldom to be found outside Lancashire and Yorkshire.

Not much is left of the old Glasgow, which is a Gaelic word for 'dark green spot', but the Cathedral now stands where the city began. St. Mungo came from Fife in the sixth century, built himself a cell and chapel on the bank of the Moleadinar Burn, became bishop, had to flee from his persecutors to

Wales, and returned after twenty-eight years of exile to put in a further twenty years before his death in 603. You will see in the crypt of the Cathedral a fine shrine which is said to mark his grave.

The present Cathedral was not, however, begun for well over six hundred years after his death. It took a further four hundred years to bring it to completion, and almost immediately after it was finished it was allowed to get into a state of neglect from which it did not recover till the last century.

The other outstanding ancient building in Glasgow is the fifteenth-century mansion called Provend's Lordship. This cross-shaped gabled house was originally part of the hospital of St. Nicholas founded in 1471 for the accommodation of twelve old men. Each storey had three rooms, and each room its own access either from an outer stair or from a timber gallery. After the Reformation it was converted into a single house, and about a hundred years ago was an inn. It was then bought for preservation and furnished with sixteenth-century stained-glass windows, Flemish tapestries, and William and Mary furniture. It is supposed that Mary Queen of Scots stayed here when she came to visit the sick Darnley nine days before his murder.

The old university stood in the High Street for 400 years after its foundation in 1451, but the new university, designed by Sir Gilbert Scott in 1870, stands high up on Gilmore Hill where you can scarcely fail to see its 300-feet-high tower.

Glasgow's history is mainly industrial, but it played a prominent part in the years of the religious persecution, but when in 1707 Scotland was granted the right of free trade with the colonies, Glasgow found something better to do, and began her most profitable trade with Virginia in tobacco. Glaswegian merchants, known as Tobacco Lords, flaunted their splendour as they walked past the old Tontine dressed in scarlet cloaks.

Then came the American war of Independence and the end of the scarlet cloak period.

But tobacco had given Glasgow her chance of developing as a port. The shallow Clyde only allowed the smallest craft to reach the city, but the channel was now deepened, and by 1775 ships drawing six feet could reach the Broomielaw, which is very near the heart of the city. I suppose Clydebank with its great succession of wharves, docks, and shipbuilding yards is to Glasgow what Princes Street is to Edinburgh. Much of it is drab and grimy, the apparently inseparable condition of the presence of iron and coal, but the products of the incessant metallic clamour and the grime are inspiring enough, for in every phase of construction you see every type of ship that sails the seas.

Glasgow's streets are set so steeply on the hillside that one longs for deep crisp snow to ski or toboggan down them.

As in Edinburgh and Chicago, you pass very quickly from terraces and houses of great dignity to tenements of unbelievable squalor, but there are about half a dozen excellent shopping streets though they are all unexpectedly narrow. Sauchiehall Street is, I suppose, the Oxford Street of Glasgow, but it has infinitely more individuality than Oxford Street. St. Vincent Street contains one of the best bookshops in the kingdom, while Gordon Street, Buchanan Street, Union Street, and Renfrew Street all have extremely good

173

shops which have the advantage of being close to one another.

But I do not visit Glasgow for its shops. It is first and last a great port, and I use it as a starting-off place for the Helensburgh tram or the steamer trip down the Clyde to Ardrishaig. You can board the steamer early in the morning at Glasgow or take the train to Gourock an hour and a half after the steamer has gone and pick it up there. I like going all the way by steamer because it gives me a chance of seeing from close quarters what the shipbuilders have got on the stocks. The shipyards stretch for miles, and the river widens very quickly once they are passed. On the northern bank at old Kilpatrick we see the place where St. Patrick embarked to convert the Irish: then come the ruins of Dunglass Castle, a stronghold of the Colquhouns, and then a curious solitary peak of basalt known as Dumbarton Rock. Fourteen hundred years ago this rock was the capital of Strathclyde which stretched as far south as Cumberland. William Wallace was imprisoned in the Rock before being taken to London in 1305, and his great two-handed sword was kept there till quite recently.

The castle was seized by Bruce, and Mary Queen of Scots embarked here at the age of six for France.

In 1571 the Rock was captured by a surprise attack in which the assailants, taking advantage of fog, scaled the 200 feet with hooked ladders and ropes and seized the garrison without losing a single man.

On the south bank we see at the foot of a hill, Port Glasgow and Greenock, the birthplace of James Watt and the scene of Burns's Highland Mary's death.

On the north side lies the fair Helensburgh and the mouth of the placid Gareloch. Helensburgh is a most

174

unexpected place. As I said, it is only a tram ride from Glasgow, but it has fine sands, overlooking a real sea, and has the great lochs and mountains of the Trossachs at its back door. I have never met anyone who stayed there, but it looks an ideal summer holiday resort.

So for that matter does Gourock which lies opposite on the south bank. Indeed we are now surrounded by popular holiday seaside resorts. On the northern shore towards which the steamer makes its way lies Dunoon, which can be as gay and festive as Blackpool and attracts enormous crowds. It is a great centre from which to explore the recesses of the Firth of Clyde. We have a further memory of Highland Mary in the memorial to her on the green slopes where the castle once stood.

Our way lies south to the island of Bute where the steamer puts in at yet another very popular resort, Rothesay, which is full of hydros and hotels. The island of Bute is only fifteen miles long by six miles broad, but it provides a happy playground for tens of thousands of Glaswegian holiday-makers who would never dream of going anywhere else.

Rothesay, however, is no new place. You may still climb up the 'bloody stairs' of the ruins of the castle which was held in turn by the Norsemen, the Scots, and the English until its demolition in 1685. Robert III who came to the throne in 1390 created the first dukedom in Scotland, and conferred the title on his eldest son, so that the Prince of Wales also bears the title of Duke of Rothesay.

Beyond Rothesay the steamer crosses the mouth of Loch Striven to enter the very narrow Kyles of Bute at Colintraive, a tiny sequestered place which is as pleasant as it sounds. Then we brush past the rocks of the Burnt Islands, and at the mouth of Loch Riddon the Kyles turn sharply south as we call in at Tighna-bruaith. We come into more open water as we leave the Kyles and look out on the islet of Inchmarnock, where the men of Bute used to maroon their innumer-able drunkards, and farther to the south see the isle of Arran with Goat Fell standing grandly up above the surrounding land. On a rough day we round Ardlamont Point with a sigh of relief, for after this we are in the calm waters of Loch Fyne, which has the reputation of producing the finest herrings in the world. Loch Fyne is one of the longest lochs in Scotland and stretches right up into the heart of Argyll beyond Inveraray. The steamer first crosses the loch to Tarbert which stands on an isthmus between East and West Loch Tarbert. East Loch Tarbert is the disembarking place for visitors to Islay and Jura which are reached by crossing Kintyre to West Loch Tarbert and there set sail over the sound of Jura, which can be very rough, to Islay which has a renowned golf-course at Machire, an hotel, fine sands, and good little fishing lochs. Jura, which is only separated from Islay by half a mile of water, is mainly remarkable for the Paps of Jura, twin peaks which stand out of the sea with remarkable effect. These two islands are now beginning to attract the tourist who is tired of finding his usual resort overcrowded and deteriorated.

The steamer's journey ends at Ardishaig, a quiet little fishing village just south of Loch Gilphead which stands at the head of one long neck in the loch. There is a good motor road from Ardishaig to Oban and the country over which we run is extremely attractive. There are a number of burns and little lochs and most of the way is over open low moorland lit up by gorse and heather. It is possible to make the round trip from Glasgow in a day by taking the train back from Oban, but nobody would hurry to leave Argyll unless he was compelled to. There is, for instance, Inveraray to see near the head of Loch Fyne. Inveraray is, like Arundel, completely feudal. Its history is the history of the Campbells of Argyll.

The present castle is only about two hundred years old and is a vast quadrangle two-storeyed house with dormer-windowed attics and a round pointed roofed tower at each corner which stands in an immense park nearly thirty miles in circumference. The most attractive feature of the estate is the number of fine avenues that we find in it.

The first Campbell to be knighted was Colin Campbell of Loch Awe in 1280. The first Earl was created in 1457. He too was a Colin Campbell. The first marquis was created in 1651 and the dukedom followed in 1701.

There is a very pleasing and comfortable inn called the Argyll Arms facing the loch which has associations with Burns, Johnson, and Boswell.

'We got', says Boswell, 'at night to Inveraray, where we found an excellent inn. Even here, Doctor Johnson would not change his wet clothes. We supped well: and after supper, Johnson, whom I had not seen taste any fermented liquor during all our travels, called for a gill of whisky. "Come," said he, "let me know what it is that makes a Scotsman happy." He owned that he got as good a room and bed as at an English inn.'

Johnson was much struck by the grandeur and elegance of the castle, but thought it too low, and wished it had been a storey higher. "What I admire here", he said, "is the total defiance of expense."

The Duke invited the pair to dinner and the Duchess was very attentive to Johnson and equally inattentive, and indeed coldly distant to Boswell.

When Boswell rather tartly quizzed Johnson with his unusual courtesy: "You were quite a true gentleman when with the Duchess", he replied, "Sir, I look upon myself as a very polite man", as a proof of which we are told that he would not return the horse lent him by the Duke without a letter of thanks.

More impressive than the castle of Inveraray is the ancient grim stronghold of Dunderave which provided Neil Munro, who was born at Inveraray, his inspiration for his fine novel, *Doom Castle*.

Dunderave stands right above the shore of Loch Fyne and has everything that you have the right to expect of a 'Doom Castle', from dungeons to battlements and the sort of exterior that makes you quite certain that it is haunted.

CHAPTER FOURTEEN

The Trossachs

ONE's first instinct is to avoid the Trossachs on the ground that they are too near Glasgow, that they have been grossly overpraised, and that they are in consequence always overcrowded.

My real complaint about the Trossachs is not so much that they have been overpraised or that they are overcrowded, as that I never know where they begin or end. The true Trossachs are only a small part of the country generally included under that heading. The word means 'bristling territory', and it is quite true that in the narrow defile that separates Loch Katrine from Loch Achray, the land bristles with hazels, birches, rowans, and hawthorns that do not quite hide the confused mass of rocky boulders.

The usual way into the Trossachs is by way of Callander which is a clean but uninspired town just on the threshold of the great lochs and bens.

Our way is under the shadow of Ben Ledi, the Hill of God, past Leny House, the home of the Buchanans, and Loch Vennachar, where you may look for but will not find the scene of the fight between Fitzjones and Roderick John. Perhaps by way of compensation you may see the kelpie who haunts the Wood of

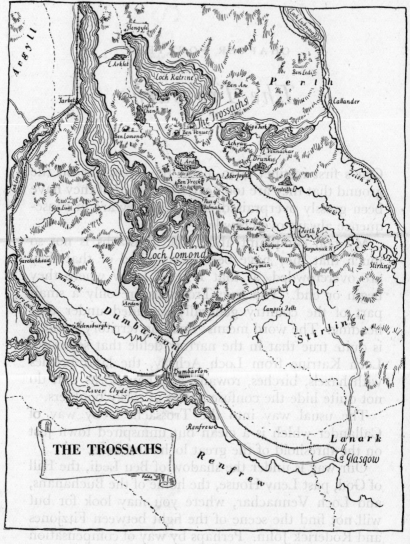

THE TROSSACHS

Lamentation and once carried off a number of playing children to drown them in the Loch.

The road runs alongside the loch for some miles, then cuts in under a fine avenue of trees to Brig o' Turk, and so to the tiny but fascinating Loch Achray which so endeared itself to Coleridge and Wordsworth as well as to Scott. Close by stands the chateau-like Trossachs Hotel which is apt to be overlooked. It looks out over the fine peak of Ben Venue (2,393 feet), but on my last visit I decided that I wanted to see the Trossachs from some point where I should meet no fellow-climbers, so I scrambled up the watery slopes at the back of the hotel to get the view from the summit of Ben A'an. This hill is only 1,700 feet high, but I found the untracked going so heavy that I have more respect for Ben A'an than for many mountains twice as high. There was a lot of bog to be crossed before assaying the final fearful-looking pinnacle from which I got a superb view of Loch Katrine just below.

The descent to the loch was even worse, for it entailed a hand-over-hand climb down the side of a wire fence through a dense wood that brought us out opposite Ellen's Isle, the cattle-pen and larder of the MacGregor who had to conceal the herds that they raided from the Lowlands in a corrie up in the hills above. The steamer runs down the loch to Stronachlachar, which means 'the mason's promontory'. The loch here narrows and ends at Glengyle, once a home of the MacGregors, an ancient house with a tiny window which Rob Roy used as a loophole for his gun. It was in the reign of Mary Queen of Scots that the MacGregors were outlawed. Somebody of importance had been murdered in Glenartney, and the murderers, whoever they were, were given sanctuary by the MacGregors. The head of the murdered man was placed on the altar, and all the MacGregors filing past laid their hands on it in approval of the murder. The Government decided that the clan should be wiped out, so they took to the hills and lived excitingly and not unprofitably on raidings and plunderings. In Charles I's reign they were treated as foreigners and their children refused baptism. Every male over the age of sixteen had to appear annually before commissioners and give security for good behaviour. Yet in Cromwell's time the Mac-Gregors fought against him, and for this act of loyalty in the Restoration they were made free men again. Later they became Jacobites, and the name of Mac-Gregor was proscribed and Rob Roy took the name of the enemy clan, Campbell, although it was a Campbell who had gone to the rescue of his wife and children when they were evicted. His sons took the name of Drummond.

At the west end of Loch Arklet we see the house whence Rob Roy abducted his bride Helen, and not far from the hotel at Inversnaid on Loch Lomond is Rob Roy's cave.

Loch Lomond is a very long narrow loch. It is twenty-one miles long and seldom more than a mile broad until you come to the southern end where it broadens out to a breadth of five miles.

It is a singularly beautiful loch, with fine peaks overshadowing it and trees fringing its shores all the way along. Ben Lomond itself, in spite of the fact that it is only just over 3,000 feet high, is most impressive. It is a mass of granite which rises into a cone with quartzite patches that make it look as if it were snow-covered when it isn't. The view from the summit stretches over sea, lochs, firths, glens, and islands to Ireland on one side and the great bens of the Grampians and Cairngorms on the other.

One of the best views of Ben Lomond is from Tarbet where the steamer calls after leaving Ardlui.

Tarbet, a common name in Scotland, means 'a place over which a boat can be drawn'. King Haakon, in the days of the last Norse invasion, had some of his galleys drawn from Loch Long to Loch Lomond, which are about one and a half miles apart. To-day cars connect Arrochar and Tarbet and their respective steamers.

There is also a fine view of the strange peak known as 'The Cobbler', which looks like one of the rugged teeth of the Cuillin escaped from Skye.

Most people start to climb Ben Lomond from Rowardennan, which is the next port of call for the steamer after Tarbet. After that we again cross the loch to Luss, an excellent centre for cruising among the thirty or so little tree-covered islands or 'inches' that occupy so much of the lower end of the loch, and also for fishing for salmon, trout, and fresh-water herring.

Luss is a protected pleasance of rose-gardens, embowered among trees, with an enviable reputation for warmth, though you can no more guarantee that the waters of the loch will remain unruffled on Loch Lomond than on any other loch. The wind has a way of springing surprises, so care is needed if you are inexperienced with sails.

The peeps through the trees as you drive along the road that runs close to the western shore of the loch provide a constantly changing vista of shapes and colours that are hardly to be excelled in any other Highland loch, but familiarity is apt to dull the edge of appetite and I can well understand that in the height of the season you cannot appreciate the views because of the immense number of motorists who block out so much of the scene. I have always been lucky in my visits and enjoyed the drive in peace. To me, Loch Lomond is as richly rewarding as any, and I seldom get any sense of its proximity to Glasgow.

This is the country of the Colquhouns whose chief lives in the Georgian house of Rossdhu, which means Black Headland. There is a fragment of their ancient castle standing nearby. The Colquhouns, as might be expected, were kept on the *qui vive* by their restless neighbours the MacGregors, though we don't hear quite such wild stories of their vendetta as we do about the MacLeod–MacDonald feuds. A particularly fierce battle, however, took place between the clans in Glen Friern in 1603 as a result of which the Mac-Gregors burnt the farms and got away with the cattle.

Among the wooded islands near Luss, you should visit Inch Tavanach, which was once the retreat of monks, and Inchlonaig, which boasts ancient yew trees planted by Robert the Bruce to supply bows for his army.

Near Balmaha, the next stopping place of the steamer, are two more interesting little islands, Inch-cailloch, the isle of the old woman, once inhabited by nuns, and Inchmurrin, which contains a ruined castle and chapel and a mysterious row of ten gigantic stones, set at intervals of eighty feet. Inchmurrin, which was formerly a deer preserve, has been put under cultivation, and now contains not only a jetty and an attractive modern house, but a poultry farm, power house, and a golf-course.

To enjoy the advantages of an island home by night

and yet be able daily to work in one's office in Glasgow sounds an ideal existence. Remoteness and accessibility are usually incompatible terms.

I wonder that more of Loch Lomond's attractive little islands have not been utilised in this way, though it would be a pity to disturb the peace of such an island as Inchcailloch which was for so long the burial-ground of the MacGregors and MacFarlanes, and is still the roosting ground of capercailzie. But the temptation to clear the ground and modernise these delectable oases must be great to the city man who longs to spend his leisure with only the lapping of water and the flight of birds to break the silence, and to rest his eyes by looking out on this exquisite combination of tree-fringed loch and high mist-crowned peaks, especially when these islands are so accessible, for Glasgow is within an hour's run of Balmaha, the jetty at the end of the loch where the River Leven runs out towards the sea.

CHAPTER FIFTEEN

Round about Stirling

IT is difficult in these days of grim austerity and semi-starvation to believe that we ever really fed as we used to feed in the Restaurant de Soleil at Gleneagles. What would I not give now for those dinners of cantaloup, lobster, partridge, and fresh peaches that we swallowed with such ease after days on the moors? Gleneagles Hotel was so self-contained and self-sufficing that many visitors to it never saw Scotland at all. They stepped out of the sleeper into the hotel and spent their holiday entirely under the hotel roof, wandering round the dress-shops, jewellers, and book-stalls between their visits to the restaurant, swimming-pools, and dance-halls, and never poked their noses outside.

The one disadvantage to this luxurious hotel is the length of the drive. It takes about half a day to get clear of the grounds on foot, and when you do get clear you have still some way to go before you reach any point of scenic or historic interest. The nearby village of Auchterarder has nothing to commend it except its name, which is lovely.

There is a glen called Gleneagles and a house of the same name, the ancestral home of the Chinnery-

Haldanes built in 1624. Its neighbour, Glen Devon, is a pleasant but scarcely exciting glen, and is certainly not typical Highland country.

Usually we made treks towards Stirling. The 'bus fare from Blackford, a village with a long tedious street, is only 2s. 3d. return, and the road runs along the side of Allan Water.

Stirling Castle stands, like Edinburgh Castle, high on a rock. It is even more impressive seen from a distance, for there is nothing else to divert the eye for miles round, as it stands above the flat surrounding country like an isolated mountain peak. The rock on which the castle stands is of basalt.

It is worth remembering that Stirling was a place of strategic importance long before Edinburgh.

Queen Margaret's son, Alexander I, dedicated a chapel in the castle and died there, as did Sir William the Lyon in 1214. Edward I had good reason to know the castle for he was continuously losing it and re-capturing it. On his last assault in 1304 he brought his Queen and her ladies to watch his guns hurling the lead that he had ripped off the roofs of churches to make breaches in the walls.

In 1314 the castle was still in English hands. Robert Bruce's brother was besieging it and had accepted the Governor's promise that it would be surrendered to the Scots on the 24th June if he were not previously relieved. That is why Edward II with his 50,000 men tried to relieve it on the 23rd and after failing to do so was compelled to fight the fatal battle of Bannockburn on the flat lands to the south of the castle on the following day.

The large English army was wedged in between two streams with no opportunity to deploy, so one half was unable to fight because the other half was in the way. Evidence is usually conflicting about these ancient battles, but the generally accepted story is that Robert the Bruce with 30,000 men killed 30,000 of the 100,000 men under Edward II. The victory was not only due to the overcrowding of the English army, but also to Bruce's device of undermining the front of his position with pits covered with turf and rushes into which the English cavalry plunged in hopeless confusion.

The next day the castle was surrendered and dismantled, only to be retaken by the English after Bruce's death when they held it for a further six years before being starved into submission.

There is a fine National Memorial to Bruce, close to the outer gateway of the castle, representing him in coat of mail facing the battlefield. Of the Keep's original four towers only two remain. After passing under the gateway we come to the Parliament House with fine oriel windows, the work of Cochrane, one of James II's favourites, who was afterwards hanged from the bridge at Lauder.

The Palace, which is the outstanding feature of the castle, was built by James V round a quadrangle known as the Lions' Den. It is easy to see that the masons were recruited from France. It is now used as a barracks, but one's thoughts fly back as usual to Mary Queen of Scots and her infant son James VI, whose christening took place in the chapel.

The bars on the windows are supposed to have been put there to prevent any possible kidnapping of the child.

In the Douglas Room you will doubtless be reminded of the supper party given by James II there to William, Earl of Douglas in 1452. Suspecting him of disloyalty and an alliance with the Earls of Crawford and Ross, he asked him to come to Stirling and at supper asked him to break his bond with these two Earls. When he refused James drew his dagger and crying, "Well, this will break it", stabbed him in the neck and chest. The courtiers gave him twenty-four more wounds and his corpse was thrown out of the window.

The view from the ramparts of the Douglas Garden just outside is superb and stretches as far afield as the high ridges of the usually snow-covered Ben Lomond, Ben Venue, Ben Ledi and Ben Vorlich, the Ochils and Sherrifmuir, and nearby across the valley rises the tree-covered Abbey Craig on the summit of which rises the tremendous tower, 220 feet high, known as the Wallace Monument, with its fine statue and sword of the warrior. From the castle walls you can see the fifteenth-century bridge that supplanted the broken one which in 1297 helped to give Wallace his greatest victory by collapsing while packed with enemy troops.

You can also see in a loop of the Forth the square tower of Cambuskenneth Abbey where lies the body of James III who was killed after the Battle of Sauchieburn. As he was fleeing he fell from his horse and was stunned just outside a mill at Bannockburn. The miller took him inside, but when he recovered consciousness he told the man who he was. "I was your king until this morning," he said. They called a priest, and when he arrived the king said, "Give me the Sacrament". "That will I do heartily," said the false priest and stabbed him to death.

What I remember best about Stirling is Mar's

Work which stands at the top of Broad Street. It still retains some of its sixteenth-century splendour in the semi-hexagonal towers flanking its arched gateway which bear two rhyming mottoes couched in the old language.

There are further reminders of the Earls of Mar, who were Governors of the castle, in the officers' mess of the Argyll and Sutherland Highlanders, round the walls of which stands a most imposing array of successive generations of the holders of this title, all with remarkably long noses.

In Castle Wynd there is a lovely old house known as Argyll's Lodging. It was begun in 1632 by the Earl of Stirling to whom James VI gave a large part of America, including Canada, but in spite of that died in poverty. It was not finished until 1672 by the Marquis of Argyll. The lodging forms three sides of a quadrangle, with turrets ending in sharply pointed roofs, and wonderfully carved chimneys and windows. It is now used as a hospital, but it retains all its exterior dignity. The High Church is unusual in that it is divided into two parish churches. It has a fine fifteenth-century open timber roof and a tower which bears the marks of shots which came from the castle by mistake.

Stirling's past lies on the heights and remains more or less undisturbed. Its present, at the foot of the hill, is that of a very vigorous industrial and shopping centre, but it is not distinctively Scottish. In Perth and Inverness the kilt is commonly worn. I have actually seen a man jeered by boys and girls for wearing a kilt and glengarry in the streets of Stirling.

There is a pleasant walk from Gleneagles over the relatively wild but not high Muir of Orchill to Crieff.

Crieff stands on the southern slopes of a hill above the Earn and has a good reputation for hotels. The wooded hill above the town known as the Knock provides a wonderful view-point from which to look out over the heart of Scotland. You can see the entrance to the Trossachs, the Grampians to the north, the flat greenlands to the south, and the hills of Ochil in the east. Just south stands Drummond Castle, which was originally built in 1491. Mary Queen of Scots spent a Christmas there. It was dismantled by Cromwell's men and partially rebuilt in 1715 but destroyed in 1745 by the Jacobite Duchess of Perth lest the Government troops should occupy it.

Beyond lies the tidy little town of Comrie, famous for its frequent earthquakes which do not, however, disturb the even tenor of the town. It owes its earthquakes to the fact that it lies on the line of 'fault' which separates the Highlands from the Lowlands. It is certainly very near the Highlands, because within a few miles we come to the lovely wooded village of St. Fillans on the shores of Loch Earn. There is a hill just opposite the very picturesque Drummond Arms called Dundurn where I have encountered herds of more than a hundred stags and hinds. Ben Vorlich frowns down on St. Fillans from an immense height and there is no mistaking the fact from that mountain's presence alone that we are now in the Highlands.

There is a pleasant wooded walk along the southern banks of Loch Earn to Ardvorlich at the foot of Glen Vorlich where the MacGregors in 1589, after murdering the King's Forester, in revenge for an imaginary injury, placed his head on a dish with a crust between his teeth and gave it to his sister when she came back from preparing their food for them.

191

Six MacDonalds of Glencoe, who lost their lives in an attempt to raid Ardvorlich, lie buried by the roadside here. At Ardvorlich House the oldest rock crystal talisman in Scotland, known as the Clach Dearg, is preserved. You can of course walk all round Loch Earn or travel by the white yacht on its surface to Loch Earnhead and back. Loch Earn is much underrated because it is so accessible. It is the last real tract of Highland scenery that we pass on our way south. Thereafter we lose at once the magic combination of long wide waters lying cupped between dark blue massive bens.

One of the most pleasing glens in this part of Scotland is the Sma' Glen which I last visited in the company of a young man from Skye who was working in a bookshop in Dundee. We went by way of Huntingtower Castle which was the scene of the Raid of Ruthven. In 1582 when James VI was sixteen, he accepted an invitation to stay here with the Earl of Gowrie and on arrival found himself trapped by a gang of nobles who demanded the dismissal of his favourites, the Duke of Lennox and Earl of Arran. When James tried to break loose, the Master of Glamis barred the way and the young king burst into tears and was told, 'Better bairns greet than bearded men'.

For a few months the Ruthven faction predominated, but in 1584 Gowrie was beheaded and James learnt his lesson. The space between the two towers of Huntingtower is called the 'Maiden's Leap' because the first earl's daughter jumped from one tower to the other to escape being caught with her lover. We then came to the bank of the Almond and passed the public school of Glenalmond, founded in 1841.

THE BRIDGE AT KILLIN, THE RIVER DOCHART, PERTHSHIRE

LOCH LOMOND. VIEW FROM ROWARDENNAN

At Buchanty we were given a prodigious meal at the post-office before entering the Sma' Glen. It is not a small glen, but a wild and beautiful one. On one side runs the high road, and on the other side of the Almond rises the razor-edged ridge of Dun Mor, a treeless and impressive height where there is a prehistoric camp.

General Wade constructed a road through the glen in 1762 of which there are still distinct traces. In the narrow pass of the glen is a huge stone which is generally believed to mark the grave of Ossian.

In a crevice of the Eagle's Rock high up on the eastern ridge is the Thief's Cave, where Alastair Bain, the notorious sheep-stealer, had his hide-out. He once foolishly lit a fire which gave away his hiding-place and his enemies tracked him to the cave, bound him, and took him away to be hanged in Perth.

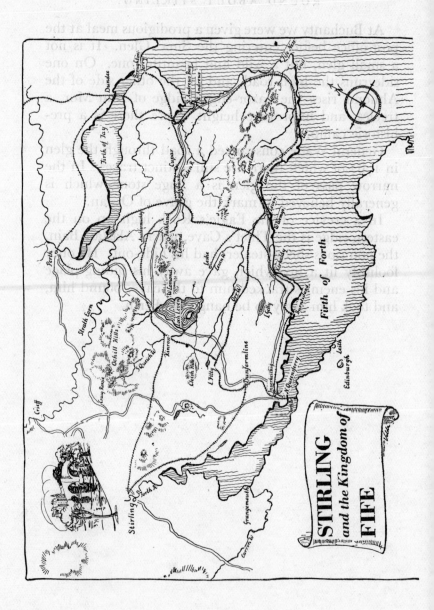

STIRLING and the Kingdom of FIFE

CHAPTER SIXTEEN

The Kingdom of Fife and St. Andrews

THE trouble about Fife is that one is forever travelling through it to get to some other part of Scotland. Each time I promise myself that on my next visit I will give up a whole holiday to its exploration. It is an extremely fertile and prosperous land, undulating and pleasing without wildness, with a glorious coastline of cliffs and sandy bays with golf-courses renowned throughout the world. It is a land of good farms and great historic antiquity.

> The King sits in Dunfermline town
> Drinking the blude-red wine.

So begins the old ballad of Sir Patrick Spens which always runs through my head whenever I visit the town that is now far better known for the benefactions of its most famous native Andrew Carnegie, who came back as a millionaire to buy the seventeenth-century mansions of Pittencrieff and turn it over to his fellow-townsmen as a museum and pleasure-park in perpetuity.

In Pittencrieff Glen stands Malcolm's Tower, built in 1066 for his Saxon Queen Margaret. They were responsible for the building of a church of which only the foundations remain. It was their son David I who founded the great Abbey church and built a very costly shrine to his mother, whose bones were removed at the Reformation in a silver casket that was afterwards traced to Spain and France and then lost sight of. Only the nave of this Abbey still stands; the western doorway is one of the finest examples of Norman architecture in Scotland. There also remains one gable of the Monastery refectory and part of the wall of the once magnificent palace which was the birthplace of Robert the Bruce's son in 1323. Dunfermline Palace was also the birthplace in 1600 of Charles I, but Charles II was the last king ever to stay there, and after his time it fell into neglect.

The new Abbey church was built about 125 years ago. On the four sides of the battlements of its 100-feet-high square tower you will see inscribed in huge stone letters, 'KING ROBERT THE BRUCE'. Bruce died at Cardross Castle of a kind of leprosy, but his body (except for his heart, which rests in Melrose Abbey) lies in Dunfermline Abbey. It is only about twelve miles from Dunfermline to Loch Leven where stands the island in which Mary Queen of Scots was imprisoned for a year before being rescued in 1568, only to be finally defeated at Langside a few days later. The keys of her prison were dropped in the loch by her rescuers and miraculously found centuries later and taken to Abbotsford. Loch Leven has of course another claim to fame. It is the finest loch in Scotland for trout.

There is another palace at Falkland with a very

196

gruesome story attached to its dungeons. In 1402 the young Duke of Rothesay was starved to death and is reputed to have been reduced to eating his own fingers. You have read all about this in *The Fair Maid of Perth*. The palace that you see to-day is not a ruin, but a trim, rather gaunt building restored first by the Bruces of Falkland and later by the Marquess of Bute, who strove hard to restore its ancient dignity. There are fine tapestries and emblazoned arms on the ceilings in many of the twelve rooms. The Chapel Royal has a richly carved screen and Flemish tapestries.

It was to this palace that Mary Queen of Scots' father came after his defeat at Solway Moss and received the news that his Queen had given birth at Linlithgow to a daughter. "It cam wi' a lass," he said of the crown, "and 'twill gang wi' a lass." Twenty years later that lass, now Mary Queen of Scots, spent a brief period of happiness at Falkland. There is a curious story of her son James VI connected with this palace. He found Alexander Rathorn asleep wearing a ribbon that he had given a little time before to his Queen. He immediately hastened to the Queen's boudoir and demanded to see his gift. By miraculous good chance, one of the Queen's ladies-in-waiting had seen the incident and seizing the ribbon restored it just in time to allay the King's suspicions.

But interesting as they are, Dunfermline and Falkland fall far behind St. Andrews, which is in many ways the most fascinating city in all Scotland.

St. Andrews is a really electrifying city. In a 'haar', or sea-mist, it is a city of mystery. But mists are not common for long on the east coast and the sun is. The Fife coast is to Scotland what the Sussex coast is to England, sun-kissed. Clouds make a point of avoiding Elie and St. Andrews, and the sun tempers the east wind for the bather from the golden sands. Only Bernard Darwin could do justice to the Royal and Ancient Golf Links, a sacrosanct course which the ordinary Englishman approaches with trembling.

My usual business, however, in St. Andrews has been to address the scarlet-gowned undergraduates of the University or the girls of St. Leonards, which is to Scotland what Cheltenham Ladies' College is to England.

I have played golf at St. Andrews, but never with quite the same carefree abandon that I play at Kingussie or Nairn. It is an intimidating course, not because of the length or difficulty of any one hole, but because of the critical scrutiny which is bestowed on one by caddie and player alike. I feel at St. Andrews as if I were on parade at Chelsea Barracks. So on the whole I prefer the bathing from those lovely sands beyond the links, and walking along the cliffs looking down on the dangerous reefs.

St. Andrews is almost as compact as Winchelsea. Four roads lead from the west to the cathedral, South Street, a gloriously wide avenue, which is entered from the only remaining gate and lined with trees, Market Street, North Street, beautified by the college tower and chapel, and the Scores, a place of large houses and schools. There are the usual wynds or narrow passages running off all these main streets.

North Street is to St. Andrews what the High is to Oxford. The original College buildings founded by Bishop Kennedy in 1450 have gone, but the vigorous spirit that was infused by that powerful chancellor, who was responsible for displacing the Douglases and

198

installing the Stewarts, remains. The present United College certainly looks as old as most Oxford colleges.

The outstanding features of the University chapel, which has some points of resemblance to St. George's, Windsor, are Bishop Kennedy's tomb, a piece of very delicate stone-work that has suffered a good deal through exposure to wind and rain, and John Knox's pulpit, which is richly carved. There are, of course, many ghosts in St. Andrews. John Knox is one of them. The chapel has been restored, but the oak roof is nearly two hundred years old and the screen of carved stone is equally impressive.

The restoration, which is unusually happy, was due to the beneficence of Dr. Harkness, who also gave the large new St. Saviour's Hall, the men students' residential hostel. The Graduation Hall was the gift of Dr. Younger.

The ruins of the castle lie off North Street. You can see on the edge of the cliffs the fragments of the older castle.

Above the gateway you can see the window from which the scheming, luxury-loving Cardinal David Beaton looked down on the preacher George Wishart being led away to be burnt.

Three months later, Melville of Halhill, Kirkcaldy of Grange, and John Leslie of Parkhill forced an entrance, surprised the guards and murdered the Cardinal, afterwards hanging his corpse from the wall for the people to see. You can see in the wall of the west tower five steps of the staircase leading to the Cardinal's rooms, and in the south-west corner is a portion of a tower with walls fifteen feet thick, and in the Sea Tower you can explore the Bottle Dungeon. It is only five feet in diameter at the top; it descends to a depth of twenty feet and expands to fifteen feet diameter at the bottom. It was here that they placed the body of Cardinal Beaton pickled in salt for seven months after his murder.

John Knox was captured in this castle a year later by French gunners who took him away to work as a slave in the French galleys.

At the Kirkhill, under the shadow of the Abbey, are the remains of an early Celtic church where a Celtic cross, coloured tiles, and stained glass have been excavated. We are now in the vast burial-ground above which stand the tower of St. Regulus and the Cathedral. Both of them were conceived in the twelfth century, but the Tower was finished two hundred years before the cathedral was consecrated in 1318 in the presence of Robert the Bruce. It must have been a wonderful building. It was 335 feet long and 63 feet wide with a central tower and side turrets. David II was crowned in this cathedral at the age of eight together with his betrothed Joanna, sister of Edward III. James V was married here to Marie of Lorraine two hundred years later.

It was not destroyed at the Reformation, but became a ruin through neglect. The seats in the wall and several stone coffins are all that are left of the Chapter House, next door to which is the Museum where you can see fragments of the stained-glass windows that once adorned the cathedral.

Close by the west gate stand the Pends, covered vaults where strangers had to wait pending their admission to the city. If you wait long enough after midnight to-day, you may meet another of St. Andrews ghosts, the Headless Nun. If you do see her and she raises her veil, you are doomed.

In South Street there is a house called 'Queen Mary's', where Mary Queen of Scots is supposed to have stayed. Her visits were happy, so her ghost doesn't haunt the place, but one of her 'Four Maries' haunts one of the houses here, perhaps one of the houses of St. Leonard's, who own 'Queen Mary's'.

The derelict St. Leonard's chapel and the previous St. Leonard's College, once a Nunnery and now a private house, stand close by.

South Street contains many very fine ancient tall houses with remarkably spacious and well-laid-out gardens. It is also the chief shopping centre, so to turn into the Quadrangle of St. Mary's College is like turning out of the High in Oxford to All Souls' or B.N.C. There is a hawthorn tree in this quadrangle that is supposed to have been planted by Mary Queen of Scots. The Tower Church, founded in 1412 and restored and rebuilt five hundred years later, is memorable for John Knox's sermons and Archbishop Sharp's memorial on 3rd May 1679. On his way home to St. Andrews with his daughter, his coach was fired on and stopped on Magnus Muir by twelve men who hacked his head to pieces for betraying the church, and then returned a prayer of thanks. His black and white monument was erected by his son.

The ruins of a chapel on the other side of the street are all that remains of the Blackfriars Monastery. Behind it stands the Madras College, founded by Dr. Bell about 120 years ago.

At the end of South Street stands the West Post or Gate which has houses built against it on either side. It is very old but the carvings over it are relatively modern.

The glory of St. Andrews does not, however, rest solely on its ancient buildings or its history. It has a magnificent setting. Away beyond the whin bushes and dunes of the four golf-courses, you can see the Sidlaws rising above the Tay and away beyond them the Grampians. Inland lies Cupar, the dignified capital of the Kingdom of Fife, and Leuchars with its Norman church and huge aerodrome. Southwards are the Royal Burghs of the Neuk towns, Crail which holds its charter from Robert the Bruce and still rings curfew as they do in St. Andrews. In the churchyard you will see the famous 'Blue Stone of Crail', shot there by the Devil as he lay in May Island. You can still see his thumb-mark in the stone. In old days the Crail natives used to kiss it on going away to ensure a safe return.

Then there are the two Anstruthers, Anstruther Eastern and Anstruther Western, separated by the little River Dreel. Here there is a fine harbour which Robert Louis Stevenson helped to design. There is a Flemish look about some of the houses above the harbour of this Royal Burgh.

Beyond the golf-course lies Pittenweem which once possessed a twelfth-century Priory, but its stones were taken to build the dower-house of the Earls of Kellie. There is a room at the base of the church tower with a barred window where Janet Corphat, suspected of being a witch, was murdered by the mob. It too boasts a fine harbour. Then comes St. Morans, the haunt of artists, with its fourteenth-century cruciform church standing up on a rocky mound but within reach of the sea spray in a storm. Nearby is the ruin of Newark Castle, once the home of Sir David Leslie and later the sanctuary of a fugitive of the Lindsay of Balcarres who was given shelter and found by a young girl in the castle.

But the place I know and like best on this part of the coast of Fife is Elie, where the golf rivals that at St. Andrews and the bathing is even better. Elie is a very gay, happy-go-lucky seaside resort, and I spent one of the happiest summers of my undergraduate days in a very care-free company in that sunny, bracing atmosphere.

Largs is, I suppose, mainly known as the home of Alexander Selkirk who provided Defoe with his material for *Robinson Crusoe*. You can see the place where his house stood and the statue to his memory.

Green Largs Law is supposed to contain a gold mine. Pagan rites used to be celebrated on its summit. There are still three megaliths at Lundin nearby, which also boasts an ancient square tower. Celtic ornaments have been excavated on Norries' Law, so the whole of this area has a strong appeal for archæologists. Beyond Wemyss, where Mary first met Darnley, we come to industrial Kirkcaldy, where Carlyle taught mathematics, and so to Burntisland, where Cromwell was induced by the natives to build up their harbour and pave their streets, and we leave the Kingdom of Fife at Inverkeithing, either by the Forth Bridge or by the ferry that plies across the Firth to Queensferry below it. It is called Queensferry because Queen Margaret, wife of Malcolm, established a free ferry here for pilgrims bound for Dunfermline and St. Andrews. This was probably a peace-offering for being given sanctuary by Malcolm when as a Saxon princess she was seeking refuge from the Normans. It is said that she did not regard her saviour well in the light of a suitor, but the fact remains that they were married.

The Forth Bridge is, of course, one of the engineering wonders of the world. It took eight years to build (1882–90) and a number of lives were lost in the process, some by white-hot rivets falling on to the builders. It is 8,295 feet long, with two main spans of 1,710 feet, and is built on the cantilever principle. The tremendous sweep of its three stupendous girders curving high above the railway line and overlooking the great naval base of Rosyth makes it easily the most dignified and impressive bridge in these islands though in length, of course, it is not to be compared with the Tay Bridge.

The way into Edinburgh from Queensferry is particularly lovely because it runs alongside the princely estate of Dalmeny, the seat of Lord Rosebery.

CHAPTER SEVENTEEN

Inverness and the North

INVERNESS, the gateway to the wonders of Ross and Sutherland, is an astonishing town. It is still so fiercely Jacobite that if by mischance you slip into the error of calling Prince Charles Edward 'the Pretender', you are in danger of being knocked down, and yet the people speak a purer English than you will hear in any town south of the Scottish border. They still retain their national dress. Everybody wears the kilt. Somebody is always playing the bag-pipes. The shops are full of dirks, claymores, sporrans, and other picturesque and often intimidating relics of the past, and the whole town breathes an atmo-sphere of Highland homogeneity. It has not been tainted or affected in the least by the passing wealthy tenants of the northern deer forests or the myriads of tourists that throng its streets.

Inverness wears a very happy air in spite of a stormy history, and most visitors agree that it is one of the most fascinating towns in the world to stay in, while everyone who lives there agrees that he wouldn't live anywhere else in the world.

With so much to see it is difficult to know where to begin. If you come to it as most Englishmen do

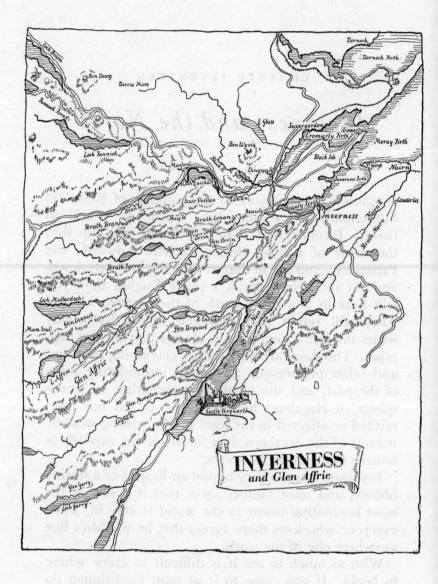

INVERNESS
and Glen Affric

over the wild moors below Strathspey your first memory is a Shakespearean one, for close to Nairn, a lovely breezy seaside resort with first-rate sands and golf-course, stands Cawdor Castle with its memories of Macbeth. You will be surprised to find that Cawdor is not a ruin. Even the drawbridge over the moat still stands and, for all I know, still works. When the family is away you may walk under its majestic towers and see the room in which—they will tell you—Macbeth murdered Duncan. It is well not to inquire too closely into this, as the present castle was built five hundred years after Macbeth was Thane of this land.

But if the Cawdor you see is not the Cawdor that Macbeth saw, Culloden Moor nearby remains much as it was on that fatal April day in 1746 when Prince Charles Edward made his last desperate stand, and the Cawdor that you see is the same castle in which Lord Lovat temporarily found sanctuary after that defeat.

Culloden is a grim bleak place and a heavy sadness still clings to it. A great memorial cairn stands above the mounds under which the Highlanders lie buried in their clans. Culloden was less a battle than a rout. The 5,000 Highlanders under Prince Charles Edward were not only half-starved and dispirited after their long retreat from Derby, they were also torn by clan jealousy. The Duke of Cumberland had 8,000 well-fed excellently disciplined troops. The battle lasted less than forty minutes. The right wing of the Highlanders had grown restive under a heavy fire and charged without orders. The MacDonalds, whose place in the line of battle through all the ages since Bannockburn had been on the right, now found themselves on the left, and stood immovable in their insulted dignity until it was too late.

Cumberland gave no quarter. The wounded and the fugitives alike were put to the sword and even on-lookers from Inverness were cut down. The English lost 310 men, the Highlanders over a thousand, and Cumberland goes down to history as 'the Butcher', while Prince Charles Edward, in spite of the degradation of his later days, retains his romantic halo.

If you want to penetrate to the very heart of Scotland, follow the route taken by the Prince after his defeat. You will find it marked on a large-scale map in the Museum in Inverness. This will lead you, among other places, to Glen Moriston, a wild and all too little known fastness, where for three weeks the seven men of Glen Moriston, in spite of their land being laid waste, lived in a cave guarding the Prince and scouring the country at great peril to find him food. They were not tempted by the £30,000 that the Government offered to anyone who would betray him.

You may, of course, reach Inverness not by way of Culloden Moor, but by water up the Caledonian Canal by way of Fort William, Loch Lochy, Invergarry, Fort Augustus, and Loch Ness, where you will doubtless peer into the depths of the black loch for signs of the Loch Ness monster. Englishmen who haven't visited the loch are apt to be sceptical about this strange beast. They should read Commander Rupert Gould's evidence on the subject and also visit that picturesque ruin, Castle Urquhart, where they may see the claw of an animal, a dinosaur of some sort, that was taken from the loch. There seems no reason at all why one of the monsters of the deep should not be imprisoned in these waters. A large number of trustworthy witnesses claim to have seen it. What is odd is the fact that nobody claimed to have seen it during the war. The nine-day wonder was eclipsed by weightier matters. The Loch Ness monster ceased to have news value after Hitler loomed upon the scene. Castle Urquhart was, by the way, a Royal Castle, seized by Edward I and the house thereafter of several governors, given eventually to the Grants for their services in 1506 against the Mac-Donalds, Lords of the Isles.

Inverness history goes back a long way. Columba came here to try to convert the Pictish King and when he found the gates shut against him, made the sacred sign and the gates flew open. That was enough to convince the King of Columba's power. Macbeth's Castle of Inverness, where he planned Duncan's death, was outside the town, but Malcolm, the husband of Margaret, built a castle on Castle Hill which lasted until Prince Charles Edward destroyed it. Mary Queen of Scots paid a visit to Inverness in 1562, but Lord Gordon refused to grant her hospitality in the castle, so she had to spend the night in a house in Bridge Street. The next day Gordon repented, but it was too late. He was executed in his own castle. There are some ancient circles and standing stones at Clava, but the most interesting place near the town is its finest view-point Tom-na-hurich, the home of the fairies, about which, if you are a true believer, the Inverness people will tell you many strange stories.

The shops are so full of colourful, picturesque and rare mementoes, the hotels and restaurants so comfortable and the people so courteous, that you will find it difficult to tear yourself away from Inverness, but having got so far north you should certainly leave enough time to explore the very varied and often wild land that lies to the north.

There is, just across the water, the Black Isle of Cromarty, a fertile low-lying land of prosperous farms, not unlike Orkney.

Beyond Strath Conan, which is beautifully wooded, lies Dingwall, where we leave the main line to discover Strathpeffer, which is unlike any place you would expect to find in the far north.

It is a mixture of Bournemouth, Buxton, Harrogate, and a Swiss winter sports centre. It lies among pine woods, with a great number of palatial hotels and hydropathics, and is full of invalids who come to take the sulphur-bath cure, and younger and more hale visitors who come in search of dancing and other gaiety.

It is a magnificent centre for walks to suit either the lazy or the vigorous. For the mountain climber, there is the vast mass of Ben Wyvis, which is an elephantine hump towering over the northern part of the town in solitary majesty. For the less strenuous, there are the Falls of Rogie, one of the most stupendous cataracts in the British Isles. To reach it you follow a well marked but usually wet track through high heather and thick bracken, over a moor alive with grouse and past a tiny loch that is full of wild duck and shelduck. The water is as black as stout and spanned by a narrow swinging bridge, which you are warned not to cross. The warning is scarcely necessary. It looks the way to instant death.

Among the pine woods I discovered a fine vitrified fort on the top of Knock Garrel, whence you look down on as green and gentle a strath as you would find in the Sussex Weald. Strathpeffer lies just off the line that runs from Inverness to Achnasheen and the Kyle of Lochalsh.

I suppose there are people who would settle down to a book even on this amazing train journey.

But I know no journey in the British Isles comparable to this for variety and grandeur. It is so lonely that the stags come down to watch the train pass. Parts of the journey pass through deep ravines with boulders overhanging the train that threaten to destroy it. There is a whole succession of wild and lonely lochs, Garve, Luichart, Fannich, Culen, and Achanalt, glittering gems set among rugged and often seemingly inaccessible peaks. Outstanding among these peaks are Sgurr Vuillin, and beyond Achnasheen the even grander peaks of Sgurr Dubh, Liathach, and Ben Eay.

The scenery grows even wilder as we leave Achnasheen and run down Glen Carron to the golden-fringed sea-loch Carron where we get our first breath-taking view of the distant jagged Cuillin hills over the water, looking at one moment like menacing thunder-clouds rising out of the sea and at another like pieces of cardboard carved into the likeness of battlements. If you leave the train at Achnasheen you will find a motor-coach waiting to take you to Loch Maree, Loch Torridon, Gairloch, Loch Broom, Ullapool, and Loch Assynt.

In this part of the North-west Highlands we reach the finest scenery in all Scotland. This is partly due to the quick change from the very soft to the very bleak. Suilven (the 'Sugar Loaf') is the wildest crag that I have ever seen and the most menacing. All the crazy peaks up here look as if they had been twisted and torn by wrathful gods. They do not invite you to climb them. Indeed Suilven is not only the most frightening of hills to look at, it is also one of the most difficult to climb, owing to the steep approaches to the main peak and the narrow serrated edges which rise like 'aiguilles'. Then there is Quineg which rises above Loch Assynt, a black rough-hewn primeval block of rock standing in a landscape without any sign whatever of life or vegetation in it.

And yet the nearby lochs are surrounded by delicate birches standing above the shining sand and primroses and violets abound on the sun-kissed banks.

It is this mixture of the very gracious and gentle with the very grim that makes this corner of Scotland so unforgettable. I suppose no sight is more ardently looked forward to than that of Loch Maree after the steep winding climb from Loch a' Chroisg to the head of Glen Docherty. And what a sight it is. A long narrow straight line of shining silver water with a host of exquisite little islets neatly bedded beneath the shadows of the great buttress of the Slioch with its finely pointed shoulders on one side and the enormous precipices and pointed peaks of Ben Eighe on the other. At the far end of the loch stands the Loch Maree Hotel, whence the road climbs over the hill past Flowerdale House, the home of the Mackenzies, along the shores of a lovely sandy bay to the village of Gairloch.

But there are those, Compton Mackenzie among them, who prefer Loch Assynt to Loch Maree. Assynt is not a sea-loch, and owes, I think, its splendour to the violently tormented peaks, notably of Suilven, which from here rises rather like the Matterhorn out of its bleak arid surroundings. But on all sides there rises above the flat black moors a whole succession of isolated mountains that look like prehistoric monsters crouching under the clouds.

If you want a real wild holiday, with first-rate fishing, solitary peak-climbing, sea-bathing, and an ever-changing panorama of really majestic scenery, make your centre at Ullapool, Lochinver, or Loch Maree. You cannot go wrong between Loch Torridon and Loch Assynt. It all beggars description as you can see from any photographs of this superb and unspoilt land.

The east coast north of Dingwall presents a very different picture. Everybody wants to visit John o' Groat's once in his life-time, and the journey by rail as far as Helmsdale clings more or less to the coast so that you get plenty of opportunity of seeing the Moray Firth. At Invergordon we pass the great naval base and at Tain, a pleasant fishing-village on the Dornoch Firth, we get a reminder of the Norse, for Tain is a corruption of Thing, 'a place of assembly'. Tain was once the shrine of St. Duthes to which James V came barefoot to pay homage. Robert the Bruce's wife and daughter were captured in this chapel by the Earl of Ross and handed over to Edward I, and later a MacNeill of Sutherland burnt up a Mowatt of Caithness and his band in this chapel where they had taken what they vainly hoped would be sanctuary.

On the other side of the firth lies Dornoch, famous for golf and the last burning of a witch in Britain (1722). It has a good modern hotel and an ancient castle.

There is a modern castle, which is all turrets and towers and windows, at Skibo, once the summer resort

of Andrew Carnegie, and a very ancient one that has
been completely modernised at Dunrobin, the home
of the Duke of Sutherland. Northward on the coast
lies Brora, with its famous salmon-fishing and golf-
course which attract more visitors than the little town
can conveniently hold, and so we come to Helmsdale,
where we leave Sutherland. Helmsdale stands above
the mouth of the Helmsdale river, and also attracts
golfers, bathers, and anglers.

There are the usual castle ruins. In this castle
in 1567, Isobel Sinclair, wishing to do away with the
heir to the earldom, poisoned by mistake the Earl,
his Countess, and her own son. Women in Helmsdale
must have a poor reputation, because in an earlier
age Sweyn, the Viking, was driven to burn a lady
called Frekark together with all her women for making
a nuisance of herself politically. Helmsdale is in the
centre of a county that is remarkably rich in hut
circles, cairns, and other relics of the Stone Age.

You get very little indication as you explore the
east coast of Sutherland of the wildness and grandeur
that lie behind; occasionally you see in the far distance
a few green isolated humps and peaks, but you are
certainly not overshadowed by their shapes, inaccessibility, wildness, and grandeur as you are at Assynt
and Ullapool. The distance across Sutherland from
east to west is seldom more than fifty miles and often
less, but as there are very few roads or villages, the
adventure is not to everyone's taste.

There are roads from Lairg to Loch Assynt and
up the north side of Loch Shin to Lexford Bridge,
but what happens to you if you try to walk across
country from Lairg direct to Assynt I can only
conjecture.

I have a feeling that the journey might not be worth the effort, as the cream of it is obviously wholly in the west.

Caithness, which we enter at the Ord of Caithness, is not mountainous at all. It is mainly a rather barren moorland plateau over which (whenever I have been there) the 'haar' or sea-mist sweeps, blotting out all the view. The coastline, however, fully redeems the lack of interest of the mainland, for there is magnificent rock scenery all the way along. This is the country about which Neil Gunn writes so well. Wick is the most important town and is really busy when the summer herring fishing is on. It is a grey, unsmiling, uninspired-looking little port, and one gets the feeling that the people live a stoical hard life.

There are plenty of tales of ancient cruelty practised in the old towers or castles that line this coast; and the sea demands a savage toll from the fishermen. So it is not surprising that the townspeople look a little grim.

The railway turns inland here for its final journey over the barren moors to Thurso, which I found to be unexpectedly lively. There are good hotels, plenty of shops, and magnificent cliff scenery overlooking Dunnet Head and the Pentland Firth. Across the bay at Scrabster the mail steamer runs daily to the Orkney.

John o' Groat's lies some miles to the east of Thurso close to Duncansby Head. It boasts a large barrack-like hotel and you may count on finding the same sort of crowd that you find at Land's End, or any other spot that "simply must be visited".

I quickly left the chattering motorists and walked down to the end of the deserted jetty and spent an hour of great delight watching flock after flock of gannets diving into the sea close by, completely un-affected by my presence.

John o' Groat's is supposed to have been a Dutch-man called de Groot who entertained seven brothers or other male relatives each year on the anniversary of their landing. As they always quarrelled as to who should take the head of the table, John built an octagonal home with eight doors and built an octa-gonal table so that each guest should enter by his own door and sit at what would be to him the obvious head of the table.

His house no longer stands. What does remain is the wild roost or race of the Pentland Firth, which has a very evil reputation, a beach that is crammed with cowrie shells, and a magnificent view from Duncansby Head over Stroma and the Pentland Skerries to the quiet and pleasant islands of the Orkney.

CHAPTER EIGHTEEN

Glen Affric

WE live in a very curious age. On every side the
Government is acquiring and exerting more and more
compulsory powers to utilise land over which we have
wandered freely for generations in order to use it as
a training-ground for tanks or to generate electric
power.

Dartmoor, many of the English lakes, the Isle of
Purbeck, many commons and heathlands, and Ash-
down Forest are already lost to the public, and many
famous Highland glens are now to follow in their wake.

I have no objection to dams as such. The dam at
Loch Laggan does not detract from its beauty. It adds
to it. But when I heard that Glen Affric was to be
transformed I felt a pang of dismay and considerable
sympathy with Lord Lovat, Cameron of Lochiel, and
all the other Highlanders who protested vigorously
against this desecration.

No one in his senses would protest against the use
of land and water for a military necessity, but the
necessity has to be proved.

No one would protest against the use of land and
water for any scheme that would bring more and
cheaper electric power within the reach of us all, but

217

we have a right to demand that such schemes should entail as little spoliation of natural beauty as possible, and we have so far had no proof that the War Office and hydro-electric scheme promoters have paid sufficient attention to the protests of those who wish to retain for the public good areas which by reason of their proposals would entirely and irretrievably lose their unique character and charm.

So far as Glen Affric is concerned, the North of Scotland Electric Board have issued a detailed statement about their proposals which deserves the widest possible publicity.

Here it is:

NORTH OF SCOTLAND HYDRO-ELECTRIC BOARD

MULLARDOCH-FASNAKYLE-AFFRIC PROJECT

The North of Scotland Hydro-Electric Board have prepared a Scheme to utilise the great water-power resources of the Glen Affric-Glen Cannich area in such a way as to leave the famous natural beauties of those Glens unspoiled.

The Board is going to contribute towards meeting the shortage of electric power in the country. They (*sic*) also intend to develop large-scale economic schemes to provide cheap power for industry in the north of Scotland and to earn revenue from which uneconomic distribution schemes in the north of Scotland may be financed.

Constructional Scheme No. 7, the Mullardoch-Fasnakyle-Affric Project, is the result.

EMPLOYMENT. Two thousand men will be required for the construction work. First priority will be given to men from employment exchanges in the district.

When the Scheme is completed, a staff of about twenty will be permanently employed. A new hamlet of electrically equipped houses, designed to fit in with their surroundings and with the other houses in the district, will be built in the neighbourhood of Cannich village.

RATES. Rates payable to the County Council in respect of this Scheme are estimated to produce ultimately £10,000 per annum, representing 1s. 5d. in the £ on the existing County rates (i.e. exclusive of Inverness City).

The rates for the whole catchment area of 124 square miles amounted last year to only some £300.

This Scheme represents more than two years of investigation and discussion. It incorporates the ideas of some of the country's most eminent engineers and architects and also the recommendations of amenity and fishery interests. The Amenity Committee and the Fisheries Committee, appointed under the Hydro-Electric Development (Scotland) Act, 1943, have been consulted throughout the preparation of the Scheme and agreement has been reached. On technical and financial grounds the Electricity Commissioners have given it their approval.

The Board's Mullardoch-Fasnakyle-Affric Project involves a dam 120 feet high at Loch Mullardoch, a tunnel diverting its waters to Loch Benevean through an underground power house, a second dam 86 feet high at Loch Benevean and a power station near Fasnakyle. It leaves Loch Affric itself entirely unaffected.

The total installed capacity of the two generating stations will be about 70,000 kilowatts and the average annual output will be about 250 million units.

The total cost is estimated at approximately £4,800,000.

This is the third Affric Hydro-Electric Scheme. The first was promoted by the Grampian Company in 1928. It was rejected by a House of Lords Committee. The second, promoted by the same Company in 1941, was approved by a Scottish Parliamentary Commission, but was finally withdrawn on the advice of the Secretary of State who promised an inquiry into the whole water power resources of the North of Scotland.

The present Scheme prepared by the Board diverges substantially from both the previous Schemes.

The 1941 Scheme would have raised Loch Benevean by 60 feet and the loch would have fluctuated by the whole of that amount. The raising of the level would have flooded up to the head of Loch Affric which would also have been affected by the fluctuation. Nor did the 1941 Scheme provide for any guaranteed flow down the River Affric from Loch Benevean as does the Board's new Scheme.

The Board's new Scheme proposes to raise Loch Benevean by no more than 25 feet, thus not reaching the level of Loch Affric. The method of operation will normally restrict the variation in the level of Loch Benevean to about 6 feet in summer and double that in winter. By comparison it may be noted that the present natural fluctuation in Loch Affric itself is about 10 feet.

A flow of water in the River Affric will be guaranteed to maintain a minimum of 15 million gallons per day below its junction with the Tomich Burn. In addition, the Board undertake to give from Loch Benevean a 'block guarantee' of 2,000 million gallons per year to be used at such times and in such quantities as may be agreed with the Fisheries and Amenity Committees.

Half a million gallons per day released from Loch Mullardoch combined with the tributaries—more than 20 in number—in the 24.9 square miles of unaffected catchment area between Loch Mullardoch and Cannich village will maintain a flow in the River Cannich, and the levels of the lochans in the Glen will be maintained by small weirs specially erected for this purpose.

Loch Mullardoch will be raised 113 feet. The 1941 Scheme would have raised it 61 feet. The increased height in the Board's Scheme will compensate for the reduction in the storage in Loch Benevean in Glen Affric.

The Fasnakyle power station, seen from the Cannich–Tomich Road, will appear as a low building on the river's bank. The sub-station, which will step up the energy to 132,000 volts for transmission, will be out of sight of the road and linked with the power station by underground cables.

NEW ROADS. The improvement of existing roads and the new sections which will have to be constructed will give much better facilities for tourists right up to the western end of Loch Benevean.

FLOOD CONTROL. Strath Glass has always been subject to violent floods. The Scheme will materially reduce this

flooding. Electric power will provide scope for the introduction of rural industries. The technical experts of the Board
will be available to assist and advise how best to apply the
cheap power to new enterprises in industry and agriculture.

Industries requiring substantial blocks of electrical power
may be attracted to the area.

Men who have a wide experience of natural beauty
say that there is no country in all the world to compare
with the Highlands of Scotland for beauty, and no
glen in all Scotland to hold a candle to Glen Affric.
I view therefore with a good deal of perturbation
any proposal to harness its waters by hydro-electric
schemes that may increase the water supply of less
lucky counties, but will inevitably mar the wild loveliness of this superb glen with dams and pipes overhead
cables and pylons.

We have fought this battle over the South Downs
and lost it. We fought it over Tummel and Rannoch
and Ericht and lost it. We fought it in Carrick and
Galloway and lost it.

There seems to be no reason why all the loveliest
pleasances in the British Isles should not quickly
become a mesh of wires, as unlovely and metropolitan
as Clapham Junction. This undoubtedly, in the eyes
of some, would be a step forward towards the mil-
lennium, a grand sign of human progress.

But what most of us who work in big cities are
asking is, 'Where now shall we spend our hard-
earned leisure and hard-earned income?' We feel
very strongly that if we are called upon to fight to
preserve our own country, somebody should be responsible for preserving it as we once knew and loved it.

It is difficult to think of anyone being willing to
lay down his life for a pylon. It is difficult to think of

anyone who would not lay down his life to keep Glen Affric free of defilement.

I have long advocated the formation in the British Isles of National Parks, small-scale Yosemites. The Cairngorm country, Exmoor, Dovedale, the Lake hills, and the Cheviot range struck me as the most obvious. But that was only because I regarded the country north of the Caledonian Canal as practically a National Park already. Now comes this bolt from the blue which threatens to make Glen Affric as commonplace as Wigan Pier.

It is quite obviously not easy to make our rulers realise that to many of us it is a matter of desperate importance to keep loveliness inviolate. Without vision the nation perishes, and vision is only kept alive by the presence of beauty.

To a large majority beauty is meaningless and those to whom it is meaningless have an understandable habit of jumping to the conclusion that it is either an affectation or an amusement in others. This notion should be corrected with some severity. More than ever is it necessary to cherish every scrap of beauty that remains.

If no one else demanded it the men from the Services would, for if you nailed down any airman or sailor or soldier to a specific object that he was fighting for, you would find that his family came first, very closely followed by some country scene, the village where he was born, the mountains which he climbed on holidays, or the burns and lochs in which he bathed or fished. Naturally the Highlander will remember with most affection some Highland glen, but you will find that he shares this affection with a vast multitude of Sassenachs. The question is what has

Glen Affric to offer that is not repeated elsewhere?
Quite easily first is its amazing blend of wildness and
gentleness.

It has the virtue of not being easily accessible, so
that it is never overcrowded, you are seldom disturbed
in your contemplation of bird or tree. If you want
the bare grandeur of high rock you can get it, if you
want a lovely loch you can get it, if you want rich
foliage and tumbling cascades, they are there too at
your right hand and on your left.

Other glens have been spoilt by too much adulation,
too frequent company. Glen Affric has managed to
preserve its splendours untarnished. It gives a good
welcome to those who reach it, because it realises
that they must be eclectic in their desires to take the
trouble to reach it.

Those for whom all glens are the same can be more
easily served nearer the main roads and railways. But
Glen Affric is for those who do not yield themselves
with unreserved panegyric to the first glen that serves.

It is not of course generally true that the farther
you go, the more inaccessible the glen, the richer the
reward in dignity and majesty, but it is true of Glen
Affric.

When you set out from Invercannich you get little
idea of the richness that lies ahead. No glen opens
with less ostentation. Its loveliness steals upon you
quietly, imperceptibly. Soon, however, the blend of
the old native forest and the young birches, range
after range of bare blue peaks still touched with snow
in high summer and the glint of sun reflected on the
water seen through trees, work the inevitable miracle.
And after the long, winding trek among the trees,
with the tumbling water never far away, to Affric

Lodge there is the stalkers' path to take to the top of
Mam Soul (*Mam Sodhail*), where you can look right
across Scotland from coast to coast and see more
rugged peaks than I have ever been able to give
names to even with my map in hand.

Here if anywhere one feels on top of the world.
Here if anywhere one gets the sense of perfect freedom.
Here if anywhere the tired worker in search of that
quietude and respite from the madding crowd may
gain refreshment and renewed strength for the battle.

To tamper with the glory of Scotland's most
glorious glen is about as evil as to demolish St. Giles'
to make the Royal Mile wider or to construct rows
of shops along the south side of Princes Street.

GLEN TROOL, KIRCUDBRIGHTSHIRE

GLEN AFFRIC, NEAR AFFRIC LODGE

CHAPTER NINETEEN

The Border

"THE finest sight that a Scotsman ever sees," said Dr. Johnson, "is the high road that leads to England." It would be much truer to say that the finest sight that an Englishman sees is the high road that leads him into Scotland.

All the approaches to Scotland, with the exception of the road to Gretna Green, are wild and romantic. The most attractive is perhaps that which enters the country by way of Carter Bar, though I have a special liking for the wild country round Deadwater. There is so vast a wealth of Abbeys, towns, ruins, and moors to be seen that it is difficult to know where to begin.

Coming to the Border from Edinburgh we should certainly pause at Peebles that lies among hills that are partly wooded, partly covered with heather. One of the oldest crosses in Scotland, the Market Cross, stands at the junction of East gate and North gate, and the tower in the burying-ground dates back to the fourteenth century.

Standing high above the banks of the Tweed nearby is the great castle of Neidpath with a turreted keep and walls ten feet thick. This sombre imposing castle was once the home of that famous eighteenth-century nobleman 'Old Q', the Duke of Queensberry, who out of spite for his successor felled all the timber. There are many other ruined castles on the banks of the Tweed which have been luckier with their trees and their owners, notably Dawyck which boasts the earliest larches and chestnuts to be planted in Scotland. The hills grow wilder and the Tweed flows faster as we follow it to Tella Glen and Tweedsmuir, and it is well worth while exploring the hills round the pass.

At Birkhill near the summit is the famous three-hundred-foot cataract of the Mare's Tail. Sir Walter Scott was very much impressed by the scenery in this neighbourhood and describes it with a wealth of detail in *Old Mortality*. We are now in the country of Hogg, the Ettrick Shepherd who sang so sweetly of the Border. His effigy stands at the side of the loch of St. Mary's where he spent so much of his time in the famous inn of Tibbie Shiels. Tibbie was an ex-domestic servant who, on being left with six children to bring up on her husband's death, turned her cottage into a hostelry that was destined to draw all Scotland's most famous learned and literary men.

The Yellow Water flows out of this loch and takes us along a brick-lined valley to Newark Castle whose tower and walls rising to four storeys still stand. And so we come to Inverleithen with the ancient Traquair House whose gates have never been opened since 1796 when the Earl decreed that they should stay closed after his wife's death until another lady should be proved worthy of taking her place. No such lady ever came to claim this honour.

There are five towns on the Border, each very different from the others. These are Selkirk, Melrose,

Kelso, Jedburgh, and Hawick. We get immediate reminders at Selkirk that we are in the land of the ancient ballads, songs of battles of long ago, that inspired Sir Philip Sidney in one account and Sir Walter Scott in another. At midsummer the people of Selkirk still carry on their ancient ceremony of riding the marches, called the Common Riding.

The town corporations bring out their standards and select a standard-bearer, and a lady to bless or kiss the flag. A procession is then formed led by a hundred or more horsemen, which follows the standard-bearer to the bank of the Ettrick, which the horsemen ford and, after riding the marches, recross the river farther down. They gallop after the procession to join in the final ceremony in the Market Square, the 'casting of the colours'. This is an intricate waving of the flags to the ancient tune of 'Up wi' the Souters o' Selkirk'. The band then plays 'The Flowers of the Forest' to remind us of the Souters of Selkirk who fell at Flodden Field.

It was a rainy dark evening in September 1513 that the English army, under the Earl of Surrey, fell upon King James's army, and by dawn inflicted on the Scots the worst defeat in their history. Of the seventy shoemakers or Souters who set out from Selkirk to defend their homes only one returned. He, however, brought back with him an English pennon which is still to be seen in the Public Library, and in the bronze figure on the Flodden Memorial you get a further reminder of this exploit.

Flodden Field itself is now an upland cornfield in the centre of which stands a simple block of granite on which are inscribed these words: 'Flodden 1513. To the Brave of Both Nations.'

The land round Selkirk is full of wizardry and romance, for in the three peaks of the Eildon Hills you see the enchanted land in which the Queen of the Fairies kept Thomas the Rhymer imprisoned for three years. Originally, according to the legend, Eildon was a single hill, but was split into three in one night by a demon for whom the wizard Michael Scot was compelled to find continual employment. Among other of the demon's activities was the building of a weir across the Tweed at Kelso. This too took him only a single night, but the spinning of ropes out of sand occupies him still.

As we wander over these enchanting and enchanted hills, snatches and fragments of the old ballads spring to our lips and we burst out singing:

> True Thomas lay on Huntlie bank;
>   A ferlie he spied wi' his e'e:
> And there he saw a ladye bright
>   Come riding by the Eildon Tree.
>
> Her skirt was o' the grass-green silk,
>   Her mantle o' the velvet fyne:
> At ilka tett o' her horse's mane
>   Hung fifty siller bells and nine.
>
> True Thomas he pu'd off his cap,
>   And bended low down on his knee:
> "Hail to thee Mary Queen of Heaven!
>   For thy peer on earth could never be!"
>
> "Oh no, Oh no, Thomas," she said
>   "That name does not belong to me:
> I'm but the Queen o' far Elfland
>   That am hither come to visit thee."

So he gave her the fateful kiss which bound him slave to her for seven years.

And till seven years were gone and past,
True Thomas on earth was never seen.

We not only sing about True Thomas. We find
ourselves looking furtively round for the green-skirted
fairy queen and her mortal lover, and if it is not True
Thomas it may be that other mortal Tam Lin who was
bewitched by the same enchantress and rescued by
the fair Janet at Miles Cross on Hallowe'en. Their
ballad is even more magical:

Janet has kilted her green kirtle
A little abune her knee,
And she has snooded her yellow hair
A little abune her bree.
And she's awa' to Carterhaugh
As fast as she can hie.

About the dead hour of the night
She heard the bridle's ring:
And Janet was as glad at that
As any earthly thing.

And first gaed by the black, black steed,
And syne gaed by the brown;
But fast she grip't the milk white steed
And pu'd the rider down.

They shaped him in her arms twa
An aske but and a snake:
But aye she grips and hauls him fast
To be her worldis make.

They shaped him in her arms twa
But and a deer sae wild:
But aye she grips and hau'ds him fast,
The father o' her child.

They shaped him in her arms at last
A mother-naked man:
She cast her mantle over him
And sae her love she wan.

'I never heard', said Sir Philip Sidney, 'the old song of Percy and Douglas, that I found not my heart moved more than with a trumpet.'

But I find my heart moved by the fairy ballads of Thomas the Rhymer and Tam Lin even more than by the fairy ballads of Otterburn and Chevy Chase.

It is of fairies and old unhappy far-off things and battles long ago that we are constantly reminded wherever we tread in this Border country.

Under the shadow of the Eildon Hills stands Bemersyde, the seat of the Haigs for over seven hundred years, of whom Thomas the Rhymer sang:

> Tyde what may betyde
> Haig shall be Haig of Bemersyde.

a prophecy that certainly increases our respect for his powers of prediction.

Nearby stand the ruins of Melrose Abbey. The nave, choir, transepts, cloisters, and chapter house, with fine and ancient windows, sculptured figures, and buttress pinnacles are still standing. It was St. Aidan who first founded a monastery at Melrose, a peninsula on the fair and broad Tweed, which was transferred together with its name by David I to little Fordell in 1136. Two hundred years later Robert the Bruce reconstructed it and the Earl of Hertford two hundred years later (in 1545) destroyed it together with three other abbeys, sixteen castles, five towns, and nearly two hundred and fifty villages. The day after it was burnt the two generals responsible for its destruction, Evers and Layton, were defeated and killed, and their bodies buried under its walls.

But the visitor is less likely to search for their burial-place than for the final resting-place of the heart of

Robert the Bruce which was at Bruce's request taken
by Lord James Douglas to be buried in the Holy
Land, but Douglas was killed on his way through
Spain by the Saracens, so it was brought home again
and buried at Melrose.

But the main object of everybody's visit to Melrose
is not so much the Abbey, picturesque and lovely as
its ruins are, but Abbotsford, the home of Sir Walter
Scott, which forms so strange a contrast to its near
neighbour Darnick Tower. Darnick stands very much
as it has stood for four hundred years. It was built
in 1425, burnt by the Earl of Hertford, and rebuilt
by Andrew Heaton in 1569. It still bears his initials
and that date above the lintel. One of the Heatons
fell at Flodden, another in the battle of Bothwell
Bridge, and it was still in the possession of the family
when Sir Walter Scott tried in vain to buy the tower
in addition to the lands on which he built his vast
mansion of Abbotsford. You will find many precious
relics in Darnick, including portraits of Queen Mary
and one of her beds and a dirk and powder horn that
belonged to Prince Charles Edward.

In many ways we cannot help wishing that Scott
had been able to occupy the old tower, with its
weather-worn battlemented square, outer gates, and
ancient twirling pin, rather than be driven to build what
Ruskin described as 'perhaps the most incongruous
pile that gentlemanly modernism ever designed'.

In point of fact we have all seen far more egregious
examples of incongruous architecture, but we are
more apt to associate Scott with ancient towers like
Darnick than with the rather bogus array of castel-
lated turrets that are so prominent a feature of
Abbotsford.

But Scott beautified the site with trees and undoubtedly took intense pleasure in watching the house of his heart's desire grow up. Abbotsford took fourteen years to build.

Here even more than at Darnick is a whole museum of relics, not only of Scott's books and clothes, but of Prince Charles Edward, Rob Roy, and Flora Mac-Donald, while the armoury contains weapons from all over the world. There is panelling taken from Dunfermline Palace, an entrance porch copied from the Palace of Linlithgow, escutcheons of famous Border families running round the cornice of the entrance hall, and carvings modelled from Melrose in the enormous library.

If the house and its contents offend some tastes by its extravagance, immensity, and over-elaboration, there can be no question of the loveliness of its situation, flanked as it is by dense woods and facing the broad Tweed in one of the most beautiful reaches. Looking down on it from a distance above, Abbotsford is not at all incongruous. It is most impressive and in complete harmony with its surroundings.

The obvious pilgrimage from Abbotsford is to Dryburgh Abbey, which provided Scott with the view that he preferred above any other in the world and most fittingly became his last resting-place. Both Sir Walter Scott and Earl Haig were buried in these ruins; Sir Walter lies under a vast stone of granite in St. Mary's aisle, together with his wife, son, and his biographer, J. G. Lockhart, while Haig lies nearby.

I was shown the mason marks of Robert Burns dated 1787, and the burial-place of a wife of one of the Erskines, who after bearing twenty-two children was presumed to have died, but after her wedding-ring finger had been cut off she not only revived but lived to be the mother of eleven more children.

Dryburgh was founded in 1150, destroyed in 1322, rebuilt, destroyed again in 1385, once more rebuilt, and again burnt by the Earl of Hertford in 1544. It came into the possession of Scott's great-grandfather in 1700, but passed out of his hands again, leaving his family only the right of burial. There now remains a ruined nave, an aisle, a transept, part of the choir, and a fine rose window in the west gable of the Refectory.

We naturally expect to get further reminders of Scott wherever we go in this neighbourhood. He had a great love for Kelso where he was for a little time at school, and it is generally agreed that he got his first love of the Border country when as a small boy he went to stay at his grandfather's farm at Sandy Knowe which is six miles out of the town near Smailholm Tower, of which he wrote: 'Here rise those crags, that mountain tower, which charmed my Fancy's waking hours.'

Smailholm, like many other Border towers, was built on a moorland crag with a small lake at its foot. The view over the undulating hills and moors from the top of the battlements is magnificent and it is easy to see how the imagination of the sensitive small boy must have been inspired by this impressive vista.

Kelso too undoubtedly played its part in fostering his life-passion for the natural beauty and romantic association of the Border country, for it stands at the junction of Tweed and Teviot and nearby are the ruins of the once most formidable of all Border castles, Roxburgh, destroyed by the Scots themselves in 1460, and the more modern seat of the Duke of

Roxburgh, Floors, a mansion of great dignity. Kelso too boasts a ruined abbey with a large square tower, the last point of defence for the besieged townsfolk, and a church in which James III was crowned after his father had been killed besieging Roxburgh.

There is still another Abbey to be visited, Jedburgh, whose square tower and long flat roof can often be seen serenely reflected in the river above which it stands embowered in trees. Jedburgh, in spite of a very stormy history, has been far less battered about than the other Border abbeys. The tower, the nave with its fine tiers of arches, and the western bay of the choir are all still standing. You may still see the house where Mary Queen of Scots was taken so ill that her life was despaired of. It is red-tiled with three gables and a stair turret.

There remains one more Border town, Hawick, which in spite of its modern industrialism preserves its Common Riding Festival which is similar to that of Selkirk and also takes place in June. But more visitors go to Hawick in search of tweeds than of observance of old-time ceremonies.

Hawick's great antiquity can be gauged, however, not only from its Festival, but even more from its moat, an artificial earthern mound about thirty feet high and over three hundred feet round the base where presumably witenagemotes or very early Parliaments or Council meetings were held.

Tower Hill was a one-time stronghold of the Douglas. It is now an hotel.

In another Douglas stronghold in the neighbourhood, Cavers, they claim to have preserved the pennon and gauntlets taken from Harry Percy at Otterburn in 1388.

In spite of the fact that Berwick-upon-Tweed is not in Scotland—it is not in England either—any visit to the Border country would be incomplete without it.

There is Berwick Market in London which attracts most visitors to London, but Berwick Market in the Border far outshines the Metropolitan one. It is a grand gathering of the hard-bitten farmers from both sides of the Border, from the Cheviot hills as well as the Lammermuirs, who bid against each other for as varied a stock of beasts and sheep as you will find anywhere. You expect to see the black-faced, long-fleeced Northumbrian sheep, but the number of small hardy black cattle from the west of Ireland is quite startling.

You can easily see how turbulent the history of Berwick has been by the absence of any ancient buildings. The walls that encompass the tower with their vast four-square projections of grass-covered bastions are Tudor and therefore built long after the Scots wars with England had finished. It changed hands no fewer than thirteen times in the three hundred years before its final capture in 1482 by Edward IV and that explains the absence of any medieval buildings. The church was entirely rebuilt during the Commonwealth period and is one of the very few churches in the country to have been built during Cromwell's Protectorate. The station stands on the site of the Great Hall where in 1291 Edward I announced that John Baliol was the rightful King of Scotland. Above this hall, in full public gaze, the Countess of Buchan was exposed for six years in a wooden cage for daring to put the crown on Robert the Bruce's head.

235

This grey city of red roofs set steeply on the northern banks of the broad Tweed is to-day a most picturesque seaside town, the haunt of fishermen, farmers, and golfers, but as we loiter on the overgrown grassy banks of the older, fragmentary walls that overlook the low-roofed cottages on the Greenses our minds turn back to a Berwick whose high-walled wynds and courts ran with blood and the flames from her burning houses lit up the sea and the night sky. There is still an austerity about her beauty to remind us that Berwick has suffered greatly.

Behind the great natural beauty of winding river and broad moorland that we get on both sides of the Border there is always a sense of the scars left on places and people by the old days of suspicion and turbulence. The church towers are fortifications as they are on the Welsh border, and the 'pele' castles that lie hidden in every fold of the hills to a depth of twenty, thirty, or even forty miles behind the actual Border show how much of the Borderer's time was spent in apprehending and preparing for sudden on-slaughts from the raiders on the other side. The exteriors of these 'pele' castles arc grim, their windows narrow slits and their walls immensely thick. They were not built for domestic cosiness but with one object only, to guarantee security. And by so doing they provide the clue to the Border country.

No wonder the Border folk believed in fairies. They had to have a little light relief.

CHAPTER TWENTY

The Buchan Country

You remember, I hope, this illuminating passage in John Buchan's memoirs:

> My chief passion in those [adolescent] years was for the Border countryside, and my object in all my 'prentice writings was to reproduce its delicate charm, to catch the aroma of its gracious landscape and turbulent history, and the idiom of its people. When I was absent from it I was homesick, my memory was full of it, my happiest days were associated with it, and some effluence from its ageless hills and waters laid a spell upon me which has never been broken. I found in its people what I most admired in human nature—realism coloured by poetry, a stalwart independence sweetened by courtesy, a shrewd, kindly wisdom. I asked for nothing better than to spend my life by the Tweed.

I was forcibly reminded of that passage as I listened in (as I hope you did) to Alan Melville's production of *The Border,* in which William Crichton of Peebles and other stalwart fishermen and shepherds from the Border country showed us exactly that realism coloured by poetry, stalwart independence sweetened by courtesy, and shrewd, kindly wisdom which Buchan praised.

They paid a high and well-deserved tribute to the

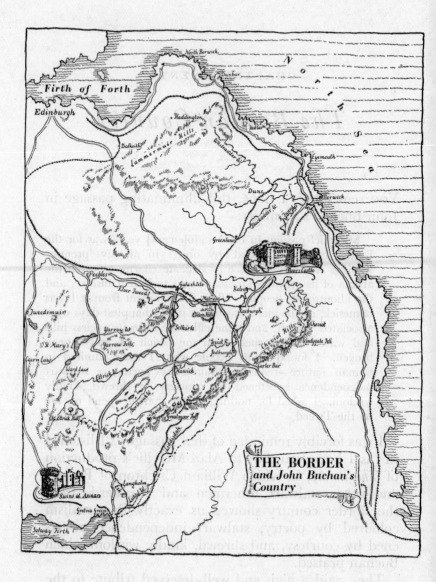

THE BORDER
and John Buchan's
Country

Firth of Forth

North Sea

Edinburgh

North Berwick

Dunbar

Haddington

Dalkeith

Lammermuir Hills

Whiteadder W.

Eyemouth

Duns

Berwick

Greenlaw

Floors Castle

Peebles

River Tweed

Galashiels

Kelso

Tweedsmuir

Melrose

Eildon Hills

Roxburgh

St. Cheviot

Yarrow W.

Selkirk

Teviot R.

Cheviot Hills

Windygate Fell

St. Mary's L.

Yarrow Fells

Jedburgh

Cairn Law

Ward Law

Ettrick W.

Hawick

Carter Bar

Ettrick Fell

Borthwick W.

Teviot W.

Liddesdale

Greatmoor Fell

Langholm

Esk R.

Liddle W.

Yalda

Ruins at Annan

Gretna Green

Solway Firth

great Borderer who was as much at home with the
road-menders as he walked along Tweedside as with
those with whom he walked in the courts of kings.

I particularly liked the salmon-poacher who claimed
not only friendship but a spiritual kinship with Lord
Tweedsmuir. He was right. Shakespeare and Buchan
were poachers by natural instinct, as they were poets
and great patriots.

Not the least of the many services that Buchan per-
formed for his country was that of communicating his
passion for the land he loved so well.

Tweedsmuir, the place, will always conjure up for
us a picture of Tweedsmuir the man, whose spirit
still haunts the moors above the Tweed.

> When we were little, wandering boys,
>   And every hill was blue and high,
> On ballad ways and martial joys
>   We fed our fancies, you and I.
> With Bruce we crouched in bracken shade,
>   With Douglas charged the Paynim foes;
> And oft in moorland noons I played
>   Colkitto to your grave Montrose.

So sang Buchan *fratri dilectissimo*, and in after years
when he took to spinning romance after romance it
was over these well-remembered hills that he sent his
heroes and villains to chase and be chased.

And, indeed, to my way of thinking there is no
other land that so catches the imagination, no other
hills and valleys that I find myself so constantly and
instantly peopling with pursuing and pursued, Campbells and MacDonalds, MacLeods and Mackenzies,
Royal Stewarts and plain Richard Hannays.

No man ever made the south-west of Scotland live
for me more vividly than Buchan in *The Thirty-Nine*

239

Steps. You remember? Hannay had somehow to make himself scarce, and quickly.

'I fixed on Galloway as the best place. It was the nearest wild part of Scotland [to London].' So off he went by the first train.

'We rambled slowly into a land of little wooded glens and then to a great wide moorland place, gleaming with lochs, with high blue hills showing northwards. . . . The air had the queer, rooty smell of bogs. . . . Over a long ridge of moorland I took my road, skirting the side of a high hill called Cairnsmore of Fleet. Nesting curlews and plovers were crying everywhere, and the links of green pasture by the streams were dotted with young lambs. [Then] I was in a wide semicircle of moorland, with a brown river as radius and the high hills forming the northern circumference. There was not a sign or sound of a human being, only the plashing water and the interminable crying of curlews. . . . I started to run. Crouching low in the runnels of the bog I ran till I had reached the rim of mountain.'

It was, however, from the top of another mountain that he looked down on the road where he met the spectacled roadman.

'Behind me was the road climbing through a long cleft in the hills, which was the upper glen of some notable river. In front was a flat space of maybe a mile, all pitted with bog-holes and rough with tussocks, and then beyond it the road fell steeply down another glen to a plain whose blue dimness melted into the distance. To left and right were round-shouldered green hills as smooth as pancakes, but to the south there was a glimpse of high heathery mountains. I was on the central boss of a huge upland country, and could see everything moving for miles. In the meadows below the road half a mile back a cottage smoked, the only sign of human life. Otherwise, there was only the calling of plovers and the tinkling of little streams.

'There was not cover in the whole place to hide a rat. I turned to the south and came to the brow of a ridge which was the containing wall of the pass. I saw the high road for maybe ten miles. Beyond the ridge I looked on a rolling green moor which fell away into wooded glens. . . .

'Away down the slope, a couple of miles away, several men were advancing like a row of beaters at a shoot. That way was shut to me, and I went by the bigger hills to the south, beyond the highway. I ran hard, crouching low except in the hollows, and as I ran I kept scanning the brow of the hill before me. Did I see figures—one, two perhaps more—moving in the glen beyond the stream?

'If you are hemmed in on all sides in a patch of land there is only one chance of escape. You must stay in the patch, and let your enemies search it, and not find you. I would have buried myself to the neck in mud or lain below water or climbed the tallest tree. But there was not a stick of wood, the bog-holes were little puddles, the stream was a slender trickle. There was nothing but short heather and bare hill bent, and the white highway.

'There in a tiny bight of road, beside a heap of stones, I found the roadman.'

I remember how keen was my disappointment on seeing the film version of *The Thirty-Nine Steps*. The film couldn't create in the way that Buchan had created that bold moorland, failed to arouse in me that state of wild excitement and suspense that I felt all the time Hannay was on the moors.

In a word, the film failed to bring out the most valuable and exciting part of this adventure, which is not the character of the people, but the character of the country. Now this is the very thing that you would expect the film to bring out most successfully.

It only goes to prove once more that photography is not necessarily art, and it was the art of Buchan to make alive for his readers the magic quality and romantic atmosphere of the Scottish scene.

No chase that I have ever read of remains so vividly in my mind as that little cameo of description leading up to that unforgettable scene with the roadman with the hangover. Yet, I wonder.

Are not the chases in *John Macnab* every bit as exciting as those of Richard Hannay in *The Thirty-Nine Steps*?

The answer is 'No'. For the simple reason that not so much depends upon the result. The deer-stalkers and salmon-poachers in *John Macnab* are only having fun. At the worst they could only be prosecuted if they were caught, whereas Richard Hannay was taking his life in his hands and was extremely lucky to get out of his escapade with a whole skin.

John Macnab has, however, one great advantage over *The Thirty-Nine Steps*. The frontispiece is a map, a map of Glenraden, Crask, and Haripol, and it serves not only to remind us of the locale of these exciting haunts, but of what we miss by not having a similar map to follow the wanderings of Richard Hannay.

What fun Buchan had in writing this golden, high-spirited adventure of the respectable, distinguished lawyer and politician in poaching their neighbour's salmon and stag after giving due warning of time and place. And what a place!

'Crask, when the traveller approaches it from the Larrig bridge, has the air of a West Highland terrier couchant and regardant. You are to picture a long tilt of moorland running east and west, not a smooth lawn of heather, but seamed with gullies and patched with bogs and thickets, and crowned at the summit with a low line of rocks above which may be seen peeping the spikes of the distant Haripol hills.

'About three-quarters of the way up the slope stands the little house—whitewashed, slated, grey stone framing the narrow windows, with that attractive jumble of masonry which belongs to an adapted farm. It is approached by a road that scorns detours and runs straight from the glen highway, and it looks south over broken moorland to the shining links of the Larrig and beyond them to the tributary vale of the Raden and the dark mountains of its source.

'From the garden behind a glimpse may be had of the policies of Strathlarrig and even of a corner of that monstrous mansion, and to the right of the tidal waters of the river and the yellow sands on which in the stillest weather the Atlantic frets.'

You remember the salmon pools that Leithen reconnoitred under the very eye of the river-keeper.

'For a fisherman it was the water of his dreams. The pools were long and shelving, with a strong stream at the head, and below precisely the right kind of boulders and out-jutting banks to shelter fish. There were three of the pools—the "Duke's", the "Black Scour", and "Davie's Pot"—and beyond, almost under the windows of the house, "Lady Maisie's", conspicuous for its dwarf birches. Then came a belt of firs, and then a long tract of broken water which was obviously not a place to hold salmon. Then he came to a noble pool. It lay in a meadow where the hay had just been cut, and was liker a bit of Tweed or Eden then a Highland stream. Its shores were low, and on the near side edged with fine gravel; the far bank was a green rise unspoiled by scrub; the current entered it with a proud swirl, washed the high bank, and spread itself out in a beautifully broken tail, so that every yard of it spelled fish.'

So much for the salmon-poacher. Now for the deer-stalker.

'At the top of the pass was a pad of flat ground, covered thick with the leaves of cloudberries. On the right rose the pinnacle ridge of Sgurr Dearg, in its beginning an easy scramble which gave no hint of the awesome towers which later awaited the traveller; on the left Sgurr Mor ran up in a steep face of screes. "Keep doun," Wattie enjoined, and crawled forward to where two boulders made a kind of window for a view to the north. The two looked down into three little corries which, like the fingers of a hand, united in the palm of a larger corrie, which was the upper glen of the Reascuill. It was a sanctuary perfectly fashioned by Nature, for the big corrie was cut off from the lower glen by a line of boiler-plates like the wall of a great dam, down which the stream plunged in cascades. The whole place was loud with water—the distant roar of the main river, the ceaseless dripping of the cliffs, the chatter and babble of a myriad hidden rivulets. But the noise seemed only to deepen the secrecy. It was a world in monochrome, every detail clear as a wet pebble, but nowhere brightness

244

or colour. Even the coats of the deer had taken on the dead grey of slaty crags.

'Never in his life had Lamancha seen so many beasts together. Each corrie was full of them, feeding on the rough pastures or among the boulders, drifting aimlessly across the spouts of screes below the high cliffs, sheltering in the rushy gullies. There were groups of hinds and calves, and knots of stags, and lone beasts on knolls or in mud-baths, and since all were restless, the numbers in each corrie were constantly changing.'

We recognise those pictures of the salmon pool and the deer-forest, generalised as they may be.

They occur in almost every glen of the Highlands.

But Buchan was no parochial Scot. He, like Sir Walter Scott, knew the loveliness of the land that lies between Carlisle and Edinburgh. You remember his story of how the minister of Woodilee left the earth for fairyland in *Witch Wood*.

You remember the prologue to that enchanting book?

'A main railway line now runs down the Aller, and the excellent summer service brings holiday-makers from a hundred miles distant. Houses and shops have clustered under the Hill of Deer. . . .

'One evening from the Hill of Deer I saw with other eyes.

'Woodilee lay right in the pass between the Scottish midlands and the south, for it was in the throat of the hills, on the march between the town and the desert. I was looking east, and to my left and behind me the open downs, farmed to their last decimal of capacity, were the ancient land of Manana, the capital province of Pictdom. The colliery headgear on the horizon, the trivial moorish hilltops, the dambroded-pattern fields, could never tame wholly for me that land's romance, and on this evening I seemed to be gazing at a thing antique and wolfish, tricked out for the moment with a sheep's coat. To my right rose the huddle of great hills which cradle all our rivers.

'It was the Woodilee of three hundred years ago. There were no highways—only tracks, miry in the bogs and stony on the braes, which led to Edinburgh on one hand and to Carlisle on the other. I saw few houses, and these were brown as peat, but on the knowe of the old Kirkton I saw the four grey walls of the kirk, and the manse beside it among elders and young ashes.

'Woodilee was no more than a tiny jumble of crofts, bounded and pressed in upon by something vast and dark, which clothed the tops of all but the highest hills, muffled the ridges, choked the glens, and over-flowed almost to the edge of the waters—which lay on the landscape like a shaggy fur cast loosely down.'

And so Buchan sees the vision of the minister in the black wood of Melanudrigill.

'The trees rose like a cloud above him, and after the open coppice of birch and hazel he seemed to be looking into deep water. . . . The ancient pines grew more sparsely than he had imagined, and beneath them were masses of sprouting ferns—primroses too, and violets. A scent of rooty dampness was about, of fresh-turned earth, and welling fountains. A little farther and he was in a glade. He stood and gazed, struck silent by its beauty. Here in truth was a dancing-floor for wood-nymphs, there was a rustling and a gleam of colour. A green gown fluttered, he saw the form of a girl. . . . He was no more the minister of Woodilee, but chance wandering youth, and he gave chase.'

And that is how David Sempill chased and caught Katrine Yester of Calidon. You remember the romantic trilogy, *Huntingtower*, *Castle Gay*, and *The House of the Four Winds*, now bound up together under the title of *The Adventures of Dickson McCunn*.

You remember the provision merchant, Dickson McCunn, setting out on pilgrimage.

'He thought of Carrick. A good, green land, with purposeful white roads and public-houses sacred to the memory of Burns; near the hills but yet lowland, and with a bright sea chafing on its shores. He decided on Carrick, found a map, and planned his journey.'

You remember his setting out and sitting on a milestone beyond Kirkmichael examining his map to determine his route.

'For he had come, all unwitting, to a turning of the ways.

'The place was high up on a bare moor, which showed a white lodge among the pines, a white cottage in a green nook by a burnside, and no other marks of human dwelling. To his left, the east, the heather rose to a low ridge of hill, much scarred with peat-bogs, behind which appeared the blue shoulder of a considerable mountain. Before him the road was lost momentarily in the woods of a shooting-box, but re-appeared at a great distance climbing a swell of upland which seemed to be the glacis of a jumble of bold summits. There was a pass there, the map told him, which led into Galloway.

'Westward there ran out a peninsula in the shape of an isosceles triangle of which the high road was the base. A railway ran parallel to the road at a distance of a mile or so, and he could see the smoke of a goods train waiting at a tiny station islanded in acres of bog.

'Thence the moor swept down to meadows and scattered copses. Beyond a village were further woodlands, not firs but old shady trees, and as they narrowed to a point the gleam of two tiny estuaries appeared on either side. He could not see the final cape, but he saw the sea beyond it, flamed with cat's-paws, gold in the afternoon sun, and on it a small herring-smack flapping listless sails.

'The peninsula was called the Cruives. The two streams which flanked it were the Laver, a clear, tumbling water springing from green hills, and the Garple, descended from the rougher mountains to the south.

'The village bore the name of Dalquharter, and the great house in the trees beyond was Huntingtower.

'He liked the way the moor dropped down to green meadows, and the mystery of the dark woods beyond. The odd names, the odd cul-de-sac of a peninsula, powerfully attracted him.'

But Huntingtower did not turn out to be the sort of place that Mr. Dickson McCunn expected, except perhaps for the old keep which stood 'some three hundred yards from the edge of the cliffs, a gnarled wood of hazels and oaks protecting it from the sea winds. It stood, a lonely shell, its three stories each a single great room connected by a spiral stone staircase.'

You remember that after the adventure of *Huntingtower*, Dickson McCunn chose a house on the spur of a Carrick moor with the sea to the west, and to south and east a distant prospect of the blue Galloway hills. Blaweary its name was, a white-washed farm with smooth, green lawns.

248

It is here that we find him at the beginning of
Castle Gay.

Castle Gay 'lies in the loveliest part of the glen of
the Callowa, in the parish of Knockraw, adjoining the
village of Starr, and some five miles from the town of
Portaway. A high wall surrounds a wild park of a
thousand acres, in the heart of which stands a grey
stone castle, for whose keep Bruces and Comyns and
Macdowalls contended seven centuries ago.'

Its creator had a very soft place in his heart for
Castle Gay.

He dedicated *The Free Fishers* to J. K. Hutchin-
son, 'in memory of our boyhood on the coast of
Fife'.

Do you remember this picture?

'Below him tucked into a nook of the coast, lay
Dysart, his childhood's home—he could see the steeple
of its kirk pricking above a jumble of russet tiles, and
the tall trees that surrounded the policies of its great
new house, where once he had bird-nested. A schooner
was tacking out with every sail set to catch the breeze.
The air was diamond-clear, and on the Lothian shore
he could make out the little towns, the thornbush
which was the cluster of masts in Leith harbour, the
Edinburgh spires on which the sun was shining, the
lift of the Castle rock, and behind all the blue back-
bone of the Pentlands.

'The looms were clacking in every cot house as he
rode through the weaving village of Gallatown; ham-
mers were busy among the nailmakers of Pathead;
the smell of a tan-pit came to his nostrils with a
pleasing pungency; when he descended the long slope
of the Path the sight of scaly fisher folk and tarry
sailor men gave him an inconsequent delight. He

stepped aboard the grimy Leith packet with the gusto of an adventurer.'

That is the best of Buchan's characters. They became infected with the lively vigour of the winds against which they run or sail. They are as cheerful as small cloud shadows skimming over the farther hill.

But it is to old Ettrick that he most often returns in his thoughts, and it is most fitting to end with his description of the land from which he took his title.

'Laverlaw', many used to say, was his notion of the end of the world. It is eight miles from a railway station, and the little village of Hangingshaw, and the road to it follows a shallow valley between benty uplands till the hills grow higher, and only the size of the stream shows that you have not reached the glen head.

Then it passes between two steep hillsides, where there is room just for it and the burn, rounds a corner, and enters an amphitheatre a mile or two square bounded by steep heather hills, with the Lammer Law heaving up its great shoulders at the far end. The amphitheatre is the park of the castle, mountain turf, diversified with patches of the old Ettrick forest, and a couple of reedy lakes. The house stands at the junction of four avenues of ancient beeches—the keep thirteenth century, most of it late sixteenth century, and nothing more modern than the Restoration wing built by Bruce of Kinross. There are lawns and pleasances and a wonderful walled garden, and then you are among heather again, for the moorlands lap it round as the sea laps a reef.

'From Hangingshaw southward there are no dwellings but hill farms and shepherds' cottages. Beyond

the containing walls of the valley lie heathy uplands
hiding an infinity of glens and burns, nameless except
to herds and keepers and the large-scale ordnance
map. The highway stops short at the castle, and
beyond it a drove road tracks the ultimate waters of
the Laver and makes its way, by a pass called the
Laxed Thrapple, to the English border. The place is
so perfect that the first sight of it catches the breath
for it is like a dream of all that is habitable and
gracious; but it is also as tonic as mid-ocean and as
lonely as the African veld.'

The splendid thing about it all is that Buchan was
so easily able to communicate the delight that he took
in his native scene that he can make even the Sassenach
share it. When I wish to revive my memories of the
Scottish scene I do not turn to the landscape-painter.
I turn to the word-painter who is able to make me
see exactly the scene I want to see in all moods and
seasons, and to convey not only the material contours
but the spiritual implications of ben and loch and glen.

Buchan has done for Scotland what Hardy did for
Wessex, heightened our consciousness of its beauty,
made us all fall far more deeply and irrevocably in
love with the land than ever before.

CHAPTER TWENTY-ONE

The Carlyle Country

THERE is one very good, if mundane, reason why every traveller by train from the south should be reminded of Carlyle more than of any other great Scots writer.

Kirk Alloway, Abbotsford, and Tweedsmuir are all off the beaten track.

Ecclefechan is on the main line of the L.M.S. You cannot miss it unless you are asleep, and few Sassenachs and no Scotsmen sleep as they cross the border at Gretna. It is a romantic moment.

Carlyle was rightly proud of belonging to a fighting Border clan. He had reason to be, in view of the fact that he owed everything to it.

The plain two-storeyed house in the long main tidy street in which he was born on 4th December 1795 still stands.

Ecclefechan has changed little in the last 150 years.

There is little reason to suppose that it will change in the next 150 years. It has a hard, austere, durable look about it. Men may indeed forget Carlyle before they forget the village that gave him birth.

His fame vacillates. He was intolerant of others. He incites dislike from others. 'Thou's gey ill to deal wi' ' said his mother—and not only his mother.

We know what he felt about the village from *Sartor Resartus*, where it figures as 'Entepfuhl'. He describes the annual cattle fair as 'undoubtedly the grand summary of the Entepfuhl child's culture, whither, assembling from all the four winds, came the elements of an unspeakable hurly-burly'.

He was presumably happy at the village school, but undeniably miserable when he was sent on, at the age of ten, to the Grammar School of Annan, where he spent two years and described his teachers as 'hidebound pedants who knew Syntax enough, and of the human soul thus much, that it had a faculty called Memory, which could be acted on through the muscular integument by appliance of birch rods'.

It was, however, from the other boys more than his masters that he mainly suffered, 'coarse, unguided, tyrannous cubs' who nicknamed him 'Tom the Tearful', and took advantage of his sensitiveness to torture and bully him. Luckily, like Anthony Trollope, he 'revolted against them, and gave them shake for shake'.

When he was still under fourteen he walked the hundred miles to Edinburgh in the month of November in order to study at the University. He walked twenty miles a day by Moffat and over Airoch Stane in the company of one other boy.

Did Carlyle ever describe it?

After staying at the University for four years he left it, as Johnson left Oxford, without a degree but with a kindled enthusiasm for mathematics.

'The man', he says, 'who has mastered the first forty-seven propositions of Euclid stands nearer to God than he did before.' As at least an equal lover of mathematics I do profoundly disagree with that. But this is no place to enlarge on the shortcomings of Euclid.

His next idea was to prepare for the ministry, and he won by open competition (what an admirable idea) the post of mathematical master at Annan Academy, a job worth about £60 a year.

His father had now left Ecclefechan and gone to live in the little three-chimneyed farm of Mainhill, about two miles from Lockerbie, where he remained till his death in 1832.

Carlyle spent his vacations there studying German and reading widely until 1816, when he became assistant master in the parish school of Kirkcaldy, in Fife, at £100 a year.

It was here that he met and made fast friends with Edward Irving and Margaret Gordon, the model for the girl Blumine of *Sartor Resartus*.

After two years more of teaching Carlyle concluded, again like Dr. Johnson, that 'it were better to perish than to continue schoolmastering', so he returned to Edinburgh as a free-lance journalist and law student. But he tired as quickly of law as he had earlier tired of theology. His health was bad. He was sleepless, dyspeptic, and troubled in mind over his irreligion.

In 1821 he met Jane Welsh, the orphan heiress of a Haddington doctor who had left her the small estate of Craigenputtock, an isolated farmstead some sixteen miles from Dumfries.

Jane was at that time passionately in love with Irving who was, however, engaged to Miss Martin. After refusing the editorship of a Dundee newspaper Carlyle became a private tutor at £200 a year to the three sons of a retired Anglo-Indian. It was in their company that Carlyle stayed at Kinnaird House, near Dunkeld, and later paid his first visit (June 1824) to London.

After throwing up this job he stayed in London to superintend the publication of his *Life of Schiller*, and in March 1825 settled with his brother Alexander on the farm at Hoddam Hill, some two miles from Mainhill.

It was there that he managed to prevail upon Jane Welsh, after considerable difficulty, to marry him.

A quarrel with his landlord led to his removal to Scotsbrig, another farm on a burn-side close to Ecclefechan. In October 1826 he married Jane at Templand, Dumfriesshire, her grandfather's house, and settled down with her at 21 Comely Bank, Edinburgh, to translate from the German and contribute to the *Edinburgh Review*.

It was in May 1928 that the young couple moved to Jane's estate at Craigenputtock and there they stayed, in spite of Carlyle's description of it as 'the dreariest spot in all the British dominions' and Jane's loneliness and unaccustomed drudgery, on and off for six years.

It was here that the young unknown American, Emerson, came to see him, and this is what Emerson has to say about Craigenputtock:

'It was a farm in Nithsdale, in the parish of Dunscore, sixteen miles distant. No public coach passed near it, so I took a private carriage from the inn. I found the house amid desolate heathery hills, where the lonely scholar nourished his mighty heart.

'He was tall and gaunt, with a cliff-like brow, self-possessed, and holding his extraordinary powers of conversation in easy command: clinging to his northern accent with evident relish, full of lively anecdotes and with a streaming humour which flouted everything he looked upon.

'Few were the objects and lonely the man, "not a person to speak to within sixteen miles except the minister of Dunscore".

'We went out to walk over long hills, and looked at Criffel, then without his cap, and down into Wordsworth's country. There we sat down and talked of the immortality of the soul. "Christ died on the tree; that built Dunscore Kirk yonder; that brought you and me together. Time has only a relative existence."'

Better still, here is Carlyle's own description of life at Craigenputtock in a letter to Goethe, written in 1828:

'Dumfries is a pleasant town, containing about fifteen thousand inhabitants. Our residence is fifteen miles to the north-west of it, among the granite hills and the black morasses which stretch westward through Galloway, almost to the Irish Sea.

'In this wilderness of heath and rock our estate stands forth a green oasis, a track of ploughed, partly enclosed and planted ground, where corn ripens, and trees afford a shade, although surrounded by sea-mews and rough-woolled sheep. Here, with no small effort, have we built and furnished a neat, substantial dwelling; here, in the absence of a professional or other office, we live to cultivate literature according to our strength, and in our own peculiar way. We wish a joyful growth to the roses and flowers of our garden: the roses, indeed, are still in part to be planted, but they blossom already in anticipation.

'Two ponies, which carry us everywhere, and the mountain air, are the best medicines for weak nerves.

This daily exercise, to which I am much devoted, is my only recreation, for this moor of ours is the loneliest in Britain.

'I came here solely with the design to simplify my life and to secure the independence through which I could be enabled to remain true to myself. This bit of earth is our own; here we live, write at will.

'Nor is the solitude of such great importance, for a stage-coach takes us speedily to Edinburgh.

'From some of our heights I can descry, about a day's journey to the west, the hill where Agricola and his Romans left a camp behind them. At the foot of it I was born, and there both father and mother still live to love me.

'The only piece of any importance that I have written since I came here is an essay on Burns. Perhaps you never heard of him. . . .'

Again, in his *Reminiscences*, Carlyle dwells lovingly on those early days at Craigenputtock:

'We went over often from Craigenputtock to Templand, one of our chief pleasures—I think almost our chief—during those moorland years. Oh! those pleasant gig-drives in fine leafy twilight, or deep in the night sometimes, ourselves, two alone in the world, the good "Larry" faring us (rather too light for the job, but always soft and willing), how they rise on me now, benignantly luminous from the bosom of the grim dead night.

'Once we had gone to Dumfries, in a soft misty December day (for a portrait which my darling wanted, not of herself!) and a bridge was found broken as we went down; brook unsafe by night: we had to try "Cluden Water" road, as all was mist and pitch darkness on our return; road unknown except in general and drive like no other in my memory. Cairn roaring on the left (my darling's side); "Larry", with but one lamp-candle (for we had put out the other, lest both might fall down) bending always to be straight in the light of that. I really anxious, though speaking only hopefully, my darling so full of trust in me, really happy and opulently interested in these equipments. . . . I saw ahead, high in the mist, the minarets of Dunscore Kirk, at last, glad sight.

'Then the drive to Boreland once, in heart of winter, intense calm frost, and through Dumfries, at least thirty-five miles for poor "Larry" and us; very beautiful that, too, and very strange, past the base of towering New Abbey, huge ruins, piercing grandly into the silent frosty sunset, on this hand, despicable cowhouse of Presbyterian Kirk on that hand (saddened contrast to Devorgilla's old bounty)—of our drive home again I recollect only her invincible contentment, and the poor old cottar woman offering to warm us with a flame of dry brook: "A'll licht a bruim coney, if ye'll please to come in!" '

'Invincible contentment.' Odd words to use of Jane Welsh, but her only chance of contentment in those days when she could drag her dyspeptic scholar away from those essays on Johnson and Burns, away from his vision of Blumine in *Sartor Resartus* to drive her over these lonely moorland wastes.

It is, however, well to accept Professor Nichol's corrective to Carlyle's 'dreariest spot'.

'On a sunny day', says Professor Nichol, 'it is an inland home, with wide billowy straths of grass around inestimable silence broken only by the placid bleating of sheep, and the long ridges of the Solway hills in front.'

'Bring your blooming Eve out of your blasted Paradise', said the outspoken Jeffrey.

The truth is that Jane loathed the drudgery of housework, and equally resented the long hours of loneliness when her husband was writing. It affected her health, it affected her temper—like that of her husband, seldom in control.

Perhaps, worst of all, the economic situation became so bad that Carlyle (a proud man) had to start borrowing.

Carlyle, accustomed to rigid economy and scrupulous attention to every detail of housekeeping, was unable to sympathise with Jane's hatred of it, and indeed described the occupation as 'the saving charm of her life'.

They left Craigenputtock. They went back. They left it again, and finally, on 10th July 1834, they settled in that small, old-fashioned house in Cheyne Walk (rent £35 a year), which Carlyle occupied for the rest of his life and is now for ever associated with the garrulous historian.

The Carlyles often left Cheyne Walk, sometimes together, sometimes separately. We owe some of the most entertaining letters in the language to Jane writing in the loneliness of Cheyne Walk to the wandering husband at Scotsbrig and other old haunts.

One particular and famous misfortune marred their early days in Cheyne Walk.

It was in the first year of their London days that a servant of John Stuart Mill burnt practically the whole of the manuscript of Carlyle's *French Revolution*, so that he had to rewrite it just at a time when he hadn't earned a penny for twenty-three months.

It was, however, the turning point, for the revised

French Revolution, published in 1837, brought him fame
and success. He never made a fortune, but he was
now able to pay his way, and the death of Jane's
brother added a further income of £200 or £300 a
year. In 1865 he was elected Lord Rector of Edinburgh University, just nineteen days before Jane died
suddenly of heart disease while driving in Hyde Park.
'All of sunshine that remained in my life went out
in that sudden moment.'

He lived for sixteen years longer and was buried
as she was in Scotland, he at Ecclefechan, she at
Haddington.

For some reason, perhaps because of Whistler's
portrait of the Sage of Chelsea, whenever most of us
think of Carlyle we think of him established as the
Great Cham of Cheyne Walk.

We owe to Froude some more interesting glimpses
of him in those early days of struggle and young
married life at Craigenputtock.

He includes a lively print of the two-storeyed farmhouse, with its three large rectangular upstairs front
windows, imposing porch looking up the hill towards
the wood, with the outhouses at the back on a lower
level. It isn't in the least like *Wuthering Heights.*
It looks bright and cheerful in spite of Froude's description of it as gaunt and hungry-looking. Indeed,
this is how Carlyle writes about it to his brother in
November 1828:

'This house, lacking some outskirt things which
must be left till spring, is really substantial, comfortable
and even half elegant. I sit here in my little library
and laugh at the howling tempests, for there are
green curtains, and a clear fire and papered walls.
The old kitchen also is as tight a dining-room as you

would wish for me. The good wife, too, is happy and contented with me and her solitude.

'You cannot figure the stillness of these moors in a November drizzle. Nevertheless, I walk often under a cloud of night, in good Ecclefechan clogs, down as far as Carstammon Burn, sometimes to Sundaywell. Jane has a pony which can canter to perfection.

'Sometimes I stroll with my axe or bill in the plantations, and when I am not writing am reading.'

Jane, when she had time, would gallop off alone down to Templand, fifteen miles away, to see her mother.

In point of fact, somewhat surprisingly, she spent their first Craigenputtock Christmas at Templand, but wrote one of her most loving of love-letters to her 'Goody', to make up for her absence.

After their first flight from it Carlyle tells his brother: 'We are minded to try if we cannot be a little more domesticated among the moors of Puttock and to feel as if the place were a home for us.'

It was of course easier for him. He had his work and enjoyed solitude. The moors improved his health. In six years it completely undermined Jane's. Carlyle was no companion. She had to steal into his dressing-room in the morning, while he was shaving, to secure that morsel of his society.

She had to do all the cooking, sewing, and scouring, to keep house, and occasionally to milk the cows. She complained very little, but Carlyle was too pre-occupied to realise that she had any cause for complaint. He adored her, but he was negligent.

Jane tried to put a brave face on it.

'For my part', she writes to Eliza Mills, 'I am very content. I have everything here my heart desires that

I could have anywhere else, except society. If the knocker makes no sound for weeks together, it is so much the better for my nerves. My husband is as good company as reasonable mortal could desire. Every fair morning we ride on horseback for an hour before breakfast. Then Carlyle takes to his writing while I inspect my house, my garden, my livestock, gather flowers, and lapfuls of eggs. After dinner I lie on the sofa, sometimes sleep. In the evening I walk on the moor.'

She only revealed to Jeffrey in sad verses her true feelings of being shut away on the lonely moor, and there must have been times when she must have found even the husband whom she so deeply loved trying beyond all endurance.

'I tell her many times there is much for her to do if she were trained to it; her whole sex to deliver from the bondage of frivolity, dollhood, and imbecility into the freedom of valour and womanhood.' It is not surprising that she found the life almost unbearable.

With the end of Craigenputtock came the end of Carlyle's apprenticeship to life. Here is Jane's picture of him written to his mother soon after they have settled in Chelsea:

'I must tell you what Carlyle will not tell of himself, that he is rapidly mending of his Craigenputtock gloom and acerbity. He is really at times a tolerably social character and seems to be regarded with a feeling of mingled terror and love in all companies.'

So we leave the strange pair in their London home, Carlyle in the throes of composing the *French Revolution*, Jane bravely standing by to provide that vivacious criticism, and that unfailing devotion which meant all the world to him, even if he was incapable except in rare spasms of giving it its due recognition and response.

So, one of these days, obey the instinct to stop off at that wayside station in Annandale and pay homage in that wide-arched, two-storeyed, plain little house in Main Street where so many relics of Carlyle are preserved, admire the fine statue set up in 1929, and spare a thought as you stand above that very modest gravestone (as inconspicuous as that which marks the resting-place of Gilbert White in Selborne) to the man who made us realise the honourable calling to which we are all summoned.

'Whatsoever thy hand findeth to do, do that with all thy might and leave the issues calmly to God.' That is Carlyle's message over the years. We know where he learnt it. It is a typical lesson of life learnt in the Border country.

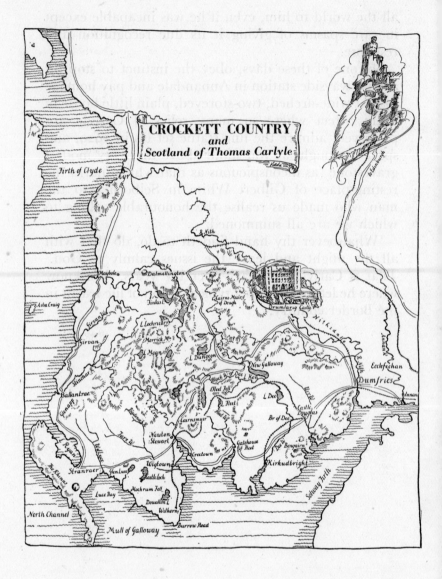

CROCKETT COUNTRY and Scotland of Thomas Carlyle

CHAPTER TWENTY-TWO

The Crockett Country

IT is, I think, true, but unfortunate, owing to the delight missed, that S. R. Crockett's books are less widely read than they used to be. It is certainly true, and even more unfortunate, owing to the delight missed, that what is called the Crockett country—that is, Galloway—is less widely visited than it deserves to be.

I have no means of knowing the reason for the failure of the Scotsman to visit it, but the Englishman certainly labours under the curious delusion that the farther north he goes the richer and wilder the scenery, though any north-bound traveller who keeps his eyes open and looks westward out of the carriage window after leaving Carlisle must wonder what lies behind those massive hills that rise out of the mist over the Solway Firth. I found, and I think most Englishmen find, the glory of Galloway and Carrick by accident.

I was staying in Ayr hunting up scenes connected with Robert Burns, and, having a little leisure, went southward by way of Dalmellington and was staggered to find that Burns had not been inspired by the magnificent combination of loch and ben, wild moorland and turbulent river, there revealed, to write some poems worthy of this grandeur.

This is certainly not the Highlands, but I found the atmosphere of Loch Trool and Loch of the Dungeon quite as attractive as, though in a quite different way from, the lochs of Perthshire and Inverness. For one thing it was surprisingly wild and lonely. For another it was full of historic association of Robert the Bruce, Border feuds, and above all of the Covenanters about whom I knew less than I did of Prince Charles Edward. I had of course read *The Raiders* and *The Lilac Sunbonnet*, both of which by the way appeared in the same year, 1894, the year before Crockett resigned from the ministry in order to devote the remaining twenty years of his life to the writing of those forty novels which gave all his readers such delight and enchantment.

Crockett was born on 24th September 1859 at Little Duchrae Farm, on the estate of Hensol, in the parish of Balmaghie in the county of Kirkcudbright.

The flooding of the river Dee in the hay season was one of the earliest things that the child remembered.

'Those Lammas floods', he tells us, 'were the terror of all the Deeside farmers. I was often startled from my bed as a boy with a wild cry, in Scots, that the Dee was out and about: a wild cry to arms against disaster and ruin.

'Into the water we went and snatched all the hay that could be saved, and plunged and groaned and struggled in our fight for our bread against the disastrous waters, until the defeated Dee rolled on placidly into Grennoch, under the pale light and the stars.'

Crockett's birthplace is situated in a green pleasance on the very borders of the wilderness of rock and heath and the mountains of the Raider country.

It was near the Boat of Rhone where the tumbling Dee joins the wider, more leisurely Ken that Crockett laid the scene for the tragic story of *The Cry Across the Black Water*.

And nearby, at Cree Brig, looking out over birches and meadows and soft uplands, Ralph Peden met Charteris at the blanket-washing in *The Lilac Sunbonnet*.

We have but to stand on any of the neighbouring knolls and cliffs to be reminded of an immense variety of associations, literary and historic. For instance, out over Bennan hill and the moorlands of Slogarie we see Burns crossing the hill to Dochenbreck, composing his immortal ode of *Scots Wha Hae*.

High on a knoll in the distance stands the castle of Kenmure where so many generations of the Gordons lived.

It is little wonder that scenes such as these should have inspired the boy to fill his mind with material that later he was to put to such excellent use in *The Lilac Sunbonnet, Lochinvar, The Raiders* and *Men of the Moss-Hags*.

The farm where Crockett was born was, like many Galloway houses of that day, a low one-storeyed cottage consisting of a kitchen and a room with a ladder leading to a loft that lacked a ceiling. Uncomfortable and small, it looked out on a winding, tree-fringed river with steep, cloud-capped heights behind of great beauty.

Crockett's was a stern introduction to life. At seven years old he was hoeing turnips in the summer, cutting them up for the sheep in the winter, and making bands for the sheaves which his mother was gathering at harvest-time.

He managed, however, to find time to read, though in those days fiction was forbidden and the selection was limited to sermons and *The Pilgrim's Progress*. Even Shakespeare and Burns were looked on with disapproval by his strict Cameronian grandparents.

Every Sunday the family had to travel nine miles to the attractive little Cameronian kirk on the hill with its pointed spire and arched windows that stood surrounded by a circle of trees on the top of a knoll at Castle Douglas.

They used to undertake this journey in a red farm-cart that lacked springs. It is not surprising to learn that the boy used to do as much of the return journey as he could on foot, taking short-cuts to meet the cart, with his grandfather sitting up in front and his grandmother behind in silk cap and apron.

Bog-Myrtle and Peat gives us vivid descriptions of the ministers of this Cameronian kirk, the famous and beloved preacher, William Symington, tall, god-like, with glowing eyes, and the small dapper, black-gloved John Kay who succeeded him.

By them and by Simpson's *Traditions of the Covenanters* his imagination was fired and he would hide himself among the hills, pretending to be a hunted Covenanter listening with mingled joy and fear for the crackling of leaves that would betoken the approach of the horse-hoofs of Claverhouse.

When he was five Crockett was sent to the school at Laurieston that adjoins the little church. He had to walk three and a half miles each way along a lonely road, his only companion his dog 'Roval'.

The education that he derived here from the Highlander, Duncan Robertson, was meagre, and consisted chiefly of memorising Latin roots, which meant nothing to him, learning the Shorter Catechism, and reading the Bible.

But his natural ability was so great that his lessons presented little difficulty to him. Indeed, his superiority in learning led to jealousy and a fight which he won. He also had fights on his way to and from school with rivals from another school that he had to pass on the Lochenbreck road.

But these excursions over the lonely moors had their compensation. There was, for instance, the lovely Loch Grennoch with its silver birch trees and hazels fringing its shores and tall hills rising behind, with here and there a lonely white-washed farmstead to inspire his latent poetic tendencies.

When he was eight the Crocketts left Little Duchrae and went to live in a cottage in Cotton Street, Castle Douglas. This, like his earlier home, was small and one-storeyed.

Crockett instantly fell in love with this new home. He loved its customs, the neighbourliness of its people, and listened with eager interest to the romantic tales of the carriers who held him with stories of encounters with highway robbers met on the wild Galloway roads between Dalmellington and Carsphairn, and other tales of spirits who lit up the dark recesses of the woods of Parton and Danevale, and of strange inexplicable cries coming up from the Dee.

Castle Douglas has changed greatly since the days when Crockett came under the influence of John Cowper, whose school he attended in his home street.

He was there for nine years, and tells us that he owed all his knowledge of the classics to Cowper, and indeed never learned much after he left this inspired teacher. On most Saturdays the boy would go up to Balmaghie to visit his relatives at Drumbreck and Glenlochar, where he came under the influence of his cousin Robert of Drumbreck, whom we know as the 'Stickit Minister'. It was he who introduced Crockett to Shakespeare, Dante, Burns, Macaulay, Carlyle, Scott, and Captain Marryatt.

Indeed, his discovery of the Waverley novels meant a revulsion against the 'penny dreadfuls' which had hitherto engrossed him, and he prevailed upon his companions to make a bonfire of their old loves.

On holidays he used to go off with his friends on dare-devil excursions, one of which included climbing the chimney of Threave Castle and walking along the top of the dangerous walls and climbing on to the hanging stone. Threave Castle is a picturesque, tall, old fortified keep standing in an island on the river among the moors.

It was during a fortnight's holiday at Colvend that he got all the material about the blanket-tramping and other incidents that he used later in *The Raiders*.

A friend tells us that one day as they were walking from Colvend to Dalbeattie he stopped in the middle of the beech avenue at Barnbarroch and then read out the line: 'The beechen bower o'er-reaching the red road, with upright bars of bole.'

He had a peculiar affection for the pleasant avenue that runs along the riverside at Castle Douglas, known as the Lover's Walk, and it was the beauty of the silver birches in this secluded walk that first inspired him to try his hand at poetry.

He also now began to paint in water-colour, one of his earliest efforts being a study of Crichhope Linn, near Thornhill.

He was equally impressed by the Carlinwark loch,

where he spent a great deal of his leisure contemplating a beauty that made a special appeal to him.

'Carlinwark', he says, 'is hardly a loch, and I have heard it called a duckpond. Well, if so, blessed be the ducks that swim in that pearl of ponds. I have crossed Lagoda, and seen less of beauty than you may see by walking open-eyed from the foot of Lovers' Walk to the clachan of Buchan—open-eyed I say—for all depends on that.'

We can read in *Kit Kennedy*, which is in large part autobiographical, more of the impression made on him by Castle Douglas, which he there calls 'Cairn Edward'. 'He slowly took in', he says of his hero, 'the vision of the little white-washed town with its smiling shops, broad streets, and comfortable merchants, all a-bustle behind their well-polished counters.

'Red carts stood tilted here and there with their shafts pointed to the sky, to the obstruction of the thoroughfare. A ceaseless tide of grey-coated, irregularly bearded farmers, and their more gaily attired women-folk, poured up and down the one main long street. There was quite a concourse at the Cross, and one could hardly elbow a way athwart the Market Hill for men and dog-fights.'

When later Crockett went up to Edinburgh University he used to spend his vacation wandering among the Galloway uplands, and made his headquarters at the farmhouse of Glenhead at the head of that most picturesque, lonely, and lovely Loch Trool, in the very heart of *The Raiders* country.

'Glenhead', said Crockett, 'I saw for the first time in the broad glare of a noonday sun—all the valley swam in a hazy blue mist, and the heat smote down from the white lift as through the glass of a hothouse.

'Then out of the coolness of the narrow, latticed sitting-room of Glenhead we step, following the slow, calm, steady shepherd stride of our friend as he paces upwards to guide us over his own beloved hills. It is hard work as we climb.

'As we mount we leave behind us to the south the green, sheep-studded sun-flecked side of Curley-wee, a name surely given to its whaup-haunted solitudes because of the wailing pipe of the curlew—"curley-wee, curley-wee, curley-wee!" Waterfalls are gleaming in the clefts, and behind us, as we rise into the realms of the blue, are Lamachan and Benanbrack. Past the side of Curley-wee it is possible to look into the great chasm of air in which, unseen, far below us lies Loch Dee. We gain the top of the ridge. Fantastic shapes, carved out of the gleaming grey granite, are all about.

'Those on the ridges look for all the world like Polar bears hunting with their long, lean noses thrust forward to scent the seals on the floes.'

Loch Valley and Loch Neldricken form, with the twin lochs of Glenhead, a water system of their own, connected with Glen Trool by the rapid torrential burn called Gairland which flashes downward through the narrow ravine which we have behind us to our left as we go upward.

Loch Enoch is the goal of our desire, a lake in cloudlands. The solemn battlemented lines rise above us so high that they are only dominated by the great mass of the Merrick.

It is hard to believe that a cliff so abrupt and stately has a lake upon its summit. Yet so it is. The fortress-like breastwork falls away in a Titanic embrasure on either side, and it is into that which lies nearest the Merrick that we direct our steps.

On the edge of Loch Neldricken lies a mass of green
and matted reeds, brilliantly emerald. In the centre
of this green bed is a perfectly defined circle of intensely
black water. It is the Murder Hole of gloomy memory.

Across a wilderness of tangled ridge, boulder, and
morass is the Long Hill of the Dungeon, depressed to
the south into the Wolf's Slock.

Now our Loch Enoch fortress is almost stormed.
At first the haze somewhat hides it. But half a dozen
steps and there we are.

Strangest sight in all this South Galloway of strange
sights is Loch Enoch, glowing like a glittering silver-
rimmed pearl out of the tangled grey and purple of
its surroundings with the strength, and tenderness, and
meaning of the human eye.

The Merrick soars away above in two great precipices and Loch Enoch spreads out beneath us in a
tangle of bays and promontories. As we sit above the
loch the large island, with the small loch within it, is
very prominent

The loch-in-loch is of a deeper and more distinct
blue, perhaps owing to its green and white setting on
the grassy, boulder-strewn island.

Probably no part of the Highlands is so free from
the presence of man as these southern wildernesses of
Galloway and here was the very fastness and fortress of
the westland Whigs in the fierce days of the killing.

Nature has got down here to her pristine elements,
and so old is the country that we seem to see the whole
turmoil of 'saps and sourocks' very much as they were
when the last of the Galloway glaciers melted slowly
away.

Right in front of us the Star Hill, Mulwharcher,
lifts itself up into the clear depths of the sky—a great

rounded cone like an old-fashioned hayrick. Beyond the levels of desolate, granite-bound, silver-sanded Loch Enoch lies a tumbled wilderness of hills.

To the left of the Star is the plateau of the Rig of Millmore, a wide and weary waste, gleaming everywhere with great tarns and shining lochans. Beyond it are the Kirrieoch hills and the pale blue ridges of Shalloch on Minnoch.

Every name is interesting here, but no name or description can give an idea of Loch Enoch itself, lifted up high, as it were, close against the sky, nearly 1,700 feet above the sea, with the giant Merrick on one side, the weird Dungeon on the other, and the grey wilderness stretching away mysteriously out into the twilight of the north.

And Crockett's description of his downward track by way of Buchan's Dungeon, the Sauch Burn, and the Shiel Burn, and Back Hill o' the Bush with its view of the green whalebacks of Corserine and the featureless range of Kells, is equally well told.

I have walked over much wild country in my time, but never over a wilder or lovelier than that which leads up into the hills by way of Black Hill o' the Bush. The main roads are more frequented, of course, by reason of the great water scheme, and German prisoners in the 1914–18 war opened up the roads south of Dalmellington, but Loch Trool remains as unfrequented and remote as ever, and anyone who wishes to visualise some of the trials endured in those desperate seventeenth-century days of the Covenanters will find in this exquisite wild country unforgettable reminders of great courage endured by brave-hearted, staunch defenders of their faith.

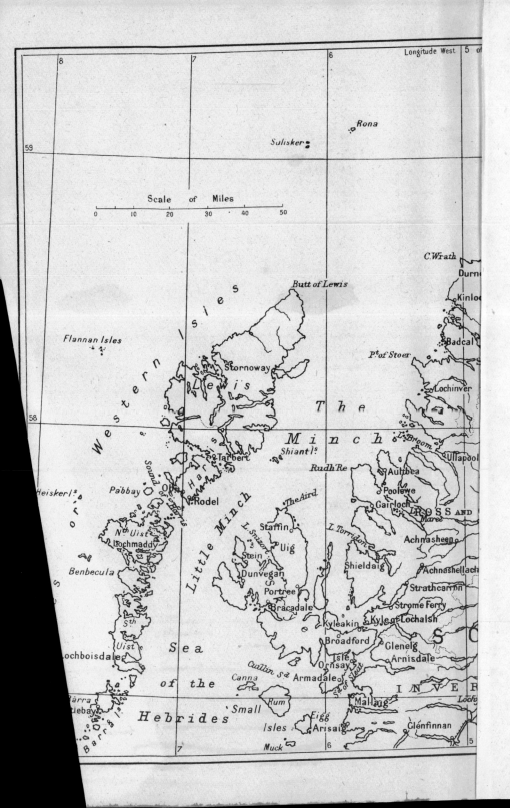